GLOBAL PERSPECTIVES ON TEACHING EXCELLENCE

Teaching excellence in higher education needs to be promoted and celebrated. However, a universal definition of excellent teaching remains elusive, and robust evidence about how it affects student learning appears to be lacking. This timely book explores the notion of teaching excellence from the viewpoint of a variety of international authors; guiding the reader to understand the complex terrain in which teaching excellence is foregrounded, and highlighting a number of key issues facing the future of global higher education.

Global Perspectives on Teaching Excellence explores:

- what is meant by teaching excellence, whether it can be measured and if so, how?
- the impact of teaching excellence frameworks, initiatives and awards.
- the new challenges for delivering global teaching excellence fit for the 21st century.

With a mix of political, theoretical and applied research foci, each chapter also includes a short critical commentary from international experts in the field to further the debate and situate the topics in a wider context. *Global Perspectives on Teaching Excellence* is essential reading for academic and education policymakers, researchers, and undergraduate and postgraduate students in education.

Christine Broughan is Professor of Higher Education at the Global Learning: Education and Attainment Research Centre, Coventry University, UK.

Graham Steventon is a Senior Lecturer in Criminology at Coventry University, UK.

Lynn Clouder is Professor of Professional Education and Academic Director of the Global Learning: Education and Attainment Research Centre at Coventry University, UK.

GLOBAL PERSPECTIVES ON TEACHING EXCELLENCE

A New Era for Higher Education

Edited by Christine Broughan,
Graham Steventon and Lynn Clouder

Routledge
Taylor & Francis Group

LONDON AND NEW YORK

First published 2018
by Routledge
2 Park Square, Milton Park, Abingdon, Oxon OX14 4RN

and by Routledge
711 Third Avenue, New York, NY 10017

Routledge is an imprint of the Taylor & Francis Group, an informa business

British Library Cataloguing-in-Publication Data
A catalogue record for this book is available from the British Library

Library of Congress Cataloging-in-Publication Data
Names: Broughan, Christine, editor.
Title: Global perspectives on teaching excellence : a new era for higher education / edited by Christine Broughan, Graham Steventon, and Lynn Clouder.
Description: Abingdon, Oxon ; New York, NY : Routledge, 2018.
Identifiers: LCCN 2017039543| ISBN 9780415793148 (hardback) | ISBN 9780415793155 (pbk.) | ISBN 9781315211251 (ebook)
Subjects: LCSH: College teaching—Cross-cultural studies. | Teacher effectiveness—Cross-cultural studies. | Education, Higher—Cross-cultural studies.
Classification: LCC LB2331 .G56 2018 | DDC 378.1/25—dc23
LC record available at https://lccn.loc.gov/2017039543

ISBN: 978-0-415-79314-8 (hbk)
ISBN: 978-0-415-79315-5 (pbk)
ISBN: 978-1-315-21125-1 (ebk)

Typeset in Bembo
by Keystroke, Neville Lodge, Tettenhall, Wolverhampton

Printed in the United Kingdom
by Henry Ling Limited

CONTENTS

LIST OF ILLUSTRATIONS

Figures

Tables

LIST OF ABBREVIATIONS

AAUT	Australian Awards for University Teaching
ACODE	Australasian Council on Open, Distance and e-Learning
AHELO	Assessment of Higher Education Learning Outcomes
ALTC	Australian Learning Teaching Council
ANTF	Association of National Teaching Fellows
ARWU	Academic Ranking of World Universities (China)
AUTCAS	Australian University Teaching Criteria and Standards
CADAD	Council of Australian Directors of Academic Development
CATE	Collaborative Awards for Teaching Excellence
CEMPE	Centre of Excellence in Music Performance Education (Norway)
CfTE	Competition for Teaching Excellence (Germany)
CPD	Continuing Professional Development
DLHE	Destination of Leavers in Higher Education
DPR	Development and Performance Review
HESA	Higher Education Statistics Agency (UK)
HEFCE	Higher Education Funding Council for England
IFNTF	International Federation of National Teaching Fellows
ISME	International Society for Music Education
ISSOTL	International Society for the Scholarship of Teaching and Learning
ITA	Inspired Teaching Awards (India)
KoKoHs	Modelling and Measuring Competencies in Higher Education (Germany)
MEQ	Module Evaluation Questionnaire
NSS	National Student Survey
NTF	National Teaching Fellow (UK)
NTFS	National Teaching Fellowship Scheme (UK)
NUS	National University of Singapore

OECD	Organisation for Economic Co-operation and Development
OLT	Office of Learning and Teaching (Australia)
PGCHE	Postgraduate Certificate in Higher Education
PTES	Postgraduate Taught Experience Survey
QAA	Quality Assurance Agency (UK)
QILT	Quality Indicators for Learning and Teaching (Australia)
SoTL	Scholarship of Teaching and Learning
STLHE	Society for Teaching and Learning in Higher Education (Canada)
TEF	Teaching Excellence Framework
TEQSA	Tertiary Education Quality and Standards Agency (Australia)
TERS	Teaching Excellence Recognition Scheme
UNESCO	United Nations Educational, Scientific and Cultural Organization
UTE	University Teaching Programme (China)

NOTES ON CONTRIBUTORS

Dawn Bennett is John Curtin Distinguished Professor and Director of the Creative Workforce Initiative at Curtin University in Australia. She is Principal Fellow of the Higher Education Academy, and convenes the Australian Learning and Teaching Fellows' network. She is also a director for the International Society for Music Education, a commissioner with the ISME Commission for Education of the Professional Musician, and co-chairs the Curtin Academy. Her research focuses on employability within higher education learning and teaching.

Michael Berry is a curriculum consultant for academic development, professional learning and curriculum renewal at Griffith University Business School, Australia. His interest and expertise in higher education derives from a long history in teacher education, curriculum development and educational leadership, including working as a school principal.

Bill Bosshardt is Professor and Director of the Center for Economic Education at Florida Atlantic University. He is also co-editor of the *International Review of Economics Education*, and Associate Editor of *The American Economist*, as well as being an internationally recognized expert and widely published in economics education.

Christine Broughan is Professor of Higher Education at the Global Learning: Education and Attainment Research Centre at Coventry University. She has a key role in equity and social inclusion research in the fields of education, ethnicity, gender, ageing, mental health and wellbeing. Christine has a proven track record in education leadership, teaching and research.

Sally Brown is an independent consultant and Emeritus Professor at Leeds Beckett University, and Visiting Professor at Plymouth, South Wales and Liverpool John

Moores Universities. She is a Principal Fellow of the Higher Education Academy, Senior Fellow of the Staff and Educational Development Association and a UK National Teaching Fellow.

Denise Chalmers is Professor Emeritus, University of Western Australia. She was awarded an OLT National Senior Teaching Fellowship on recognizing and rewarding university teaching in 2015 and an Australian Award for University Teaching Citation in 2014. She has demonstrated leadership and innovation in higher education for over twenty-five years.

Lynn Clouder is Professor of Professional Education and Academic Director of the Global Learning: Education and Attainment Research Centre at Coventry University. She was Director of a HEFCE funded Centre for Excellence in Teaching and Learning (CETL) from 2005–2010 and was awarded a National Teaching Fellowship in 2007. Currently, she enjoys researching, and mentoring colleagues/ postgraduate students.

Glenda Crosling is Professor and Head of the Centre for Higher Education Research at Sunway University in Malaysia, and Adjunct Associate Professor in the Office of the Deputy Provost (Learning and Teaching), Monash University, Australia. She has researched and published widely on the enhancement of the learning, teaching, curriculum and assessment in higher education.

James Derounian is Principal Lecturer in Applied Social Sciences at the University of Gloucestershire. He has a thirty-seven-year career in community engagement and academia and was awarded a National Teaching Fellowship in 2007. His research, consultancy and teaching range across active and blended learning, community and rural development.

Roberto Di Napoli is Professor of Higher Education Practice and Scholarship, and Head of the Centre for Educational Development and Innovation (CEDI) at St George's Institute of Medical and Biomedical Education, University of London. He is Visiting Professor at the Università of Teramo (Italy) and has been Educator in Residence at the National University of Singapore. His scholarly interests lie in the field of higher education identities and professionalism.

Celia Duffy has held senior positions in the performing arts and academia for over twenty years. As a professor and member of the senior leadership team at the Royal Conservatoire of Scotland, she led an ambitious Curriculum Reform project aiming to redefine the contemporary conservatoire learning experience, and she continues to be active in the sector as a consultant, teacher and Board chair.

Ron Edwards is Professor and Vice Chancellor of Asia Pacific University (APU), a private university in Kuala Lumpur, Malaysia, responsible for the quality of learning and teaching. His previous leadership roles were at Monash University (Australia and Malaysia), and RMIT (Vietnam). He has authored over forty articles and chapters in refereed journals and scholarly books.

Suki Ekaratne is a marine ecologist turned educational developer. In both of these disciplines he has taught and held professorial appointments in several countries, including Sri Lanka, UK, US, and Hong Kong. He has also authored book chapters, held journal editorships, delivered keynotes and received awards such as the International Consortium for Educational Development's 'Spirit of ICED' award.

Sandeep Gakhal works as a research assistant for Coventry University Research Solutions (CUReS) and primarily contributes to research and consultancy work in student satisfaction. She has a BA joint honours in English and Social and Applied Psychology and an MSc in Organisational Psychology and Business. Sandeep is experienced in both educational and health services research.

Mark Gan is a senior education specialist at the Centre for Development of Teaching and Learning, National University of Singapore. He has been engaged in research on assessment over the last six years, with a particular focus on developing students' use of peer feedback for learning.

Johan Geertsema is Associate Professor directing the Centre for Development of Teaching and Learning at the National University of Singapore. His PhD is in English; current research interests include: the complexities of academic identities and cultures in relation to teaching in/across the disciplines; teaching achievement; recognition and reward; and communities of practice.

Aline Germain-Rutherford is Associate Vice President, Teaching and Learning, at University of Ottawa and previously Associate Vice President of the Language Schools and Graduate programmes of Middlebury College. She has led research projects on faculty development and multicultural issues in post-secondary education, and has a 3M National Teaching Fellow Award.

Ross Guest is Dean (Learning and Teaching) and Professor of Economics at Griffith University, Australia. He is a National Senior Teaching Fellow, the Editor-in-Chief of the *International Review of Economics Education*, a textbook author and winner of a national teaching citation. He has published a number of articles on economics education.

Vicky Gunn is Professor and Head of Learning and Teaching at the Glasgow School of Art. She has led research on several national-level teaching enhancement projects with both QAA Scotland and the Higher Education Academy, and has a penchant for policy development in higher education at institutional and national levels.

Cécile Hardebolle is an academic developer at the École Polytechnique Fédérale de Lausanne. Originally trained as an engineer, she worked as a researcher and lecturer in Computer Science at a French grande école (Supélec, Paris) and she has taught in several French engineering institutions including Polytechnique and Centrale Paris.

Scott Harrison is Professor and Director of Queensland Conservatorium, Griffith University, Australia. He has taught in primary, secondary and tertiary environments, with over twenty years of experience including performance, opera and music theatre as both singer and musical director. He is co-editor of the *International Journal of Music Education*, and holds an Australian Award for University Teaching and a Fellowship for the Australian Office for Learning and Teaching.

Owen Hicks is Emeritus Professor, University of Western Australia, formerly responsible for academic development, and is a life member and past president of HERDSA. As an Australian Learning and Teaching Council senior consultant, he engaged with a wide cross-section of academics. He recently completed volunteer university assignments in East Timor, China and Vietnam.

Chng Huang Hoon is Associate Professor (English Language) and Associate Provost (Undergraduate Education) at the National University of Singapore. Her interests are in gender and education. She currently serves on various editorial and advisory boards including the Taylor Institute, University of Calgary and *International Journal for Academic Development*.

Lynne Hunt is Emeritus Professor at University of Queensland, Australia. She won the 2002 Australian Award for Social Science Teaching, the Prime Minister's Award for Australian University Teacher of the Year, and an Australian Executive Endeavour Award in 2009. She co-edited *University Teaching in Focus* (2012) and *The Realities of Change in Higher Education* (2006).

Siara Isaac is an academic developer specializing in science and engineering at the École Polytechnique Fédérale de Lausanne, and concurrently pursuing a PhD characterizing the epistemic development of engineering students. Originally trained as a chemist, she has taught in Canada, China and France.

Mark Israel is Adjunct Professor of Law and Criminology at Flinders University, and a visiting academic at the School of Social Sciences, University of Western Australia. He chairs the Academic Board of the Australian School of Management, and is an Australian Learning and Teaching Fellow and Principal Fellow of the Higher Education Academy in the UK.

Erika Kustra is Director, Teaching and Learning Development, University of Windsor, Canada and Chair of the Educational Developers Caucus. She has been an educational developer for over nineteen years, co-authoring guides and leading multi-institutional projects on teaching culture and educational development. Erika has received university and national awards for teaching and leadership.

Ingrid Le Duc works as an academic developer at the École Polytechnique Fédérale de Lausanne. She completed her PhD in Social Psychology at the London School of Economics and has taught in England, Mexico and Switzerland. Her current research interests focus on how current educational standards meet teachers' real concerns.

Kathy Luckett is an associate professor at the University of Cape Town, South Africa. She has an undergraduate degree in English, History and Religious Studies and holds postgraduate qualifications in Education, Linguistics, Social Policy and Social Science Research Methods. She has consulted to the Council on Higher Education in South Africa on higher education policy, academic planning, quality assurance, and teaching and learning policy.

Katarina Mårtensson is a senior lecturer and academic developer at Lund University, Sweden, since 2000. Her research focuses on strategic educational development, academic culture and leadership. She has been co-editor of the *International Journal for Academic Development*, and is currently co-President of the International Society for the Scholarship of Teaching and Learning.

Marianne Merkt holds a professorship for academic development at Magdeburg-Stendal University of Applied Sciences. She is Head of the Centre for Academic Development and Research in Higher Education and representative of the German Association of Academic Development. Her research embraces professionalization of academic teachers and developers, enculturation of students and digitalization in teaching and learning.

Phil Race is Emeritus Professor at Leeds Beckett University and Visiting Professor at the University of Plymouth. He publishes widely (and keynotes) on teaching, learning and assessment in higher education. His best-known books include *Making Learning Happen* (SAGE Publications 2014) and *The Lecturer's Toolkit* (Routledge 2015).

Torgny Roxå is an academic developer at Lund University, Sweden, since 1988 working in Strategic Educational Development. He has won the Lund University award for distinguished pedagogical achievements and has served as external examiner at Oxford University. He is currently appointed Distinguished Scholar at McMaster University in Canada.

Mary Runté is Associate Professor in Policy and Strategy in the Faculty of Management at the University of Lethbridge, Alberta, Canada, where she teaches on social responsibility in business and society drawn from an extensive background in the voluntary sector. Her research interests focus on non-profit and business collaboration.

Robert Runté is Associate Professor in Educational Foundations (Sociology) and Student Evaluation at the University of Lethbridge. Before joining the University, he spent a decade in the Department of Education where he observed first hand some of the policy shifts described in his chapter. He is also Senior Editor at Five Rivers Publishing.

Alan Soong is an academic developer at the Centre for Development of Teaching and Learning, National University of Singapore. He has been working in the area of academic development and educational technology in higher education since 2002. Alan's research interests include academic development and blended learning in higher education.

Bjørn Stensaker is Professor of Higher Education Studies in the Department of Education, University of Oslo. His special research interest lies in governance, leadership and organizational change in higher education on which he has published widely in international journals and books.

Graham Steventon qualified as an architect and gained a PhD in Sociology at Warwick University before becoming a senior lecturer in Criminology at Coventry University in 2002. He uses creative approaches to teaching and assessment (role play; immersive virtual contexts; podcasting; concept mapping) and has researched and presented internationally on pedagogy. He co-edited two previously published books (Routledge 2012 and 2016) on higher education.

Pedro Teixeira is Associate Professor, Economics, Vice Rector at the University of Porto, and Director of the Centre of Research on Higher Education Policy. He specializes in the economics of higher education and history of economic ideas and has edited several volumes in these fields.

Roland Tormey is Coordinator of the Teaching Support Centre in the École Polytechnique Fédérale de Lausanne, Switzerland where he also teaches courses in Learning Sciences. A sociologist by training, he was previously Head of Teacher Education at the University of Limerick, Ireland.

Beatrice Tucker is Associate Professor and Director, Curtin Learning Institute, and has led the development and implementation of Curtin University's online student evaluation system and the Teaching Excellence framework, which outlines criteria and standards for academics. She is responsible for the Scholarship of Teaching and Learning, learning spaces and educational support.

Caroline Wilson is a social scientist involved in the design, analysis, reporting and presenting results of surveys of students, staff and others associated with student experience at Coventry University. She is an experienced evaluator with a PhD and subsequent work focusing on mechanisms to encourage and monitor voluntary behaviour change.

FOREWORD

Vicky Gunn

Christine Broughan, Graham Steventon and Lynn Clouder have seized a moment to produce this collection on teaching excellence. While excellence is a familiar term for those of us who work in higher education, the Editors recognized a significant, contextual change was afoot. The frameworks that are emerging in such circumstances arguably redefine what excellence is when associated with teaching.

Excellence as a category of aspiration and analysis is unquestionably supported, but at the same time its definition remains elusive and ambiguous. The phrase 'teaching excellence' has quite rightly become regarded as a site of contestation. In particular, the book focuses debate on who sets the rules for defining and measuring teaching excellence and cautions against ranking superiority that promotes a monolithic, Westernized model of higher education. Authors explore the tension between academics and policy makers that drive at the very core of what 'teaching is and is for'.

As notions of excellence are attached to frameworks which aspire to specific and often limited interpretations of the collective moral good of higher education (particularly in terms of socio-economic mobility, equality and diversity, and continued wealth creation within globalization), necessary disquiet rumbles on in the scholarship. Moreover, as such laudable aims come to be evidenced through a governmental dependence on uni-dimensional metrics for automated decision-making around resources, even university senior management teams, their planners and business analysts have grown increasingly nervous. Research demonstrates that these metrics tell us more about perceptions of satisfaction, the production of value within the knowledge economy for the individual in a narrow manner, and a reductive conception of success in graduate employment. This book offers a rebalance of teaching excellence that is much more authentic and rich; sensitive to the nuances of values, discipline and cultural specific issues and the need for the recognition of input and throughput, as well as outputs.

Ultimately, what this book offers is the ability to accurately, robustly and sensitively demonstrate the value of co-creation of university teaching excellence; something lacking from most teaching excellence frameworks. The authors look to the relational aspects of higher education's teaching and learning. Each chapter demands that we re-engage fully in debates, policies, and practices regarding teaching excellence, and by doing so maintain a scholarly and robust approach as to how universities are to be judged.

INTRODUCTION: A NEW ERA FOR HIGHER EDUCATION

Christine Broughan, Graham Steventon and Lynn Clouder

The idea for this book started as many good ideas start, over coffee with individuals who are more than just colleagues; like-minded people who share a passion for, and aspire to achieve, excellence in higher education. Against a backdrop of a progressively competitive and technological global market in which higher education is often viewed as a commodity with students exercising consumer choices, teaching excellence has become the latest national policy concern and means of institutional differentiation. With the need for more graduates to meet the workforce demands of an increasingly connected and diverse world comes the questioning of higher education's capacity to deliver in terms of raising standards, addressing mediocrity and delivering excellence.

Central to the debate is what teaching excellence actually means and who should define it: policymakers, institutional managers, teachers, or students? Some would argue that teaching excellence has always been the raison d'être of higher education, but its elusiveness in terms of agreed values, behaviours and measures has been both a source of frustration and appeal to the sector and beyond. There are clear tensions between those who need to demonstrate efficient and effective use of the public (or private) purse and teachers who wish to retain academic autonomy, yet their ultimate goal is the same: to produce excellent graduates. Nationally, governments and institutions have begun to recognize the need to understand and celebrate teaching excellence, resulting up to now in a relatively fragmented plethora of frameworks for setting standards across the sector (for example: South Africa National Award; Australian Awards for University Teaching; UK Teaching Excellence Framework; Indian National Science Academy Awards). What is being achieved through these developments, however, is that by measuring and valuing teaching quality, such awards and frameworks are, to some extent, bringing teaching into line with research excellence, benefiting those institutions that have specialized in the former.

It is clear, nonetheless, that teaching excellence is a highly complex phenomenon and this is no more evident than when trying to establish simple metrics by which to measure it. The first aim of this book, therefore, is to explore teaching excellence from a variety of voices whose views shape how teaching is measured and valued in order to develop more nuanced understandings of the ontological and epistemological notions underpinning teaching – whose interests does it/should it serve and how do we know what it is? We reflect on the implementation of various national and international teaching quality frameworks and teaching excellence awards, and offer suggestions as to how such initiatives, implemented sensitively and appropriately to enhance the learning gain of students, might serve to drive up excellence across the sector. However, we also highlight the dangers of universal policy approaches that use proxy measures defined by metrics to inform national and international league tables that may, in fact, encourage standardized, superficial practices rather than genuine quality.

Since excellence can mean many things to different people, we do not seek to offer a panacea. Instead, this book offers a unique contribution by placing different subject positions side by side, guiding the reader to understand the complex terrain from which teaching excellence is foregrounded and exploring issues at macro-, meso- and micro-contextual levels. Key to the debate is the need for governments to engage with stakeholders in order to ensure that the implementation of proxy measures and incentives, such as teaching excellence frameworks and national teaching fellowship awards, is decisive, has validity, and is supported by the sector. The book critically explores the complexity of trying to measure teaching excellence and highlight the impact of such measurement. In particular, it examines the efficacy and efficiency of a reductionist approach offered by current metrics and explores meaningful alternatives. For example, should metrics be used to differentiate forms of teaching excellence, or to benchmark standards, or both? We question the set of circumstances required to ensure that all teaching is excellent across the national and global sector which at the same time avoids us hurtling towards a monolithic view of higher education provision. A managerial perspective will address the issues and practicalities of implementing teaching excellence initiatives. In particular, we explore the impact of job design and contract types on teaching excellence, suggesting that the rise of peripatetic teaching places the previously taken for granted principles of academic citizenship in communities of practice under strain.

Book structure

The book has been arranged around five thematic areas and each chapter is accompanied by a short critical commentary written by a specialist in the field with the remit to extend the debate and set the chapter into a wider, national and international context. First, in defining excellence, Sandeep Gakhal explores definitional variations and scrutinizes international examples for similarities and differences. She critically examines the constructs of a number of international frameworks alongside staff and student perceptions of teaching excellence, describing the tensions that exist between staff and student ideas of proxy measures of teaching excellence.

Continuing the discussion of measuring teaching excellence, Caroline Wilson questions the ability of metrics to accurately measure what they purport to measure, and queries whether measuring serves to improve or deflect from teaching excellence. Critical to the debate is whether a unit of analysis for teaching excellence should be sought that avoids division between individual and institutional levels. She suggests that a basket of measures can provide an indication of the quality of teaching and its impact on the learning gained by students, but that it is difficult to disaggregate the impact of the university experience from other external factors when measuring student performance.

The impact of the external environment and the importance of understanding local conditions are picked up by Lynne Hunt and Owen Hicks. They present a convincing argument against the tendency to work towards one global, simplistic pinnacle of excellence and promote the adoption of a model that is more mindful of socio-cultural and economic contexts. Consequently, they suggest that the pursuit of excellence in terms of global rankings is, for the majority, a futile exercise. Using examples from teaching in provincial universities in China, Vietnam and Timor-Leste, they question the assumption that most students experience a global higher education and suggest this is something afforded only to the privileged few. This point is key in light of the evidence that suggests that significant areas for growth in higher education is in those provincial universities that appear 'off the radar' in terms of global ranking.

The second theme considers organizational and structural issues and Glenda Crosling explores teaching excellence in the global context of transnational teaching and the risks and benefits this might bring to institutions. She suggests that when delivered appropriately, transnational programmes can enhance the curriculum, teaching and educational experience of all students, regardless of their geographic location. What becomes clear is that teaching excellence is situated both historically and culturally, and it is these contexts that feature in Mary and Robert Runté's examination of four discourses on the purpose of higher education. The shift from higher education as a playful place to become enlightened and explore boundaries, to a remit of producing students ready to enter professional careers, has significant impact on what determines excellent teaching. Measures of teaching excellence, Runté and Runté argue, need to align with student expectations.

Torgny Roxå and Katarina Mårtensson note that the achievement of teaching excellence in academic micro-cultures is dependent on organizational structures that recognize and reward excellence. While such structures will always involve a combination of collegiality, managerialism and bureaucracy, it is the relative weight that is important and they caution against models that primarily promote managerial governance since collegial academic micro-cultures are most likely to produce sustainable excellent teaching practices.

How well culture can foreground teaching excellence is addressed by Denise Chalmers and Beatrice Tucker as they describe a national strategy implemented in

Australia. The Australian teaching excellence framework was developed to support institutions' development rather than 'measure' performance *per se*. The framework has been adopted in Canada, Iceland, Sweden, South Africa and Malaysia.

In our third theme of rewards, recognition and development, Mark Israel and Dawn Bennett examine national teaching awards implemented in the UK, Australia, New Zealand and Canada. They question how much impact National Teaching Fellow awards have had in terms of acting as agents of institutional change, and go further to suggest that institutions themselves do not really value, or take seriously, such schemes.

Another potential to drive excellence is through institutional training and development programmes and looking at the pivotal role of staff training and development in supporting teaching excellence, Siara Isaac, Ingrid Le Duc, Cécile Hardebolle and Roland Tormey argue that teaching excellence should be about the *process* of scholarly improvement rather than *outcome* focused. They suggest that to meet the needs of the 21st century, teaching excellence should be driven by learner analytics in order to inform decisions and support academics.

Johan Geertsema, Chng Huang Hoon, Mark Gan and Alan Soong take up the mantel of questioning what needs to be done in order to achieve the wholesale delivery of teaching excellence across institutions. They explore whether education-based employment tracks have the ability to deliver teaching excellence, finding no evidence to suggest that 'teaching only' contract staff members are better at teaching than other staff. As such, they warn against the segmentation of academic roles and raise concerns regarding the fragmentation of work due to non-tenured positions. Teaching excellence for these authors means retaining the principles of academic citizenship that enables academic freedom and the promotion of a community of learners.

As part of a theme on teaching excellence case studies, Michael Berry and Ross Guest acknowledge the clarity offered by national frameworks in terms of strategic priorities and criteria for measuring teaching excellence, but stress the importance not to lose sight of discipline specific nuances that will influence how teaching excellence is valued and defined. They describe the benefits of a locally implemented teaching excellence recognition scheme in an Australian Business School, while Scott Harrison uses the example of the performing arts to show how teaching excellence is weighted heavily by the teacher's lineage (their professional performance credentials, accolades, awards and reputation) and how successful alumni are in the industry. Caution therefore must be exercised when comparing student evaluations across disciplines. A multifaceted approach is more likely to improve the validity and reliability of teaching excellent measures.

Whilst it is recognized that national schemes and league tables appear to dominate the current discourses around teaching excellence, James Derounian encourages readers not to forget the *art* of teaching. He describes teaching as a performance; one that encourages students to experience the 'thrill of the unexpected', disrupting unimaginative teaching practices and exploring different world views to stimulate student learning.

Finally, in a theme of teaching excellence futures, Caroline Wilson and Christine Broughan conclude by drawing together comments from an international range of academics, with authority in the field, to explore the tensions and issues that are likely to impact on teaching excellence in this new era of higher education.

Acknowledgements

We would like to thank Coventry University for supporting us in our endeavour to present this edited book on teaching excellence; in particular, Ian Dunn for being our inspirational leader and Lindsay Dickson, Gabriela Chitroceanu and Sabrina Jefferies for keeping us in order.

1

WHAT IS TEACHING EXCELLENCE?

Sandeep Gakhal

Introduction

Over the last two decades teaching excellence has become of increasing global concern in higher education (Gunn and Fisk 2013; Land and Gordon 2015) and yet there is no general agreement as to what it constitutes (Gunn and Fisk 2013; Greatbatch and Holland 2016). Hence, this chapter seeks to: (i) explore and draw similarities and comparisons between the ways in which teaching excellence is defined globally; (ii) provide a critique of the conceptions used within a number of teaching excellence initiatives and how well these align with teachers' and students' perceptions of teaching excellence; (iii) examine future implications for the higher education environment in terms of the way in which teaching excellence is defined and, in turn, measured. A case study is presented that examines the UK's Teaching Excellence Framework (TEF) using Kelly's (1955) repertory grid.

The findings of the repertory grid case study emphasize tensions between the way in which teaching excellence is defined by teachers and students, and how well these align with the proxy measures used to assess teaching excellence within the TEF. These findings are in line with previous studies (see, for example, Vielba and Hillier 2000, in Skelton 2005) and highlight inconsistencies between teachers' and students' perceptions of teaching excellence and proposed models of measuring teaching excellence. Furthermore, concerns exist around the proxy metrics used within the TEF as it is suggested that they are providing a skewed representation of teaching excellence (Robinson and Hilli 2016). Consequently, questions are raised as to whether the implementation of initiatives, such as the TEF, will actually result in driving up teaching excellence. Despite this, the chapter concludes that national initiatives, such as the TEF, are increasingly likely to acquire sector dominance in the future. Such initiatives, which are discussed in the chapter, focus on comparative measures between institutions as a means of promoting teaching excellence and benchmarking teaching quality across institutions. In this context, teaching excellence becomes defined by easily identifiable and harvestable data that relies on objective measures of performance. As a result, initiatives of this kind are at risk of promoting a monolithic view of teaching excellence.

Defining teaching excellence in the 21st century

Various definitions of 'excellence' and 'teaching' exist. Macfarlane (2007) usefully distinguishes between different stages of teaching: (1) pre-performance – involving all tasks undertaken prior to the teaching, such as preparing teaching materials; (2) performance – comprising teaching undertaken in various settings, such as lectures, seminars and workshops; (3) post-performance – involving all tasks following the teaching activity including providing learners with guidance and support. Sangoleye and Kolawole (2016) suggest that teaching can be defined as a variety of instructional methods designed to promote deep learning and conceptual change such as effective questioning. Furthermore, Fitzmaurice (2010) suggests that teaching involves building and nurturing a safe and supportive environment, which stimulates learning. The definitions provided suggest that the teacher's performance cannot, and should not, be measured in isolation.

As with definitions of teaching, there are also differences in the way that excellence is defined. According to Brusoni et al. (2014: 27), 'excellence is a highly relative concept, it implies a judgement that evaluates if and to what extent something or someone possesses some definite intrinsic characteristics to be considered excellent (in relation to oneself and others)'. In other words, excellence is relational and influenced by those whose interests are being served, measured or judged at any given period (Brown 2011; Brusoni et al. 2014).

Taking into consideration the various definitions of what is meant by 'teaching' and 'excellence' as individual concepts, it comes as no surprise that there is no agreed definition of 'teaching excellence' as discussed earlier (Gunn and Fisk 2013; Greatbatch and Holland 2016) and it is questionable as to whether this is something that we should aspire to. Teaching excellence can be interpreted and assessed in various ways (Hammer et al. 2010). Elton (1998: 9) argues that teaching excellence is 'multi-dimensional' and Skelton (2005: 4) perceives it as a 'contested and value-laden concept'. The rapid growth of global higher education has resulted in institutions continuously striving to review and improve the quality of their teaching and research (Üstünlüoğlu 2016), for example in Australia (Dinham 2013) and India (Gafoor and Shilna 2013), in order to positively impact on student learning outcomes (Archibong and Nja 2011).

Individual teaching excellence

Within the literature, teaching excellence has been primarily concerned with determining what constitutes excellence in teaching (Chen et al. 2012). Although there is no universal agreement, there are some commonalities, including an emphasis on personal attributes/expertise of the teacher and student development

(Gibbs 2008; Brusoni et al. 2014). For example, students' perceptions of effective teaching in a Nigerian university were mostly found to be characterized by the ability to assess their level of comprehension and respond to questions sufficiently (Aregbeyen 2010). In a Slovenian university, first year students were found to be primarily concerned with a teacher's ability to deliver content in a clear, coherent and engaging manner; however, third year students were more concerned with the teacher's ability to develop students' in-depth knowledge of the subject area, promote independent learning and instil critical thinking skills (Šteh et al. 2014). Research has also shown differences in perceptions of excellent teaching between and across cultures (Keeley et al. 2012); for example, Chinese students tend to favour more structured, goal-orientated teaching in comparison to Japanese students who value more interpersonal teacher/student relationships (Liu et al. 2015; Keeley et al. 2016).

Institutional and national teaching excellence

Numerous institutional and national initiatives exist to encourage and support teaching excellence (Land and Gordon 2015; Greatbatch and Holland 2016). These include auditing and accrediting courses (Mohd. Deni et al. 2014), staff development programmes (Lemass and Stace 2010), and gathering students' feedback on teaching (Flodén 2016). Accrediting agencies, such as the Malaysian Qualifications Agency (MQA) and South Africa's Higher Education Quality Committee (HEQC), aim to ensure that higher education programmes are delivered to the highest standards (Luckett 2010; Mohd. Deni et al. 2014). However, although auditing and accrediting courses provides a standardized and consistent approach to the way in which programmes are managed and delivered, they do not necessarily lead to improved teaching quality in practice (Mohd. Deni et al. 2014), or better student outcomes (Luckett 2010). Similarly, despite the seemingly global obsession of collating and analysing student feedback (Denson et al. 2010; Flodén 2016), some studies suggest that it does not, by itself, lead to improvements in teaching practice. For example, Blair and Noel (2014) investigated student evaluations from five courses, delivered by the same teacher during 2011–2012 and 2012–2013, and findings indicated little evidence of improvements in teachers' practice as a result of the feedback provided (Lemass and Stace 2010). Likewise, many institutions offer professional development programmes to foster effective teaching skills and yet they are often disregarded by academic staff (Lemass and Stace 2010).

Predominately, teaching excellence initiatives have focused on recognizing and rewarding individual teaching excellence (D'Andrea 2007; Skelton 2007). In many countries, various teaching award schemes have been introduced (Brown 2011) which underpin different definitions of teaching excellence as illustrated in Table 1.1 (Gibbs, 2008); for example, the National Teaching Fellowship Scheme (NTFS) in the UK (Higher Education Academy 2015); the Australian Awards for University Teaching (AAUT) in Australia (Australian Government Department of Education and Training 2017); the Inspired Teaching Awards in India (Indian Honour 2017).

TABLE 1.1 Different conceptions of teaching excellence underlying teaching award schemes

1.   No conception
2.   Exhibiting certain behaviours in a skillful way
3.   Implementing a student focus effectively
4.   Engaging in the scholarship of teaching
5.   Exploiting benefits from disciplinary research
6.   Developing students
7.   Creating effective learning environments
8.   Good citizenship
9.   Innovating in teaching
10.   Developing the teaching of others
11.   Corporate definitions of excellence
12.   Leadership in teaching
13.   Collegial definitions of excellence

Source: Adapted from Gibbs (2008: 6 & 7)

Leibowitz, Farmer and Franklin (2012) also provide a range of examples of the different types of criteria used within teaching awards to measure teaching excellence.

In Australia, an increasing number of higher education institutions have adopted the former Australian Learning Teaching Council's (ALTC) set of criteria at an institutional level to recognize and reward excellent teaching within their institutions (Devlin and Samarawickrema 2010). This wide-scale adoption suggests that the criteria have had a positive impact on teaching excellence; however, the authors do not present evidence demonstrating formal measures of impact. Furthermore, the authors contend that the ALTC criteria should be revised and re-worked in order to respond to rapid changes in higher education.

Whilst some teaching excellence initiatives emphasize the role of the individual teacher, others focus on influencing teaching excellence at the institutional level. A national initiative, introduced in Germany in 2010, specifically intended to serve the latter. The Competition for Teaching Excellence (CfTE) encouraged higher education institutions to apply for the award of excellence in teaching. Submissions were assessed against a diverse set of criteria and successful institutions obtained additional funding (Brockerhoff et al. 2014). The CfTE advocates a multifaceted concept of teaching excellence which is viewed through various structural (for example: curriculum design) and cultural (for example: staff development programmes) activities designed to enhance teaching quality within an institution (Brockerhoff et al. 2014). Given that there has been no formal evaluation of the CfTE, it is difficult to conclude whether or not it has impacted positively on teaching quality (Brockerhoff et al. 2014).

Following the massification of higher education and a deterioration in teaching quality, the Ministry of Education in China introduced the University Teaching

Programme (UTE) to monitor and assess teaching quality across higher education institutions (Yin and Wang 2015). All institutions within the first five-year cycle (2003–2008) of the programme were assessed on criteria based on the following eight principles (Yin and Wang 2015: 1033):

(1) guiding principles of university operation
(2) teaching staff
(3) teaching conditions and the utilization of teaching facilities
(4) subjects and teaching
(5) teaching management
(6) academic atmosphere
(7) learning outcomes
(8) special features

Assessment was standardized and based on an independent review. Institutions were awarded a rating of excellent, good, pass or unqualified for their overall quality of teaching (Yin and Wang 2015). A review of the first cycle of the programme found a high proportion of institutions were rated as excellent which contradicted widely held views of reduced teaching quality (Jiang 2010; Yin and Wang 2015; Greatbatch and Holland 2016). Yin and Wang (2015) reported that the programme neglected to assess the direct learning outcomes of students and that the criteria employed within the programme should be revised to take this into consideration. The programme also appeared to be more concerned with quality standards/criteria, benchmarking the performance of higher education institutions, rather than the aspiration of achieving excellence per se. In light of the critique of the first round of evaluations, the second (2012–ongoing) is more concerned with the impact of teaching and learning processes on student learning outcomes (Greatbatch and Holland 2016).

In 2016, the UK government introduced the Teaching Excellence Framework (TEF) to monitor, assess and enhance teaching quality in higher education, offering both financial and reputational incentives (Department for Business Innovation and Skills 2016; Department of Education 2016). The TEF serves as a single measurement of teaching quality on which the overall performance of institutions can be ranked (Bishop 2016). Within the TEF, teaching excellence is defined under the following umbrella headings: teaching quality, learning environment, student outcomes, and learning gain as illustrated in Figure 1.1 (Department of Education 2016).

Higher education institutions will be assessed against the following core metrics, although further metrics are likely to be introduced (Department of Education 2016; Robinson and Hilli 2016): (1) National Student Survey (NSS) – satisfaction with teaching, assessment and feedback and academic support; (2) Destination of Leavers in Higher Education survey (DLHE) – the number of graduates in employ-ment (and in highly skilled positions)/further education; (3) Non-continuation figures/drop-out rates (HESA). As well as the core metrics, institutions are also able to provide non-prescriptive evidence to support their case for the best possible TEF

Aspects of quality (to be assessed)	Teaching quality includes various contexts i.e. seminars and tutorials and involves both academic and support staff	Learning environment includes the availability and effectiveness of learning materials and resources to support students' learning	Student outcomes and learning gain relates specifically to graduate employment outcomes and the educational gains made by students from various backgrounds
Evidence	Core metrics		
	Teaching on my course (NSS scale 1) Assessment and Feedback (NSS scale 2)	Academic Support (NSS scale 3) Non-continuation (HESA)	Employment/further study (DLHE) Highly-skilled employment/further study (DLHE)
Additional evidence (provider submission)			
Statement of findings	Brief description of the reasons for the award given including particular strengths		
Overall outcome	The TEF rating awarded		

FIGURE 1.1 Teaching Excellence Framework

Source: Adapted from Department of Education (2016: 18)

rating (Department of Education 2016; Robinson and Hilli 2016). Given that the TEF is in its preliminary stages and is first of its kind within the UK, its efficacy in driving teaching excellence is yet to be established.

Critique of different conceptions of teaching excellence within the teaching excellence initiatives

Teaching excellence initiatives have primarily focused on recognizing and rewarding individual teaching excellence (D'Andrea 2007; Skelton 2007). Although there are various award schemes with different types of assessment criteria, teaching excellence appears to be typically defined within a single list of criteria with awardees primarily demonstrating and/or providing evidence of specific levels of expertise, competencies and achievements (Leibowitz et al. 2012). Shephard et al. (2010) address concerns and potential dangers of an over-reliance on narrow or rigid conceptions of excellence used within national teaching awards in terms of impacting on the way in which teaching excellence is understood, and in turn inhibiting the way in which it is practised in higher education.

National initiatives, such as the TEF and the UTE programme, appear to promote a monolithic view of teaching excellence which relies on predetermined measures of performance or outcomes. They also: (1) demonstrate the collective responsibility of the whole institution to achieve teaching excellence; (2) enable comparisons to be drawn across institutions; (3) act as a means for stimulating competition and improvements through rewards and incentives. However, such initiatives have come under criticism. The first criteria employed within the UTE programme, as discussed earlier, was condemned for its lack of emphasis on teaching and learning processes, particularly due to its inefficiency in assessing the impact of student learning outcomes, and has since been adapted in the second round of evaluations (Ying and Wang 2015; Greatbatch and Holland 2016).

In its preliminary stages TEF has already come under criticism with Robinson and Hilli (2016: 155) highlighting that it is primarily driven by outcomes/measures of performance and that 'teaching is more than can be counted or measured'. This suggests the need for a more accurate representation of teaching excellence that is otherwise being addressed within the TEF (Robinson and Hilli 2016). Specifically, the criteria presently underpinning the TEF appear to lack consideration of factors which have been found to contribute to high quality teaching in education, such as subject-matter expertise (Ashwin 2017). Therefore, if measures within the TEF do not reflect reality then institutions will chase false summits and the sector risks institutional gaming (Ashwin 2017) because the costs of receiving a poor rating in terms of rankings are too high.

There are some exceptions to initiatives which rely on pre-determined measures, with the Competition for Teaching Excellence (CfTE) in Germany appearing to go some way to mitigate a standardized measure and definition of teaching excellence. Brockerhoff et al. (2014) point out the diverse nature of the CfTE criteria in taking into consideration achievements as well as future aspirations to improve teaching quality. The criteria also emphasize a collective institutional approach to achieving teaching excellence, which is presented as a multi-faceted concept that manifests itself through various structural and cultural activities integrated within an institution intended to drive quality. However, Brockerhoff et al. also acknowledge that the diversity of conceptions may also prove to be problematic as it becomes difficult to compare and generalize across disciplines and institutions.

UK Teaching Excellence Framework case study

In the UK, the implications of introducing a teaching excellence framework to monitor and assess teaching quality at an institutional level have yet to be realized. However, the framework has already come under criticism of its use of proxy measures to define teaching excellence (Robinson and Hilli 2016), as discussed earlier. Findings from previous research have specifically highlighted differences between students' and teachers' interpretations of teaching excellence and proposed models of teaching excellence (Skelton 2005). For instance, Vielba and Hillier (2000 in Skelton 2005) revealed variations between students' and teachers' perceptions and selection criteria underpinning teaching excellence within the National Teaching Fellowship Scheme (NTFS). Students and teachers placed greater emphasis on personal attributes, for example, being passionate and enthusiastic and possessing subject-matter knowledge rather than evidence of contributions to high-quality resources and teaching and learning initiatives (Vielba and Hiller 2000 in Skelton 2005). Furthermore, using a repertory grid methodology (Kelly 1955), Hillier and Vielba (2001) similarly revealed that students and teachers focused on personal attributes of a teacher and the quality of their levels of engagement and interactions with students when describing teaching excellence. Given that the TEF is the first initiative of its kind in the UK, and in light of the financial and reputational implications that it will have for the higher education sector (Department for Business Innovation and Skills 2016; Department of Education 2016), it is important to explore teachers' and students' views about whether the TEF has the potential to drive up teaching excellence across the higher education sector.

Hence, repertory grid interviews were undertaken with students and teachers across various UK institutions in order to (a) elicit their views about teaching excellence in terms of the ways in which it is/can be measured, and (b) explore how well these interpretations align with the proxy metrics of teaching excellence within the TEF. The repertory grid methodology is an interviewing technique initially developed by Kelly (1955) for patients to provide information on their issues and develop ways to address them through defining and exploring constructs that were significant to them. It has since been adopted in various fields, and is used to elicit individuals' thoughts about a given topic termed as constructs (Bernard and Flitman 2002). The elements are referred to as the items being described or discussed and are typically presented to participants in a series of triads, which are distinguished by two ends of a continuum ('similar pole' and 'contrast pole'). For example, two siblings may be similar in that they are ambitious while the third is different because they lack ambition.

In this case study, the elements under focus were metrics used to measure/ represent teaching excellence. The metrics selected were institutional and national measures of teaching excellence, particularly those used with the TEF to draw out a number of items that were relevant in the present time. Examples of elements included: National Student Survey (NSS), Postgraduate Taught Experience Survey (PTES), Module Evaluation Questionnaires (MEQ), Higher Education Academy National Teaching Fellowships (NTFs), Staff Continuing Professional Development (CPD), Staff Development and Performance Review (DPR), and Staff Postgraduate Certificate in Higher Education qualification (PGCHE). Around fifty elements were included in total. Students and teachers were asked to identify two elements which they thought were similar in some way (mark with an S), and one which they thought was different from the other two in some way (marked with an X) as shown in Figure 1.2. Critically, they were then asked to describe the rationale for their choice and it is this rationale that elicits the factors that are key to the individual when defining teaching excellence.

Through the repertory grid various interpretations of each of the elements, that is measures of teaching excellence, were elicited by the students and teachers. This highlights the complexity of defining, and in turn, measuring teaching excellence. Table 1.2 illustrates examples of teachers' similar constructs grouped by themes. When describing how each of the elements were similar, teachers grouped them

	DPR outcomes	Student attendance	Good honours degree	Staff PGCHE	HEA National Teaching Fellowships	Staff CPD	MEQ	NSS	PTES	
Student focused		S	S			X				**Staff focused**

FIGURE 1.2 Example of repertory grid

TABLE 1.2 Examples of teachers' similar constructs grouped by themes

Student outcomes	Staff development/ excellence	Quality assurance/ reward & recognition	Influenced by the institution
No. & type of contact hours/Grade Point Average (GPA)	HEA National Teaching Fellowships/Staff Promotion	External evaluation/ Independent panel review	Teaching & Learning Research/Student ratings (Rate my Professor)
Retention & continuation/Degree completion	Reflections on practice/DPR outcomes	External examiner role/Professorship in teaching and learning	Module mean mark & deviation/peer teaching observation feedback
Retention & continuation/Student attendance	Staff CPD/Staff PGCHE qualifications	Staff student ratio/ Academic services spend	Student learning gain or value added/student extra-curricular engagement

predominately as similar due to being of the opinion that they could be directly influenced by the institution, such as student ratings, through for example, teaching and learning processes. Table 1.3 illustrates examples of students' similar constructs also grouped by themes. Students typically described the elements as being similar due to their association with student-centred methodologies and desirable student learning outcomes.

TABLE 1.3 Examples of students' similar constructs grouped by themes

Student-centred/student outcomes	Student satisfaction	Staff excellence
Student learning gain or value added/module mean mark & deviation	Student ratings (Rate my Professor)/Retention & continuation	Teaching awards/degree completion
Good honours degree/MEQ	Staff student ratio/student ratings (Rate my Professor)	Teaching awards/student attendance
Student extra-curricular engagement/degree completion	PTES/alumni ratings	Degree completion/student ratings (Rate my Professor)

Both students and teachers who participated in the repertory grid exercise adopted more psychologized rather than performative discourses of teaching excellence, which involves the quality of teacher–student relationships. Skelton (2005) describes four ways in which teaching excellence is conceptualized within the higher education sector, with psychologized being the most prominent and performative growing in popularity. In contrast to psychologized discourses of teaching excellence, performative discourses focus on institutions' measurements of performance such as continuation rates, capacity to recruit students from an international higher education market and produce highly skilled graduates which contribute to the social and economic growth of society (Skelton 2005). Whilst these discourses are not mutually exclusive it does raise questions regarding the alignment of definitions of teaching excellence at the macro-, meso- and micro-level.

Although both students and teachers recognized the intended purposes and value of the TEF, they felt that its core metrics did not adequately define teaching excellence, which in turn supports previously raised questions around whether the TEF has the potential to drive up teaching excellence. Furthermore, the findings are in line with earlier research which highlights an ongoing conflict between psychologized and performative understandings of teaching excellence.

Conclusion – implications for policy and practice

This chapter has explored similarities/comparisons between the ways in which teaching excellence is defined globally, provided a critique of the definitions used within teaching excellence initiatives, and investigated how well these align with the perceptions of teachers and students. It has established that teaching excellence does not appear to be a stable aggregate but something that is socially and culturally constructed (Brusoni et al. 2014) and influenced over time (Greatbatch and Holland 2016). It seems inevitable that, to some degree, individuals, institutions and the government/state will always differ in their focus on the way that teaching excellence should be defined and, in turn, measured. In this respect issues of power and whose interests are being served (such as those of students or institutions) remains a contentious issue some two decades after being raised by McLean (2001).

Teaching excellence within the literature has very much focused on what is recognized as excellence in teaching by institutional and national teaching award schemes introduced worldwide. Despite definitions varying within and between these award schemes, they are typically characterized by a specific set of criteria (Leibowitz et al. 2012) raising potential concerns around constricting the way in which teaching excellence is understood (Shephard et al. 2010). National initiatives such as the TEF, in which teaching excellence is characterized through measures of performance or outcomes, allow for effective benchmarking of teaching quality across institutions where previously this has not been possible. Using the teaching excellence framework as a case study, conclusions from the repertory grid exercise confirmed previous research findings (see, for example, Skelton 2005) of a conflict between students' and teachers' perceptions of teaching excellence and proposed models of teaching excellence. These perceptions are difficult to assess and translate into measurable outcomes of performance required for quality assurance purposes (Hillier and Vielba 2001; Skelton 2005). Although national initiatives such as the TEF enable comparisons to be drawn between institutions and then subsequently ranked, it is apparent that they potentially run the risk of teaching excellence becoming promoted as a tick box exercise (Ashwin 2017), moulding the way in which teaching excellence is viewed and subsequently practised (Burke et al. 2015). Despite this, it appears that in light of the growing challenges of massification (De Courcy 2015; Üstünlüoğlu 2016), rapid changes in teaching practices to support modern day learning (De Courcy 2015), and the need to instill work-readiness and employability skills within graduates (Williams 2013; Burke et al. 2015), for many countries these kinds of national teaching excellence initiatives will be the way forward. It remains to be seen how well they will contribute to the fair and accurate assessment of teaching excellence across the higher education sector.

References

Archibong, I. A. and Nja, M. E. (2011) 'Towards improved teaching effectiveness in Nigerian public universities: instrument design and validation', *Higher Education Studies*, 1(2): 78–91.

Aregbeyen, O. (2010) 'Students perceptions of effective teaching and effective lecturer characteristics at the University of Ibadan, Nigeria', *Pakistan Journal of Social Sciences*, 7(2): 62–69.

Ashwin, P. W. H. (2017) 'What is the Teaching Excellence Framework in the United Kingdom, and will it work?', *International Higher Education*, 88: 10–11.

Australian Government Department of Education and Training (2017) *Australian awards for university teaching*. Online. Available at www.education.gov.au/australian-awards-university-teaching (accessed 23 February 2017).

Bernard, T. and Flitman, A. (2002) 'Using Repertory Grid Analysis to gather qualitative data for information systems research', *Proceedings of the 15th Australasian Conference on Information Systems, ACIS 2002*, 98.

Bishop, D. (2016) *Clarity of purpose in the TEF and the REF*. Online. Available at www.timeshighereducation.com/blog/clarity-purpose-tef-and-ref (accessed 16 March 2017).

Blair, E. and Valdez Noel, K. (2014) 'Improving higher education practice through student evaluation systems: is the student voice being heard?', *Assessment & Evaluation in Higher Education*, 39(7): 879–894.

Brockerhoff, L., Stensaker, B. and Huisman, J. (2014) 'Prescriptions and perceptions of teaching excellence: a study of the national "Wettbewerb Exzellente Lehre" initiative in Germany', *Quality in Higher Education*, 20(3): 235–254.

Brown, M. E. (2011) 'Standing up for teaching: the "crime" of striving for excellence', *Journal of Pedagogic Development*, 1(2): 52–57.

Brusoni, M., Damian, R., Sauri, J. G., Jackson, S., Kömürcügil, H., Malmedy, M., Matveeva, O., Motova, G., Pisarz, S., Pol, P., Rostlund, A., Soboleva, E., Tavares, O. and Zobel, L. (2014) 'The concept of excellence in higher education', *Occasional Papers 20*, Brussels: European Association for Quality Assurance in Higher Education (ENQA).

Burke, P. J., Stevenson, J. and Whelan, P. (2015) 'Teaching "excellence" and pedagogic stratification in higher education', *International Studies in Widening Participation*, 2(2): 29–43.

Chen, J., Brown, G. T. L., Hattie, J. A. C. and Millward, P. (2012) 'Teachers' conceptions of excellent teaching and its relationships to self-reported teaching practices', *Teaching and Teacher Education*, 28(7): 936–947.

D'Andrea, V. M. (2007) 'National strategies for promoting excellence in teaching', in A. Skelton (ed.) *International perspectives on teaching excellence in higher education: improving knowledge and practice*, 169–182, London: Routledge.

De Courcy, E. (2015) 'Defining and measuring teaching excellence in higher education in the 21st century', *College Quarterly*, 18(1). Online. Available at http://files.eric.ed.gov/fulltext/EJ1070007.pdf (accessed 16 March 2017).

Department for Business Innovation and Skills (2016) *Teaching Excellence Framework: technical consultation for year two*, May 2016. Online. Available at www.gov.uk/government/uploads/system/uploads/attachment_data/file/523340/bis-16-262-teaching-excellence-framework-techcon.pdf (accessed 16 March 2017).

Department of Education (2016) *Teaching Excellence Framework: year two specification*, September 2016. Online. Available at www.gov.uk/government/publications/teaching-excellence-framework-year-2-specification (accessed 16 March 2017).

Denson, N., Loveday, T. and Dalton, H. (2010) 'Student evaluation of courses: what predicts satisfaction?', *Higher Education Research & Development*, 29(4): 339–356.

Devlin, M. and Samarawickrema, G. (2010) 'The criteria of effective teaching in a changing higher education context', *Higher Education Research & Development*, 29(2): 111–124.

Dinham, S. (2013) 'The quality teaching movement in Australia encounters difficult terrain: a personal perspective', *Australian Journal of Education*, 57(2): 91–106.

Elton, L. (1998) 'Dimensions of excellence in university teaching', *The International Journal for Academic Development*, 3(1): 3–11.

Fitzmaurice, M. (2010) 'Considering teaching in higher education as a practice', *Teaching in Higher Education*, 15(1): 45–55.

Flodén, J. (2016) 'The impact of student feedback on teaching in higher education', *Assessment & Evaluation in Higher Education*, 1–15. Online. Available at http://doi.org/10.1080/02602938.2016.1224997 (accessed 16 March 2017).

Gafoor, K. A. and Shilna, V. (2013) *Need for equipping teachers for quality higher education: exploring how teachers in Kerala perceive quality practices in higher education*. Online. Available at http://files.eric.ed.gov/fulltext/ED545359.pdf (accessed 16 March 2017).

Gibbs, G. (2008) *Designing teaching award schemes*, York: Higher Education Academy.

Greatbatch, D. and Holland, J. (2016) *Teaching quality in higher education: literature review and qualitative research*, Department for Business, Innovation and Skills. Online. Available at www.gov.uk/government/uploads/system/uploads/attachment_data/file/524495/he-teaching-quality-literature-review-qualitative-research.pdf (accessed 16 March 2017).

Gunn, V. and Fisk, A. (2013) *Considering teaching excellence in higher education: 2007–2013: a literature review since the CHERI Report 2007*, York: Higher Education Academy.

Hammer, D., Piascik, P., Medina, M., Pittenger, A., Rose, R., Creekmore, F., Soltis, R., Bouldin, A., Schwarz, L. and Scott, S. (2010) 'Recognition of teaching excellence', *American Journal of Pharmaceutical Education*, 74(9): 164–176.

Higher Education Academy (2015) *National Fellowship Teaching Scheme. Celebrating excellent practice and outstanding achievement*. Online. Available at www.heacademy.ac.uk/individuals/national-teaching-fellowship-scheme (accessed 16 March 2017).

Hillier, Y. and Vielba, C. (2001) *Perceptions of excellence: personal constructs of excellence in teaching and learning*, paper presented at the Institute of Learning and Teaching Annual Conference held July 2001 at University of York.

Indian Honour (2017) *Inspired teacher awards*. Online. Available at www.indianhonour.com/inspired-teacher-awards (accessed 16 March 2017).

Jiang, K. (2010) 'Undergraduate teaching evaluation in China: progress and debate', *International Higher Education*, 58: 15–17.

Keeley, J. W., Christopher A. N. and Buskist, W. (2012) 'Emerging evidence for excellent teaching across borders', in J. E. Groccia, M. A. T. Alsudairi and W. Buskist (eds) *Handbook of college and university teaching: a global perspective*, 374–390, Thousand Oaks, CA: SAGE Publications.

Keeley, J. W., Ismail, E. and Buskist, W. (2016) 'Excellent teachers' perspectives on excellent teaching', *Teaching of Psychology*, 43(3): 175–179.

Kelly, G. A. (1955) *The psychology of personal constructs*, New York: W. W. Norton & Company.

Land, R. and Gordon, G. (2015) *Teaching excellence initiatives: modalities and operational factors*, York: Higher Education Academy.

Leibowitz, B., Farmer, J. and Franklin, M. (2012) *Teaching excellence awards in South Africa: a national study*, HE Monitor, 13. Online. Available at www.che.ac.za/media_and_publications/higher-education-monitor/higher-education-monitor-13-teaching-excellence (accessed 17 March 2017).

Lemass, B. and Stace, R. (2010) 'Towards teaching and research parity: a teaching quality and reward framework', *Perspectives: Policy and Practice in Higher Education*, 14(1): 21–27.

Liu, S., Keeley, J. W. and Buskist, W. (2015) 'Chinese college students' perceptions of characteristics of excellent teachers', *Teaching of Psychology*, 42(1): 83–86.

Luckett, K. (2010) 'A "quality revolution" constrained? A critical reflection on quality assurance methodology from the South African higher education context', *Quality in Higher Education*, 16(1): 71–75.

Macfarlane, B. (2007) 'Beyond performance in teaching excellence', in A. Skelton (ed.) *International perspectives on teaching excellence in higher education: improving knowledge and practice*, 48–59, London and New York: Routledge.

McLean, M. (2001) 'Rewarding teaching excellence. Can we measure teaching "excellence"? Who should be the judge?', *Medical Teacher*, 23(1): 6–11.

Mohd. Deni, A. R., Zainal, Z. I. and Malakolunthu, S. (2014) 'Improving teaching in higher education in Malaysia: issues and challenges', *Journal of Further and Higher Education*, 38(5): 656–673.

Robinson, W. and Hilli, A. (2016) 'The English Teaching Excellence Framework and professionalising teaching and learning in research-intensive universities: an exploration of opportunities, challenges, rewards and values from a recent empirical study', *Foro de Educación*, 14(21): 151–165.

Sangoleye, S. A. and Kolawole, C. O. O. (2016) 'A critique of selected instructional strategies in higher institutions in Nigeria', *Journal of Education and Practice*, 7(7): 78–84.

Shephard, K., Harland, T., Stein, S. and Tidswell, T. (2010) 'Preparing an application for a higher-education teaching-excellence award: whose foot fits Cinderella's shoe?', *Journal of Higher Education Policy and Management*, 33(1): 47–56.

Skelton, A. (2005) *Understanding teaching excellence in higher education: towards a critical approach*, London: Routledge.

Skelton, A. (ed.) (2007) *International perspectives on teaching excellence in higher education: improving knowledge and practice*, London: Routledge.

Šteh, B., Kalin, J. and Mažgon, J. (2014) 'The role and responsibility of teachers and students in university studies: a comparative analysis of the views expressed by pedagogy students', *Zbornik Instituta za pedagoska istrazivanja*, 46(1): 50–68.

Üstünlüoğlu, E. (2016) 'Teaching quality matters in higher education: a case study from Turkey and Slovakia', *Teachers and Teaching*, 23(3): 367–382.

Williams, J. (2013) *Consuming higher education: why learning can't be bought*, London and New York: Bloomsbury.

Yin, H. and Wang, W. (2015) 'Assessing and improving the quality of undergraduate teaching in China: the Course Experience Questionnaire', *Assessment & Evaluation in Higher Education*, 40(8): 1032–1049.

Critical friend commentary

Kathy Luckett

It is not surprising that some scepticism has been expressed by the scholarship of the teaching and learning community in the UK about the validity of the information on teaching excellence to be provided by the Teaching Excellence Framework (TEF), as Gakhal notes (see also Ashwin 2017), and particularly its potential to improve the quality of teaching. I argue first that the reasons for this scepticism can be located in the limitations of an externally driven accountability model of quality assurance to adequately conceptualize teaching (and learning) and thus to engage with the self-understandings and life-worlds of academics, and second that the TEF's evaluation methodology will lead to compliance rather than improvement, and social reproduction rather than transformation. These remarks are informed by a critical/social realist perspective (Archer 1995; 2000; 2003; Bhaskar 2016) and framed by my teaching in a southern context where definitions of teaching excellence must include dealing with difference and diversity, which may well involve challenging the social and institutional norms and structures that historically have caused difference and inequality.

While there is no agreement on definitions of teaching excellence, teaching is widely understood to be a complex intentional activity that draws on personal identities, cognitive and communicative powers, emotions and motivations – that is the agency of both teachers and learners (Packer and Goicoechea 2000). But learning is not entirely an outcome of agency. Teachers and learners are thrown into pre-existing socially and culturally structured worlds that shape and constrain their interaction. Learning is an emergent property from complex human interactions that may or may not emerge because it occurs in open systems where its emergence may be enabled or blocked by a range of contingent factors located in its context. All of this emphasizes the intentional, concept- and context-dependent nature of teaching. If we want to improve or change teaching practice, we must have a hermeneutic starting point – namely engage with the reasoning and self-understandings of teachers. This is particularly pertinent in Southern contexts where definitions of excellent teaching are linked to working for social justice and social transformation; where academics are challenged not only to teach for critical and transformative conceptual change in their students, but also to interrogate their own assumptions and practices (Leibowitz and Bozalek 2016). In these contexts, excellent teaching entails engaging with the self-understandings of academics and developing high levels of reflexivity in order to self-transform and then challenge the social structures, institutional hierarchies, cultural norms and epistemic assumptions that have shaped inherited teaching practices.

References

Archer, M. (1995) *Realist social theory: the morphonogenetic approach*, Cambridge: Cambridge University Press.

Archer, M. (2000) *Being human: the problem of agency*, Cambridge: Cambridge University Press.

Archer, M. (2003) *Structure, agency and the internal conversation*, Cambridge: Cambridge University Press.

Ashwin, P. (2017) 'What is the Teaching Excellence Framework in the United Kingdom, and will it work?', *International Higher Education*, 88: 10–11.

Bhaskar, R. (2016) *Enlightened common sense: the philosophy of critical realism*, London: Routledge.

Leibowitz, B. and Bozalek, V. (2016) 'The scholarship of teaching and learning from a social justice perspective', *Teaching in Higher Education*, 21(2): 109–122.

Packer, M. J. and Goicoechea, J. (2000) 'Sociocultural and constructivist theories of learning: ontology, not just epistemology', *Educational Psychologist*, 35: 227–241.

2

WHAT OUTCOMES ARE WE TRYING TO ACHIEVE FROM EXCELLENT TEACHING AND WHY ARE THEY SO DIFFICULT TO MEASURE?

Caroline Wilson

Introduction

Imagine you are sitting on a plane and see an advertisement on the headrest in front of you that inspires you take a holiday at the destination shown. The performance of advertisers and marketers is measured according to tangible uplifts in bookings at the time the adverts are live. But what if your circumstances do not allow you to take your holiday at this inspiring destination for the next four or five years? Some outcomes take time to come to fruition. Educational institutes may be unable to capture the measurable achievement of future peacemakers, lifesavers, innovators or leaders until (too) long after graduation to claim credit. Further, these same future achievers will have been moulded by experiences at home, school, or with subsequent employers that all contribute to their feats. As Broadbent (2007) argues, it is impossible to disentangle the provision of education from the participant involvement of the student, who is the key to the process and any creditable outcomes. Issues of gestation and entanglement arise when trying to identify and measure excellent teaching as localized cause and effect: as if the student is being involved in some kind of experiment and affected by the experience in some measurable way.

This chapter assumes that teaching excellence is desirable in that it is socially beneficial, aiding the development of human capital and boosting economic productivity (Braun and Bily 2013). But it seeks clarity over the frequently proxy, or indirect, measures often used in the absence of direct measurements of the desired phenomena to assess 'excellence'. It also explores the nature of the 'outcome variable' which is the result of excellent teaching: is it the proportion of students who achieve 'good degrees', however that may be defined, or graduate employment statistics? Or is it, as Bryson (2015) argues, about what a student is 'becoming', both as a learner and as a future professional, which may, or may not, be fully captured by measuring the difference, or distance travelled, between student achievement on entry and on graduation?

The chapter reviews the international literature for how others have modelled the measurement of teaching excellence and critiqued the performance of such modelling both from a policy stance and empirically. The chapter then examines the ongoing investigation of alternative direct measures of teaching excellence and concludes by highlighting some of the outstanding issues and challenges presenting the measurement of teaching excellence.

Current models of measuring teaching excellence

According to the Organisation for Economic Co-operation and Development (OECD) (2013), higher education has a critical role to play in global economic prosperity and social well-being in the 21st century, due to the current and future reliance on skills and human capital. This demand for skills has led to a rapid expansion of the higher education sector through growth in existing provision, and also to the establishment of new types of providers (ibid.). Sector growth is likely to continue by as much as 400 per cent by 2030, requiring weekly openings of a new university somewhere in the world (Global High Level Policy Forum 2015). Growth brings concurrent increases in cost and changes in funding are driving the desire for universities to deliver 'more, more explicitly, and to deliver demonstrable quality' (Stensaker and Sweetman 2014: 251). The definitions of teaching excellence are fully explored by Sandeep Gakhal in Chapter 1 of this edition, as is the lack of agreed criteria due to the heterogeneity of institutions, of degrees and ways of teaching, of students and of contexts. A current definition that appears prominent is the function of teaching excellence as a measure to judge quality. One way to judge quality is the systematic collection of information (Patton 2008). Good evaluation, in the form of monitoring programmes and student behaviour, with explicit indicators and measures of success, is an essential responsibility of university leadership because it leads to improvement (Thomas 2012).

Evaluation of university output as a result of (excellent) teaching can be viewed at several levels, for example: course or department, campus or state or system (Sullivan et al. 2012). This latter macro-level of evaluation generally requires aggregated data at the campus rather than individual teacher level (ibid.). It is this macro-level which is the concern of this chapter, as it is this level which is currently exerting new formal pressures on the sector to demonstrate improved performance. When teaching excellence becomes part of a bigger framework to judge quality across, rather than within a single university, there is a tendency to focus on 'crude metrics' rather than on supportive judgements that allow individuals to make 'thoughtful improvement' (London Mathematical Society 2015: 3–5). As a result, this chapter does not consider methods suitable for course or department level assessments of quality, such as peer observation of teaching or the role of the external examiner.

Currently, macro-level assessments of teaching excellence rely on proxy 'input' measures such as learning environment and resources, and 'output' measures such as rankings (OECD 2013). Inputs are defined by the OECD as the resources used

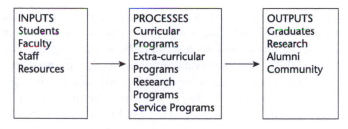

FIGURE 2.1 Systems view of the higher education system
Source: Chinta et al. (2016)

to achieve outputs, which are the products and services of interventions (to encourage students to achieve) and lead to outcomes, the short and medium term effects, and impact, the long term effects (OECD 2010), although it should be acknowledged that these terms are often used inconsistently (Simister 2010).

While such a linear model is argued to be an appropriate performance evaluation model for higher education institutions, there is little guidance for choosing appropriate metrics and benchmarks for such a model (Chinta et al. 2016). Figure 2.1 shows such a linear model adapted for higher education, and although inconsistent in terminology, has a similar linear path to that described above with indicative inputs (for example, students entering the system), and value-added processes transforming those inputs (for example, learning processes) which generate outputs (for example, graduates).

Using the model in Figure 2.1, (excellent) teachers are a key input and their efforts through delivery of classes, for instance, are key processes. The model can be elaborated by greater focus on the factors which lead to quality learning, frequently conceptualized as comprising the student experience or student engagement. While sometimes used interchangeably and referring to similar or overlapping concepts, Kandiko (2012) argues that there is a critical difference: while experience infers activities and opportunities which the students are offered, engagement involves students having responsibilities as learners rather than considering themselves as passive receivers. Excellent teaching has a central role in both these overlapping concepts. Although engagement is, at face value, personal to the student, the curriculum should be designed to promote engagement, develop a sense of belonging, foster relationships between students and teachers, and build students' capacities to ensure they are able to fully participate in their learning (Thomas 2012). Experience and engagement are thus distinct process variables that would be desirable to measure in an evaluation model. Experience is frequently assessed via student surveys. Indicators of engagement can be evidenced by observed behaviour, such as attendance or use of university facilities, and also by figures for retention and completion (Thomas 2012).

The evaluation model can be enhanced by greater elaboration of the outputs of excellent teaching. These have been broadly categorized as: grades or degree classifications, self-report surveys, standardized tests, qualitative measures of student development, such as portfolios, or a mixture of these methods (McGrath et al. 2015). Other methods of evaluating teaching and learning include labour market outcomes, quality assurance and accreditation, benchmarking and comparison (Braun and Bily 2013). There are several proposals for exactly what standardized tests and other ways of evidencing achievement should look for. It is argued that students cannot learn the knowledge they need for an uncertain and rapidly changing future, but that there are competencies which will be essential to help them cope with this uncertainty (Buckingham Shum and Crick 2016). Table 2.1 summarizes these competencies from various authors.

The reviewed literature suggests that the earlier discussed outlined linear model is too simplistic for the purposes of fully assessing the quality of teaching and learning. Based on the literature, Figure 2.2 proposes that experience, in terms of learning opportunities, course structure design and support on offer to students, underpins achievement. This creates the foundation for students to engage with their study and results in attainment. Figure 2.2 also shows the metrics associated with each of these three features, which broadly align with the linear model comprising *inputs* such as contact hours, *outputs* such as continuation, and *outcomes*, such as employment. It also illustrates that not all teaching is excellent. 'Threshold quality teaching' is what universities should routinely provide and is distinct from excellent teaching, although the difference between the two is insufficiently articulated (Gunn and Fisk 2013: 10).

It should be acknowledged that however improved or detailed, a linear model cannot fully capture the complexity of a holistic student experience (Bryson 2015), or how the manner of delivery is as important as what is delivered (Thomas 2012).

Critiques of the linear input-output-outcome model

This section reviews some of the examples of teaching excellence metrics discussed so far in terms of their efficacy as a means to monitor and evaluate the progress of students on their journey through their studies and beyond. It also explores evidence of the degree to which such metrics measure what they purport to measure. Controversies around current metrics appear to fall into three categories. The first is how to untangle university provision from other factors. The second is whether the metrics and rankings measure what they intend to measure. The third is the impact of being measured and whether the act of measurement serves to improve or deflect from improved performance.

Student engagement was identified in the previous section as having a positive relationship with knowledge acquisition and cognitive growth. This hypothesized relationship presents the first entanglement issue in assessment of university performance. Many factors associated with engagement are within the student's control in terms of quantity, as in hours of attendance, and qualitatively, as in the extent to which students choose to take an active part in what the university has to offer (Dollinger et al. 2008; Ramsden 2013). Other student-oriented factors include their levels of motivation (Barkley 2010), levels of trust in self/others, belonging,

TABLE 2.1 Review of competencies needed by future graduates

Critical thinking;	Solving complex problems;	Mindful agency;	Cognitive;	Critical thinking;	Content knowledge;
Creativity;	Thinking critically;	Sense-making;	Methodological;	Discipline knowledge;	Ability to complete tasks;
Collaboration;	Effective (intercultural) communication;	Creativity;	Technological;	Problem solving;	Use knowledge, skills and personal, social and/or methodological abilities;
Metacognition;	Collaborative working;	Curiosity;	Interpersonal;	Teamwork;	
Motivation	Adaptability;	Belonging;	Systemic (ability to understand whole systems);	Communication;	Citizenship or confidence;
(Lai and Viering 2012)	Effectiveness;	Collaboration;	Linguistic	Professional skills, ethics and values;	Respect for diversity
	Independent learners	Hope;	(Gonzalez and Wagenaar 2008)	Creativity and learning to learn	(McGrath et al. 2015)
	(National Research Council 2011)	Optimism;		(Braun and Bily 2013)	
		Orientation to learning			
		(Crick et al. 2013)			

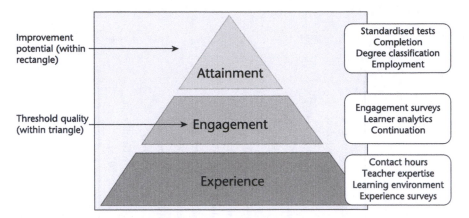

FIGURE 2.2 Proposed evaluation model to evidence teaching excellence

and social capital (Zepke 2015). The student is thus not an 'inert input' but part of the process, as are others, such as professional bodies, employers and community groups (Broadbent 2007: 195).

Similarly there are other metrics used to measure teaching excellence that can be difficult to separate from external factors. Raw employment data does not measure an institution's capability at creating employable graduates. The former can be subject to a range of factors including gender, those associated with the student's home region, age, ethnicity and subject of study (Blyth and Cleminson 2016). Raw data on employment can also be affected by developments extraneous to higher education, such as the state of the labour market, and the recruiting behaviour of employers (McGrath et al. 2015).

The second category of critique is around whether proxy metrics are adequate to measure what they intend to measure. Proxy measures of learning are 'efficient' (McGrath et al. 2015: 46) as they are readily available and do not involve the cost and time commitment of new initiatives. A literature review conducted recently in the UK found that the most common measures used to assess teaching quality included test scores and retention rates, student surveys and feedback from employers (Strang et al. 2016). The review found a 'striking lack of evidence' (ibid.: 5) for the presumed causality between the measures or indicators used and whether these truly capture the dependent variable; what students have learned or become. Of the twenty-five indicators identified in the review assumed to assess teaching quality, eighteen were supported by very weak measurement data.

Student surveys are frequently used as a proxy metric of teaching quality. A student's overall evaluation of services received as part of their educational experience has found to contain seven dimensions (for example: input quality, curriculum, academic facilities, industry interaction, interaction quality, support facilities and non-academic processes) (Jain et al. 2013). However, student evaluations of teaching appear to be biased by preconceptions of quality which reinforce the dominant culture: a breakdown of national student satisfaction data compared with staff data show that students are more likely to be satisfied when taught by teachers who are white, full professors and holding doctorates (Bell and Brooks 2016).

The notion that student satisfaction equates with success has been challenged by the observation that satisfaction is not the core objective of a university. Providing a high quality education may at times be challenging rather than satisfying (Lawson et al. 2012). A weakness of using student opinion as a proxy for excellence is that, at the point they are asked, new graduates are not always fully aware of the benefits of their experience and how it will help them in their careers (Hervey and Wood 2016). A longitudinal case study of law students re-interviewed several years after graduation found that previously unpopular learning methods were much more appreciated when their employability value became clear (ibid.). Attaching too much weight to immediate and short term student satisfaction may lead to the avoidance of forms of teaching that students find challenging. Moreover, achieving student satisfaction might be at odds with other competing priorities, such as an agenda to widen participation in that dissatisfaction is likely to be higher among some non-traditional students (Nevill and Rhodes 2004; Neves and Hillman 2016). Arguably student satisfaction is such a crude indicator as to give only a partial picture of performance, and which is more useful as an internal monitoring measure identifying issues to follow-up rather than a measure of success (Lawson et al. 2012).

Counting contact hours has also been criticized as an indicator of quality, with a quantitative approach failing to account for the quality of contact and what is achieved as a result of it (Docherty 2011). Contact time may be available but not taken up if perceived by students to lack quality (Macfarlane 2016). Furthermore, subjects with an emphasis on practical skills tend to involve higher amounts of contact time, so it would be difficult to make cross-discipline comparisons (Quality Assurance Agency 2011). One of the key functions of higher education is to support students in establishing their own autonomy as independent learners, where quality might be implied by a gradually reduced requirement for contact hours (Docherty 2011).

Retention of students through to completion of their programme of study is another proxy output measure of quality which is associated with student success. In an analysis of data from nineteen higher education institutions in Colombia, no relationship was found between retention rates and test scores required to graduate (Martínez et al. 2015). A relationship was found between retention and a composite 'accreditation score' based on several institutional output indicators, such as student-teacher ratio, teacher innovation and administrative efficiency (ibid.). This serves to reinforce the lack of certainty of a linear model in which output measures can be presumed to help predict outcomes.

The third area of controversy around metrics is the impact of being measured and the potential to deflect from improved performance. A tension exists between the desire of stakeholders outside of the classroom for clear evidence that students are acquiring knowledge and skills as a result of their studies, and those inside the classroom who may feel that this monitoring activity serves institutional and other external demands rather than improving the learning experience (Borden and

Peters 2014). The use of a fixed set of indicators risks a calculating, transactional approach in which metrics and performance can be manipulated (Broadbent 2007; London Mathematical Society 2015).

The limitations of proxy and partial measures of teaching excellence perhaps explain why a frequent method to judge the quality of teaching and learning is not to rely on single indicators, but to make assessments using a 'basket of measures' where several indicators are bundled together to calculate an overall performance score (Greatbatch and Holland 2016: 5). These include global and elite ranking systems such as Academic Ranking of World Universities (ARWU) calculated by Shanghai Jiao Tong University, the QS World University Rankings and the Times Higher Education (THE) World University Rankings. The THE ranking is the only one of those listed which includes a substantive (30%) of its criteria to teaching factors: survey data about the higher education institution's reputation, staff to student ratio, doctorate to bachelor ratio, the proportion of academic staff with doctorates and institutional income (Greatbatch and Holland 2016). However, as is clear from this list, all of the teaching data is a proxy for, rather than direct information about, quality of teaching. Although influential both to institutional reputation and student choices (Gibbons et al. 2015), such rankings are more frequently based on research metrics than those assessing teaching (Greatbatch and Holland 2016). This is because research metrics are better established and there are too many differences in expectations of teaching in different parts of the globe. In addition, there is the allied challenge of collecting internationally comparable data, and also a lack of an agreed direct method to assess the added value provided by teaching (Liu and Cheng 2005; Shin et al. 2011). Compared to these global rankings, national league tables commonly offer a more proportionate share of metrics associated with teaching, including ratings of teachers by students, study hours, accessibility of teachers, accessibility of class discussion, library, study abroad, attainment of generic skills, retention and employment/further study on graduation (Shin et al. 2011).

Ranking of universities as an indicator of excellence is popular with those outside the university system because the results are easy to understand and make it simple to differentiate between institutions (Williams and de Rassenfosse 2016). The counter argument is that without significant financial and other resources, it is very difficult for most universities to improve their ranking status, and that institutions ought to pull back from giving rankings the outsized priority they currently enjoy (Altbach and Hazelkorn 2017). Becoming distracted by the pursuit of status that rankings imply leads to ignoring parts of the university mission that contribute not at all, or only weakly, to rankings, and to shift focus away from local and even national purposes in favour of global standing (Tilak 2016).

A further criticism of rankings is their vulnerability to the weightings chosen and the way data is prepared for statistical analysis. Williams and de Rassenfosse (2016) examined alternative interpretations of the data used for the THE and Shanghai Jiao Tong (ARWU) rankings of universities. These were found to give preference to a certain type of performance, especially excellence in scientific research. The researchers argue that rankings become less useful the greater number of universities they include and the more diverse types of provision that they accommodate (Williams and de Rassenfosse 2016). Furthermore, although easy to understand, the rankings of lower league performers can be too stable. Commonly aggregated to compare all universities against the best, the scores of mid-table university performance relative to the best becomes increasingly less distinct, leading to many institutions scoring the same and seeing insufficient year on year movement. Critically, the problems of linearity are also found with league tables. Even when some of the metrics used to rank universities are focused on teaching excellence, they are not aligned to measures of student attainment, the central product of teaching excellence. More than 3,000 students from seventeen universities in Colombia were tested at first and final years and evidence was found of improvement in critical thinking, problem-solving and communication skills (Saavedra and Saavedra 2011). There was no correlation between the changed test scores and other measures typically used in rankings (selectivity, share of faculty with PhD, share of full-time faculty and expenditure per student), suggesting that these proxy indicators of institutional quality are not actually providing students, parents, funders and other stakeholders with a guide to which institution delivers the biggest gain in relevant skills (ibid.).

Rankings may be flawed in the extent to which they identify excellent teaching, but they are powerful. The damage to universities of performing poorly in such exercises is not just reputational; rankings can be used as a decision tool leading to re-allocation of resources towards the successful, and as a basis for allocating funds to the detriment of missions not fully represented in gathered ranking data (OECD 2013). As an example, the Teaching Excellence Framework in the UK (introduced in Chapter 1) seeks to rate university provision as a result of assessing of a basket of metrics and to recognize and reward excellent learning and teaching by giving greater freedoms to high performing institutions (Department for Business Innovation and Skills 2016). A number of other countries have devised similar comprehensive quality assurance systems, such as Brazil and Colombia (Melguizo and Wainer 2015; see also Coates 2014 for a collection of critiques of individual countries' experiences of using student learning outcomes as quality assurance measures).

The direction of travel towards audit-type uses of performance indicator measures is argued by some to present a substantial risk to autonomy. Universities thrive when they are autonomous; free to contribute to local life and the economy, with the most successful higher education systems internationally being self-directed, able to respond more swiftly and more flexibly to changing market conditions and newly presented opportunities (Eastwood 2014). Autonomy is critical to innovation, giving freedom to identify and develop international collaborations that do not immediately respond to the criteria for excellence (Borysiewicz 2016), a point which highlights again the problem of gestation introduced at the start of this chapter: that future excellence in a fast-changing world may not be identified using current criteria. When autonomy is absent, it can lead, at extremes, to the most senior levels of university management having to be too responsive to political vested interests rather than operating for global and or local benefit (Appiagyei-Atua et al. 2015).

As with rankings, the 'one size fits all' outcomes assessment of such audits risks inappropriate and inaccurate conclusions being drawn, and failure to take into account the diversity of missions in higher education globally (Corbett Broad and Davidson 2015). Positive outcomes of university missions, such as the promotion of social engagement or citizenship of students, is a case in point: social engagement is argued to be an attitude that can only be assessed as an outcome of higher education over an extended period of time, sometime after graduation (van den Wijngaard et al. 2015).

Direct measures evidence for and work in progress

Given the criticisms reviewed in the previous section about current, frequently proxy, measures of assessing successful outcomes of higher educational learning, policymakers, employers and students are all looking for a reliable way to benchmark the learning of students directly in a way which successfully transcends disciplines and international boundaries (OECD 2013). Learning outcomes are natural quality assurance tools as they set out a pre-defined objective about what a student is expected to know, understand or be able to do after a period of learning (Stensaker and Sweetman 2014). Several initiatives have tried to discover optimum ways to test both generic learning outcomes and those that are domain-based. The ongoing KoKoHs research programme in Germany is discovering how best to conduct such dual assessment with students of clusters of disciplines such as engineering, economic and social sciences, teaching and educational sciences. This clustering according to disciplines is argued to be neither too narrow nor too broad, and has been recommended to be scaled up to include more domains of learning (Zlatkin-Troitschanskaia et al. 2014).

In addition to the challenge of how to devise student assessments suitable for domain-based and generic learning outcomes, there is a further challenge of how to devise assessments which work across cultural as well as subject boundaries. The Bologna Process describes a project to ensure comparability in the standards and quality of higher education qualifications in Europe. Aligned to this, the Tuning approach was developed to assess generic and subject specific competences as identified by each subject area (González and Wagenaar 2008). Credits are awarded when specific learning outcomes have been met and are portable across the institutions of participating countries.

Such regional level frameworks are, however, insufficiently universal to serve a modern globalized education system. Students are increasingly able to study and then work without consideration of country or education system boundaries, and also to use technology to adopt new ways of learning across different locations and times (Osman et al. 2010), enabling and encouraging the building up of a personalized portfolio of learning as and when required (Sharples et al. 2006). The OECD set up an Assessment of Higher Education Learning Outcomes (AHELO) study to develop a global platform of assessing higher education learning outcomes (OECD 2013). Its remit was to look at how to accommodate different education approaches yet still assess the development of graduates in ways that were internationally comparable. Experts associated with AHELO argued against using 'raw scores' and instead called for a value-added analysis, adjusting test results to take into account different contexts and also to control for students' prior academic achievement. Accounting for context attempts to accommodate the fact that a student's proficiency at the end of their degree is the sum of more than just the effectiveness of their institution but also of previous learning and life experiences (Braun and Bily 2013). This was found problematic for at least one of the seventeen participant countries. Brazil has a system of standardized tests for undergraduates at entry and graduation and participated in AHELO, but was unable to provide any context for prior achievement, and thus was not able to demonstrate the value added by the university (Melguizo and Wainer 2015). A further problem identified has been student participation in what is an additional assessment activity that is not part of, nor contributes towards, their degree. The AHELO scheme in Australia offered \$50 vouchers for participation but still saw participation rates as low as twelve per cent in one institution (Edwards and Pearce 2014).

Final recommendations by the AHELO project team included a recommendation that any attempt to benchmark learning outcomes directly needs to continue to be only one of several components by which an institution should assess performance (Braun and Bily 2013). The project's proposals failed to be adopted due to lack of interest from universities and some countries (Morgan 2015), and also because of issues around the soundness of the measurement used, especially the difficulty of finding sufficient commonality of curriculum on which to test and compare students across disciplines (Altbach 2015). It was also accused of 'coloniality'; favouring existing dominant (white, Eurocentric) ideas of the political economy, knowledge production and power relations (Shahjahan 2013).

The use of the term 'learning outcomes' in the AHELO project was criticized as a description of *generic* student achievement (Corbett Broad and Davidson 2015) because of its existing use to *differentiate* outcomes according to discipline and degree type. At a programme level, learning outcomes are a statement of what students of a particular programme should be able to do, and are set by academics looking for evidence of gaining expertise in a particular subject (Coates and Mahat 2014). The term 'learning gain' has been preferred as a description of what has been learned in a manner comparable *across* disciplines (McGrath et al. 2015). More definitive than notions of 'value-added' which could incorporate attainment of any of the competencies illustrated in Table 2.1, learning gain has been defined as a measurable improvement in student performance between two stages of their studies, or 'distance travelled' (McGrath et al. 2015). It also differs from some other concepts of assessment in that it requires data from two sets of reliable and valid tests.

Attempts to define and measure learning gain continue, with various options being tested. These include use of students' credentials to compare their attainment scores on entry, for example, the Universities Central Admissions System (UCAS) tariff points, with their received class of degree, and also a basket of student self-assessed progress (measured at application stage and during their last year in higher education) in the development of generic skills such as written communication, spoken communication, numeracy skills, computer literacy and self-confidence (Behle 2016). It should, however, be remembered from earlier in this chapter that learning gain is not a measure of teaching, but of learning, which is a shared responsibility of the university and of the engaged student. To equate learning gain with excellent teaching is to ignore the role of the student and issues identified earlier in this chapter as being within a student's control; such as in hours of attendance, and the extent to which students choose to take an active role. Conversely, it is also possible for a motivated student to learn well despite poor teaching, and lack of support or guidance. Despite this, learning gain as a concept looks like a more promising dependent variable to assess the product of excellent teaching than others discussed in the previous section.

Conclusion

The introduction to this chapter posed the problem of disentangling factors that contribute to student learning alongside excellent teaching. Assessments of learning gain, measured from two given points in time look, in principle, a promising means of separating out some entanglement factors, but not those associated with the efforts of the individual student. However, learning gain is also only an 'indicator' of what might follow, and it is likely that universities will not be able to formally lay claim to the achievements of long term future peacemakers, lifesavers, innovators and leaders (especially as the situation at university which led to their flourishing may have changed in the intervening period). These two examples illustrated the complexity of attempting to measure, and judge the measuring of, excellence.

Whilst there may never be a metric that accounts for achievements of graduates long into the future, there needs to be as much confidence as possible that the higher education system is capable of supporting such flourishing potential. This chapter has reviewed current dominant ideas and practices around measuring teaching excellence, which is to use several available metrics to make a judgement about a course, faculty or institution. The current position has two historic practical drivers: the availability of metrics at course or institution level, and the lack of general agreement on excellent teaching at an individual level. However, it is perhaps the macro-level where the most pressure currently exists for better performance data as a result of the rapid growth in both the numbers of students and the cost of higher education globally. A further rationale for focusing on this level is that excellent teaching is not just the concern of the teacher, but heavily influenced by macro factors such as policy, facilities, equipment, administration and regulation (see also Chapter 1 by Sandeep Gakhal).

This review has highlighted sufficient questions over metrics in current use to recommend that they deserve both caution, in the extent to which they inform policy decisions, and further research into their efficacy. The review evidences a case for the argument that metrics, when used to inform rankings, favour certain types of provision and discourage missions whose contribution is less easy to quantify, such as widening participation to non-traditional students, or a commitment to engendering social citizenship. Research is required to further investigate the detail of the linear model presented in the inputs/outputs model sketched out by Chinta et al. (2016) and elaborated in this chapter. In this broad linear model, metrics for inputs are used as indicators, or predictors, of progress towards the desired outcome of excellent teaching, which is a student with enhanced capabilities gained as a result of learning. Specifically, future research should focus on investigating whether preference might be given to some measures, with others being abandoned or given reduced weight.

Reviewing Figure 2.2, a proposed evaluation model to evidence teaching excellence, it would appear that higher education needs better ways to monitor and measure student engagement that might provide a more accurate indicator of future success than student experience, which is argued to play too dominant a role in some rankings at present. Further work is also needed to devise successful direct methods of measuring student achievement in ways which adapt to mobilized learning and allow a student to have their achievements recognized globally. In the future, further metrics will be developed as technology allows the capture and interrogation of more data about student, teacher and institutional behaviours. Caution will be required in use of these 'big data' metrics, since such data is usually gathered ad hoc rather than from a representative sample and can be open to misinterpretation (Gent 2016). It is important to note that, just because data become available, it does not mean they should be used to indicate performance. The example of contact hours is a case in point: it can readily be measured by quantity but not by quality; and, as observed earlier, when students reach more independent levels of study, even its quantitative value should be questioned as an indicator of teaching excellence. Finally, in terms of research, work is needed to assess the relationship between excellent teaching input and student learning gain, recalling that the former is a joint enterprise involving support systems of a university and the teacher, and that the latter is also dependent on the efforts of students.

The principle of gathering data in order to improve performance is recognized as best practice. So far, no single direct measure of student achievement has been found to be sufficiently comprehensive to identify excellent teaching. As such, baskets of measures will continue to be of use for benchmarking. However, selection of, and weight given to data in such baskets needs to be clear to all who use it about what is being measured and to what extent it is, in reality, offering a judgement about research quality or excellent teaching. It also needs to consider whether the chosen metrics favour a particular set of disciplines or an established Westernized university system.

It is recommended that the advice of McGrath et al. (2015) be adhered to, in that whatever global or national metrics are used, they are reviewed by an individual institution's stakeholders (the professional bodies, employers, community groups, policymakers and students), who are best placed to advise which existing or additional metrics should be used as the starting point for contextual discussion about improvement at the local level. In this way the diversity of needs and goals of these stakeholders are likely to be taken into account. Thus, measures to assess the quality of teaching and learning can be of use both as a means of judging performance against similar types of provision elsewhere, *and* as a resource for critical reflection on teaching and learning. The value of this latter exercise is potentially far higher as a means to increase quality if those within institutions find the data collected can inform their decisions.

While there is a case for using a range of measures to benchmark teaching excellence, the current climate means that a strong political will is needed to avoid a reductive approach to simple rankings, or a single indicator from which important stakeholders, such as future students, or an institution's partners, are expected to make decisions. This chapter has highlighted the disproportionate priority and mistaken perceptions that these measured metrics already receive. This priority is likely to increase if the impact of such assessments moves beyond affecting reputation. To use a selected set of performance metrics to make funding decisions or limit access to certain markets is to give too much credence to indicators that are likely to inhibit diversity of provision. As others have argued, the focus on data risks stifling academic creativity and promotes homogeneity of provision which neglects local or even national need or opportunity. It would be an irony if attaching so much power to performance metrics led to a stifling of learning and innovation at the very institutions such qualities are supposed to nurture.

References

Altbach, P. (2015) 'AHELO: the myth of measurement and comparability', *University World News*, 367. Online. Available at www.universityworldnews.com/article.php?story= 20150515064746124 (accessed 20 March 2017).

Altbach, P. and Hazelkorn, E. (2017) 'Why most universities should quit the rankings game', *University World News*, 442. Online. Available at www.universityworldnews.com/article. php?story=20170105122700949 (accessed 20 March 2017).

Appiagyei-Atua, K., Beiter, K. and Karran, T. (2015) 'The capture of institutional autonomy by the political elite and its impact on academic freedom in African universities', *Higher Education Review*, 47(3): 48–74.

Barkley, E. (2010) *Student engagement techniques: a handbook for college faculty*, San Francisco, CA: Jossey-Bass.

Behle, H. (2016) *Measuring learning gain*, paper presented at the Society for Research into Higher Education (SRHE) Annual Conference, 7–9 December 2016, Celtic Manor, Newport, South Wales.

Bell, A. R. and Brooks, C. (2016) *Is there a magic link between research activity, professional teaching qualifications and student satisfaction?* SSRN, 1–32. Online. Available at https:// papers.ssrn.com/sol3/papers.cfm?abstract_id=2712412 (accessed 20 March 2017).

Blyth, P. and Cleminson, A. (2016) *Teaching Excellence Framework: analysis of highly skilled employment outcomes*, London: Department for Education.

Borden, V. and Peters, S. (2014) 'Faculty engagement in leaning outcomes assessment', in H. Coates (ed.) *Higher education learning outcomes assessment*, 201–212, Frankfurt am Main: Peter Lang Publishing.

Borysiewicz, L. (2016) 'Without autonomy universities risk losing the public's trust says Sir Leszek Borysiewicz, Vice-Chancellor of the University of Cambridge', News,

University of Cambridge. Online. Available at www.cam.ac.uk/news/without-autonomy-universities-risk-losing-the-publics-trust-says-sir-leszek-borysiewicz-vice (accessed 20 March 2017).

Braun, H. and Bily, C. (2013) *OECD assessment of higher education learning outcomes: further insights – volume 3*, Paris: OECD.

Broadbent, J. (2007) 'If you can't measure it, how can you manage it? Management and governance in higher educational institutions', *Public Money and Management*, 27(3): 193–198.

Bryson, C. (2015) 'Clarifying the concept of student engagement', in C. Bryson (ed.) *Understanding and developing student engagement*, 1–22, Abingdon: Routledge.

Buckingham Shum, S. and Crick, R. D. (2016) 'Learning analytics for 21st century competencies', *Journal of Learning Analytics*, 3: 6–21.

Chinta, R., Kebritchi, M. and Ellias, J. (2016) 'A conceptual framework for evaluating higher education institutions', *International Journal of Educational Management*, 30(6): 989–1002.

Coates, H. (ed.) (2014) *Higher education learning outcomes assessment*, Frankfurt am Main: Peter Lang Publishing.

Coates, H. and Mahat, M. (2014) 'Advancing student learning outcomes', in H. Coates (ed.) *Higher education learning outcomes assessment*, 15–32, Frankfurt am Main: Peter Lang Publishing.

Corbett Broad, M. and Davidson, P. (2015) *Open letter to the Secretary-General of OECD*, 7 May 2015. Online. Available at www.acenet.edu/news-room/Documents/Letter-to-OECD-on-AHELO.pdf (accessed 20 March 2017).

Department for Business Innovation and Skills (2016) *Teaching Excellence Framework: technical consultation for Year Two*, May 2016. Online. Available at www.gov.uk/government/uploads/system/uploads/attachment_data/file/523340/bis-16-262-teaching-excellence-framework-techcon.pdf (accessed 20 March 2017).

Docherty, T. (2011) 'Compromising higher learning, measure for reified measure', *Times Higher Education Supplement World University Rankings*, 14 April 2011. Online. Available at www.timeshighereducation.com/comment/columnists/compromising-higher-learning-measure-for-reified-measure/415822.article?sectioncode=26&storycode=4158 22 (accessed 20 March 2017).

Dollinger S. J., Matyja, A. M. and Huber, J. L. (2008) 'Which factors best account for academic success: those which college students can control or those they cannot?', *Journal of Research in Personality*, 42(4): 872–885.

Eastwood, D. (2014) 'Through a glass darkly: what the future of higher education might be', keynote address at the British Council for Education, DePaul University. Online. Available at www.birmingham.ac.uk/Documents/university/VC-Speeches/Through-a-glass-darkly.pdf (accessed 21 March 2017).

Edwards, D. and Pearce, J. (2014) 'Outcomes assessment in practice: reflections on two Australian implementations', in H. Coates (ed.) *Higher education learning outcomes assessment*, 69–88, Frankfurt am Main: Peter Lang Publishing.

Gent, E. (2016) 'Beware of the gaps in big data', *E & T Engineering and Technology*. Online. Available at https://eandt.theiet.org/content/articles/2016/09/beware-of-the-gaps-in-big-data/ (accessed 21 March 2017).

Gibbons, S., Neumayer, E. and Perkins, R. (2015) 'Student satisfaction, league tables and university applications: evidence from Britain', *Economics of Education Review*, 48(September): 148–164.

Global High Level Policy Forum (2015) *Online, open and flexible higher education for the future we want. From statements to action: equity, access, and quality learning outcomes*, 9–11 June 2015,

UNESCO, Paris. Online. Available at https://iite.unesco.org/files/news/639206/Paris%20Message%2013%2007%202015%20Final.pdf (accessed 21 March 2017).

González, J. and Wagenaar, R. (eds) (2008) *Universities' contribution to the Bologna Process: an introduction*, 2nd edn, Bilbao: Universidad de Deusto. Online. Available at www.unideusto.org/tuningeu/images/stories/Publications/ENGLISH_BROCHURE_FOR_WEBSITE.pdf (accessed 21 March 2017).

Greatbatch, D. and Holland, J. (2016) *Teaching quality in higher education: literature review and qualitative research*, May 2016, London: Department for Business, Innovation and Skills. Online. Available at www.gov.uk/government/uploads/system/uploads/attachment_data/file/524495/he-teaching-quality-literature-review-qualitative-research.pdf (accessed 21 March 2017).

Gunn, V. and Fisk, A. (2013) *Considering teaching excellence in higher education: 2007–2013: a literature review since the CHERI Report 2007*, York: Higher Education Academy.

Hervey, T. and Wood, J. (2016) '"Now I understand what you were trying to do, I see that this was the best module I had at University": student learning expectations reviewed eight years later', *European Journal of Current Legal Issues*, 22(3): 1–27.

Jain, R., Sahney, S. and Sinha, G. (2013) 'Developing a scale to measure students' perception of service quality in the Indian context', *The TQM Journal*, 25(3): 276–294.

Kandiko, C. (2012) *Engagement versus satisfaction: approaches to measuring the student experience*, paper presented at the Society for Research into Higher Education (SRHE) Annual Conference, 12–14 December 2012, Celtic Manor, Newport, South Wales.

Lawson, A., Leach, M. and Burrows, S. (2012) 'The implications for learners, teachers and institutions of using student satisfaction as a measure of success: a review of the literature', *Education Journal*, 21 September 2012, 138: 7–12.

Liu, N. C. and Cheng, Y. (2005) 'The academic ranking of world universities', *Higher Education in Europe*, 30(2): 127–136.

London Mathematical Society (2015) *Assessing the quality of higher education: written submission to the BIS Select Committee, from the London Mathematical Society*. Online. Available at www.lms.ac.uk/sites/lms.ac.uk/files/BISselectcommittee%20LMS%20response_29October2015.pdf (accessed 22 March 2017).

Macfarlane, B. (2016) *Freedom to learn: the threat to student academic freedom and why it needs to be reclaimed*, Abingdon: Routledge.

Martínez, A., Borjas, M., Herrera, M. and Valencia, J. (2015) 'Relationship between measures of academic quality and undergraduate student attrition: the case of higher education institutions in the Colombian Caribbean region', *Higher Education Research and Development*, 34(6): 1192–1206.

McGrath, H. C., Guerin, B., Harte, E., Frearson, M. and Manville, C. (2015) *Learning gains in higher education*, Santa Monica, CA: Rand Corporation.

Melguizo, T. and Wainer, J. (2015) 'Toward a set of measures of student learning outcomes in higher education: evidence from Brazil', *Higher Education*, 72(3): 1–21.

Morgan, J. (2015) 'OECD's AHELO will fail to launch, says education director', *Times Higher Education World University Rankings*. Online. Available at www.timeshighereducation.com/news/oecds-ahelo-will-fail-launch-says-education-director (accessed 22 March 2017).

Neves, J. and Hillman, N. (2016) *The 2016 Student Academic Experience Survey*, York: Higher Education Academy.

Nevill, A. and Rhodes, C. (2004) 'Academic and social integration: a survey of satisfaction and dissatisfaction within a first-year education studies cohort at a new university', *Journal of Further and Higher Education*, 28(2): 179–193.

Organisation for Economic Co-operation and Development (2010) *Glossary of key terms in evaluation and results based management.* Online. Available at http://www.oecd.org/dac/evaluation/2754804.pdf (accessed 22 March 2017).

Organisation for Economic Co-operation and Development (2013) *Assessment of higher education learning outcomes (AHELO): Feasibility Study Report, Vol 1: design and implementation,* Paris: OECD.

Osman, M., El-Hussein, M. and Cronje, J. C. (2010) 'Defining mobile learning in the higher education landscape', *Educational Technology & Society,* 13(3): 12–21.

Patton, M. Q. (2008) *Utilization-focused evaluation,* 4th edn, Thousand Oaks, CA: SAGE Publications.

Quality Assurance Agency (2011) *Explaining contact hours.* Online. Available at www.qaa.ac.uk/en/Publications/Documents/contact-hours.pdf (accessed 22 March 2017).

Ramsden, P. (2013) *Leadership for a better student experience: what do senior executives need to know?,* London: Leadership Foundation for Higher Education.

Saavedra, A. R. and Saavedra, J. E. (2011) 'Do colleges cultivate critical thinking, problem solving, writing and interpersonal skills?', *Economics of Education Review,* 30(6): 1516–1526.

Shahjahan, R. A. (2013) 'Coloniality and a global testing regime in higher education: unpacking the OECD's AHELO initiative', *Journal of Education Policy,* 28(5): 676–694.

Sharples, M., Taylor, J. and Vavoula, G. (2006) 'A theory of learning for the mobile age', in R. Andrews and C. Haythornthwaite (eds) *The SAGE handbook of e-learning research,* 221–247, Thousand Oaks, CA: SAGE Publications.

Shin, J. C., Toutkoushian, R. K. and Teichler, U. (2011) *University rankings: theoretical basis, methodology and impacts on global higher education,* Dordrecht, NL: Springer.

Simister, N. (2010) *Outputs, outcomes and impact,* Bishkek, Kyrgyz Republic: INTRAC.

Stensaker, B. and Sweetman, R. (2014) 'Impact of assessment initiatives on quality assurance', in H. Coates (ed.) *Higher education learning outcomes assessment,* 237–262, Frankfurt am Main: Peter Lang Publishing.

Strang, L., Belanger, J., Manville, C. and Meads, C. (2016) *Review of the research literature on defining and demonstrating quality teaching and impact in higher education,* York: Higher Education Academy and RAND Europe.

Sullivan, T. A., Mackie, C., Massy, W. F. and Sinha, E. (2012) 'Why measurement of higher education productivity is difficult', in T. A. Sullivan, C. Mackie, W. F. Massy and E. Sinha (eds) *Improving measurement of productivity in higher education,* 37–60, Washington D. C.: National Academies Press.

Thomas, L. (2012) *Building student engagement and belonging in higher education at a time of change: final report from the What Works? Student Retention and Success programme,* York: Higher Education Academy.

Tilak, J. B. G. (2016) 'Global rankings, world-class universities and dilemma in higher education policy in India', *Higher Education for the Future,* 3(2): 126–143.

van den Wijngaard, O., Beausaert, S., Segers, M. and Gijselaers, W. (2015) 'The development and validation of an instrument to measure conditions for social engagement of students in higher education', *Journal of Social Work Education,* 40(4): 704–720.

Williams, R. and de Rassenfosse, G. (2016) 'Pitfalls in aggregating performance measures in higher education', *Studies in Higher Education,* 41(1): 51–62.

Zepke, N. (2015) 'Student engagement research: thinking beyond the mainstream', *Higher Education Research & Development,* 34(6): 1311–1323.

Zlatkin-Troitschanskaia, O., Kuhn, C. and Toepper, M. (2014) 'Modelling and assessing higher education learning outcomes in Germany', in H. Coates (ed.) *Higher education learning outcomes assessment,* 213–236, Frankfurt am Main: Peter Lang Publishing.

Critical friend commentary

Bjørn Stensaker

A more globalized higher education sector is constantly introduced to new expectations and demands concerning how the sector can contribute to the economic, cultural and social development of our societies. While quality in higher education has been high on the agenda for a number of decades, the notion of excellence – especially in teaching – has emerged as a dominant new term to which the sector needs to be accountable. Whether the term excellence actually adds much to the discussions so far on quality can be questioned. Both concepts trigger the same questions; quality/excellence of what, for what?

Both concepts can be said to be multi-dimensional, containing a range of different understandings and meanings, and both also present a fascinating paradox; everyone agrees they are important, but most people disagree on how they should be defined (Harvey and Knight 1996). While governments, institutions, the media and researchers launch numerous attempts to find ways of attempting to measure the concepts, few question the validity of the concepts themselves. Of course, as the sector is caught up in struggles to attract students, staff, resources, and to strengthen reputation, it is increasingly difficult not to be part of this game, especially due to institutional legitimacy risks (Brockerhoff et al. 2014). In playing the game, the many possible indicators and measures of excellence can easily create an information overload, especially since many stakeholders, including students, have quite nuanced and multifaceted preferences and wishes concerning the content and outcome of their education (Jungblut et al. 2015).

The alternative is to take a more reductionist approach and focus on the sort of single metrics many global university rankings are characterized by, but for which they have been criticized (Craig et al. 2014). While this kind of reductionism rightly can be questioned, there are other kinds of reductionist approaches that might be more attractive. One of these might be to combine ideas about excellence and university missions/purpose as a response to concerns about lacking system diversity in mass higher education systems (Brockerhoff et al. 2014). Another idea might be to bring back issues of trust and trustworthiness in the assessment discussion (Stensaker and Maassen 2015), and experiment with more process-related measures as we know that they tend to stimulate student learning. Many people see creativity as part of the excellence concept, so perhaps that thinking should be applied to the assessment of the concept.

References

Brockerhoff, L., Stensaker, B. and Huisman, J. (2014) 'Prescriptions and perceptions of teaching excellence: a study of the national "Wettbewerb Exzellente Lehre" initiative in Germany', *Quality in Higher Education*, 20(3): 235–254.

Craig, R., Amernic, J. and Tourish, D. (2014) 'Perverse audit culture and accountability of the modern public university', *Financial Accountability & Management*, 30(1): 1–24.

Harvey, L. and Knight, P. T. (1996) *Transforming higher education*, Buckingham: SRHE and Open University Press.

Jungblut, J., Vukasovic, M. and Stensaker, B. (2015) 'Student perspectives on quality in higher education', *European Journal of Higher Education*, 5(2): 157–180.

Stensaker, B. and Maassen, P. (2015) 'A conceptualization of available trust-building mechanisms for international quality assurance of higher education', *Journal of Higher Education Policy and Management*, 37(1): 30–40.

3

BOUNDED EXCELLENCE

Lynne Hunt and Owen Hicks

Introduction

This chapter critically analyses the concept of teaching excellence, noting that it is now a measurable phenomenon and a component of the professionalization of teaching that has elevated the teaching function in universities. Since the 1990s, excellence in university teaching has emerged as an organizational goal in Western universities. However, the codification of teaching excellence also risks narrowing its scope to a single, simplistic, pinnacle of excellence to which all should aspire. So the purpose of this discussion is to encourage multi-pinnacled and inclusive concepts of 'bounded excellence' relevant to local socio-cultural and economic contexts. To illustrate the need for complex and contextualized understandings of teaching excellence, the chapter draws on observations of university teaching in China, Vietnam and Timor-Leste.

The discussion interrogates understandings of teaching excellence in higher education and explores the evaluation, measurement and quality assurance of university teaching. It also addresses the distorting influence of international university league tables, arguing that such rankings are unfit for the purpose of enhancing students' learning opportunities and counterproductive of opportunities to work with diverse meanings of teaching excellence. It concludes that excellence is not just a measure of outputs, but also of inputs and throughputs because this addresses the excellence of individual teachers as well as the quality of support provided to them by their universities. Furthermore, attention to inputs and throughputs accommodates variance in the resource base of universities in different countries and creates opportunities to assess teaching and learning in terms of being the best possible in a particular context. In short, this chapter challenges reductionist measures of teaching outcomes and proposes multi-pinnacled conceptualizations of teaching excellence that enhance the 'art of the possible' for university teaching and learning around the world.

Relative and absolute understandings of teaching excellence

Consider examples of our earliest identified universities, such as Bologna, Prague, Oxford, or the ancient academies of Taixue in China, and the Quoc Tu Giam in Vietnam. The oldest universities in continuous operation were established around 900 years ago. Did they demonstrate excellence in teaching? If so, what was the nature of that excellence? Is the excellence that might have been claimed then comparable to the excellence of today's so-called best universities? Will the universities of the future aspire to similar definitions of teaching excellence? Is teaching in today's universities better than it was 900 years ago, and will institutions of the next millennium mock the perceived excellence of today – and is such excellence reducible to a given score? Such questions challenge the pursuit of absolute definitions of teaching excellence and set the scene for the relative and multi-pinnacled understandings of teaching excellence explored in this chapter.

Owen (one of the chapter authors) worked in a Chinese and a Vietnamese university for a total of four and a half years. Conversations with staff and students of these two provincial universities alerted him to cultural variations in perceptions of teaching excellence, which he sought to clarify by asking two questions: 'which are the best universities?' and 'what is teaching excellence?' Unsurprisingly, the answers from staff and students were bounded by their horizons. Students assumed that excellence in teaching was what occurred at the best institution they knew. For Chinese students, this meant the perceived best institution (not their own) in the province. Staff responded similarly, perhaps because most had been educated within the province. Few had read or thought about excellence in teaching but assumed it occurred in institutions that had a good reputation in the region. They were also aware of the best teachers in their own institution so, axiomatically, teaching excellence was what these teachers did. Few of the Vietnamese students had travelled outside their province and their culturally established veneration of teachers made it difficult for them to acknowledge excellence or the lack of it. There was an assumed quality in what teachers provided to their classes. Reference to measures of excellence appeared alien to their culture; Vietnamese teachers gave little thought to excellence. The best universities were seen as those few national or international institutions where the children of prominent members of the community were educated.

Measures of teaching excellence

In their review of teaching evaluation, Chalmers and Hunt (2016) chart how measures of excellence proliferated in the western world over the twentieth century. Smith (2008) synthesized them into a 4-Quadrant (4Q) approach based on the sources of information: self-assessment; peer review; student input; and student achievement. In brief, teaching excellence may be evaluated by what others (peers and students) think of teaching and how well students succeed. This is useful, but says little about what teaching excellence means.

Over the last quarter of a century, research into university teaching gained momentum through the scholarship of teaching and learning (SoTL) movement. This substantiated understandings of excellence in university teaching. For example, Bain's (2004: 15–18) study of award winning teachers identified the characteristics of good teachers who: 'know their subjects . . . treat their lectures, discussion and problem based sessions . . . as serious intellectual endeavours . . . [and they] challenge students to grapple with ideas, rethink their assumptions, and examine their mental models of reality'. Good teachers are reflective practitioners with a repertoire of effective teaching strategies and skills in curriculum development and evaluation. The Australian University Teaching Criteria and Standards framework (Chalmers et al. 2014) synthesizes the complex dimensions of good university teaching into seven criteria:

1. Design and planning of learning activities
2. Teaching and supporting student learning
3. Assessment and giving feedback to students on their learning
4. Developing effective learning environments, student support and guidance
5. Integration of scholarship, research and professional activities with teaching
6. Evaluation of practice and continuing professional development
7. Professional and personal effectiveness

In brief, Western definitions of teaching excellence refer to a mélange of reflective teaching practices, curriculum development and evaluation skills that require a supportive context including professional development, an infrastructure of learning technologies, and quality assurance processes associated with course development and the moderation of marks. This highlights the difference between being an excellent teacher (being the best I can be) and teaching excellence as a broader concept requiring a bundle of coordinated activities and resources.

In the 1990s, national quality assurance agencies emerged in some countries that required universities to evaluate teaching processes and outcomes. This resulted in public reporting on teaching and students' learning experiences seen, for example, in the Australian Quality Indicators for Learning and Teaching (QILT) (2017) website. This increase in governmental interest in university teaching has been driven by the massification of higher education and corresponding increases in government investment as the higher education sector has expanded. Governments want accountability for expenditure and they also want to assure the quality of tertiary teaching and learning to protect international and domestic students in a globalized market. Most Western universities now report routinely on matters such as student progression, retention and satisfaction with course experiences. Critics argue that such formal processes are destructive of the real purpose of measuring teaching excellence, which, as Chalmers and Hunt (2016: 26) argue: 'should be part of a reflective cycle that leads to: improved opportunities for students' learning; enhanced curricula; and career development'. However, Newton (2002: 42) doubts the connection between measures of teaching and quality enhancement initiatives because, 'The evaluation game can lead to tokenism, reputation management and image control'.

Another risk in measurements of teaching is that they may lead to standardized rather than culturally appropriate definitions of excellence. One driver of the trend to standardization is the growing importance of international rankings. These are based largely on just a few research-intensive universities and more on research outcomes than on teaching. This has attracted growing criticism, but there is some evidence of change. For example, the Times Higher Education (THE) World University Rankings now claim to provide global performance tables based on all the core missions of universities including teaching. The extent to which teaching is still a poor cousin to research remains an open question, but the THE rankings that once encompassed a mere 400 universities now include 980 institutions (THE 2016). Even so, this is still narrow in scope because it implies that there are only 980 world class universities, and these drawn from approximately one in every eight nations of the world. At best, this is a partial representation of higher education. If a conservative figure of 9,000 is taken as the number of higher education institutions worldwide, then these rankings include approximately ten per cent of the total, with more than ninety per cent not even considered (Hicks 2016: 5). For this large majority of institutions, the question is not how well will they be ranked, but will they be ranked at all? So, the argument in this chapter is that international rankings of university teaching distort international perceptions of teaching excellence and risk being counterproductive of positive outcomes for students, the majority of whom are studying in unranked, less prestigious and often poorly resourced universities. What meaning can teaching excellence have in these contexts?

Teaching excellence in a global context

It is now customary to characterize the context of higher education in terms of globalization. Musselin (2011: 461) went so far as to claim: 'It is probably impossible to nowadays find a policy statement on higher education that does not start with a sentence close to "In a globalised world . . . higher education plays a critical role'''. In terms of teaching and learning, globalization has a number of implications. Firstly, many universities are now tasked with producing graduates who will be global citizens. A second implication for university teaching and learning is cross-border education. The United Nations Educational, Scientific and Cultural Organization (UNESCO) Institute for Statistics (2014) noted an unsurpassed demand for higher education as universities compete globally to attract students. However, given an estimated total of 130 million university students worldwide (Maslen 2012), the 2.8 million studying abroad is only around two per cent. Projecting university student populations to 2025, Maslen (ibid.) suggests a doubling of the 2012 total number to 260 million, and a trebling of the number of students studying abroad to circa 8.4 million. Nonetheless, this still represents only a little over three per cent. So, for ninety-seven per cent of the world's student population, cross-border education may be less important than it is made out to be.

Many institutions are still not positioned as global institutions. Universities Worldwide (2017) identifies 9,464 universities in 206 countries, while Ranking Web of Universities (2017) claims approximately 26,000 institutions from 253 countries and independent territories. The International Association of Universities (2017) claims 605 member institutions from 120 countries, with twenty-four per cent drawn from Asia and the Pacific. It is difficult to reconcile these figures, especially where definitions of what constitutes a university vary. Even so, current analyses of globalization can be criticized for focusing only on those universities that have a high national or international profile. So, this is the context for our three case study institutions in Timor-Leste, China and Vietnam. None of them is listed on any of the aforementioned websites.

International case studies of university teaching

These case studies draw on participant observation in three higher education institutions in northwest China (NWC), central Vietnam (CV) and Timor-Leste (TL). The differences between them draws attention to weaknesses inherent in any broad discussions about Asia, which, as Marginson (2010: 42) observed, is no more than a geo-political construct comprised of considerable international and intra-national diversity that extends to differences between universities; there is no single concept of a university. There are many different missions, structures and organizational cultures associated with distinctive traditions and models of higher education. These multiple 'ideas' are nested in historical and national contexts, and have specific conditions of possibility.

The purpose of the case studies is pragmatic because they can 'provide ideas, suggestions, or imagery that might sensitize outsiders to issues they may have not considered' (Wals et al. 2004: 347), and in this chapter, that means ideas about teaching excellence in international contexts. The information is clustered around themes to highlight the collective realities of the institutions rather than their separate identities. Owen spent eleven, twenty-three, and eighteen months respectively in these institutions, between 2004 and 2014, as a volunteer with roles including senior advisor, lecturer and English teacher/trainer.

The institutions are relatively small provincial universities, with student populations of approximately 350, 6,000 and 14,000. Two have growing populations while student numbers at the third are nationally controlled and relatively stable. The major focus of all three is on teaching and learning rather than research. Two of the institutions have pre-graduate (college) and graduate level programmes while the third also has a small postgraduate cohort of students. The TL and NWC student populations are drawn from across each nation, while CV students are almost exclusively from the local province. Here, teacher training programmes attract the largest numbers of students. Academics at each institution are typically locally born and educated. Only a small proportion has completed higher degrees outside of their respective provinces. Very few have doctoral qualifications, and opportunities for international study leave are almost non-existent. At one of the institutions, sickness was a major problem, with absenteeism of staff and students significantly affecting learning opportunities. At another, civil unrest saw times when students and staff were unable to attend. The universities in China and Vietnam are little known beyond the provinces in which they are located. In contrast, TL had considerable local standing, but it is not the premier institution of this small country. All three institutions are virtually off the map to the western world and each is severely under-resourced. They do, however, represent many thousands of similar institutions spread across all nations that currently have an underdeveloped higher education sector. So what sort of meaning might be attached to teaching excellence in such contexts?

Students' and teachers' perceptions of teaching excellence at NWC and CV were bounded by culture and a limited awareness of higher education beyond narrowly drawn geographical boundaries. At TL, excellence, in any absolute sense, was simply not considered in an institution where both staff and students were much more engaged in survival issues: getting to and from class safely; ensuring rooms were sufficiently equipped for teaching; struggling in a multi-lingual learning environment where four languages might be used across different classes; battling with intermittent power supply for the few unreliable electronic devices available as teaching aids; establishing and maintaining basic information systems and regulations to enable the continuing functioning of the institution. Some staff also battled to sustain an income because their institution, on occasion, ran out of funds. Low and intermittent salary meant seeking additional outside work to support the family.

Regarding curricula and course structure, the dominant feature of most courses observed in NWC and CV was their dependence on textbooks. Any coherence in curricula was dependent on the quality of the books. Yet in NWC it was not the teachers who chose the texts but an administrative arm of the university, who chose from nationally produced and approved publications. In the Foreign Languages Department at NWC, course content and learning activities were determined by what was contained in the text. Texts for English major degree programmes were typically developed at the national level under collaborative foreign (usually US) and Chinese authorship. In both NWC and CV, components of ideology and political theory were part of all undergraduate programmes and students were required to participate in military training. At TL there was little evidence of a coherent curriculum at programme level. Course material was generated from whatever limited sources lecturers could access. Typically this reflected the learning experiences of the teachers when they were students. Courses were sometimes built from what lecturers could assemble from overseas university websites.

The basic teaching and learning resource was the set text, which in some cases students bought as part of a package when they enrolled. Basic classroom materials were almost non-existent. Poor quality class sets of texts, often bound photo-copies, were sometimes made available by the library. Paper-based source material was occasionally provided to students to be photocopied at their own expense. At NWC each class had a small student-managed budget from which class photo-copying was occasionally funded. Learning and teaching resources were severely limited; for example, at TL there were two data-projectors carried from room to room as required, and two photocopiers. Equipment was dated and often unusable due to lack of maintenance and frequent power outages. At TL, the IT equipment comprised old computers donated by an overseas bank. At NWC, typically twenty/ thirty per cent of students had laptop computers, often shared with fellow students in their dormitories. Almost all students had mobile phones, about a third of which were smartphones. At NWC and CV, access to the internet was provided free on campus. It allowed students to do basic searches and very limited downloading of learning materials. However, the internet was slow and intermittent. To compensate, CV students sat at the gates of the university in the evening 'poaching' internet connection from the coffee shop opposite.

Approaches to teaching and learning at TL were determined idiosyncratically according to the background and experience of individual staff. These varied considerably from a teacher-centred information transfer, typical of Indonesian trained staff, to a more interactive student-centred approach from staff trained elsewhere. At NWC the approach to teaching and learning reflected the Confucian heritage of teachers and students. It was respectful, structured and prescriptive. It appeared teacher-centred and included students memorizing and hopefully developing an understanding of material from texts. Similarly, at CV, students were exposed to limited material and encouraged to learn set pieces. Some teachers showed knowledge and understanding of student-centred learning and this was reflected in some class exercises.

What might be considered teaching excellence, in Western terms, was observable on occasion. Staff in the three institutions did an incredibly good job given the constraints. With limited resources and training, sometimes small miracles occurred. Perhaps the term constrained excellence, but excellence nonetheless, is apposite. Sometimes students were highly engaged in their learning. A good example was seen in a final-year class of CV English-major degree students in an English Literature module, presenting critiques of famous British and North American writers. With the process facilitated by their teacher, small groups sourced audio-visual material from the internet then led the rest of their class through a lively interrogation of some of the greatest (Western) literary works of our time, even reflecting on what such writing meant for them. These were students who had hardly been out of a rural province in Central Vietnam, never been in a library, the likes of which are taken for granted in Western countries, and never been to the movies! A 'foreigner' could easily find some fault in the students' work and the teacher's involvement. But it was outstanding, perhaps even excellent teaching.

A multi-pinnacle approach

So what insights do the three interwoven case studies offer about teaching excellence in international contexts? One inevitable conclusion is that any analysis of teaching excellence in international contexts must question the extent to which it is possible to sustain teaching excellence, at individual and institutional levels, when some universities are well funded and others are not. What does this mean for students and their teachers and what does it imply about international benchmarking and rankings of university excellence? Are some institutions immediately excluded? Should all universities be 'in it to win it' or stay out of processes based on non-level playing fields? After all, any international competition is unwinnable, as Marginson (2010: 26) pointed out: 'while the world class university movement beckons to all Asia Pacific universities, few have the funding levels and personnel enabling them to compete effectively, and in an English language science system [which] excludes swathes of non-English speaking Asia'.

These are important considerations for teaching excellence because, as Hicks (2016: 23) observed, the global growth in student numbers is occurring largely in non-ranked teaching-focused universities. They are not research intensive and most offer courses not intended to lead to further study. Indeed, the Organisation for Economic Co-operation and Development (OECD) (2012: 20) noted that: 'At the highest levels of tertiary education, about 1.6 per cent of people complete advanced research programmes in OECD countries'. It could be argued that this percentage would be even lower if all countries of the world were included. This suggests that, like rain without thunder, a change has crept unnoticed into the higher education sector with undergraduate teaching emerging as the dominant function. So, when examining international perspectives on teaching in higher education, it might be productive to explore those institutions that do the teaching, such as the three described in this chapter. What implications do they have for promoting teaching excellence?

The three case studies in this chapter suggest the need to define concepts of teaching excellence in terms of the socio-cultural, geographic and economic contexts of particular institutions. This implies that teaching excellence is a relative concept. It becomes 'bounded excellence' conditioned by each institution's worldview and conceptualized from the locally known and understood. This indicates a need for a multi-pinnacle, rather than standardized, approach to assessments of teaching excellence.

While not wanting to commodify teaching in higher education, a consideration of perspectives on what is an excellent automobile may be edifying. The primary purpose of a car is transport, but do we recognize a single make or model as excellent and attempt to replicate that model so that everyone can have that 'excellent' car? Different cars are suited to different purposes, and budgets. Some are excellent in some conditions and perform poorly in others. Because of available resources in some locations, cars may be designed with different constraints and to meet different consumer demands. Imagine the reality if all car manufacturers in the world aspired to produce the same excellent vehicle! While this is a preposterous notion, consider the dangers: the conformity/uniformity; the moderation of expectations; the fragility of a single product market; the lock-in effect of economic but identical production; the difficulty of effecting change if, or when, excellence in the car was found wanting. Not to mention the highly variable opportunities to maintain and run the vehicle in specific sites around the world. If university teachers are the drivers they need good maintenance teams and resources to support them.

One approach to assuring standards in teaching, whilst avoiding standardization, may be to foster the local implementation of national or even global standards. Chalmers and Hunt (2016: 13) concur on the need for local adaptation of processes to enable teaching excellence; for example, they argue that 'Peer-review models and practices are not readily transferrable between institutions. They really need to be tailored to the needs and circumstances of particular institutions, disciplines, and curricula contexts'. Similarly, measures of excellence need to be diverse and locally relevant, focusing on both teaching and the context of teaching. These include measures of inputs, outputs, and throughputs because, as Scott (2005) points out, evidence indicates that students want and need the full support of teachers along with university services to maximize their opportunities for learning. This means that 'faculties, libraries, administration, student support, and learning technology services must all coordinate their work through 'joined-up' policies, plans and procedures' (Hunt and Chalmers 2017: 377).

Hunt and Chalmers' (2017) discussion is based on McInnes et al.'s (2012) five principles of action, which are: (1) Shape the strategic vision that puts student learning and student experience at its core; (2) Inspire and enable excellence; (3) Devolve leadership of learning and teaching; (4) Reward, recognize and develop teaching; and (5) Involve students. Without this full organizational commitment to teaching excellence there is a risk that students will not receive the best education available to them. The five principles for action represent a capacity-building approach described by Hunt (2006) in terms of the type of community-development deployed by global development organizations, which as a minimum require: financial support; useful policy; the reorientation of services to support teaching; participatory planning and decision-making; identified change leaders; incentives such as teaching awards and grants; professional development; and inter-sectoral collaboration at university, regional and national levels. Measures of teaching excellence based on local adaptations of these dimensions would demand a rethink of teaching excellence frameworks, and require a more sophisticated, multi-pinnacled conceptualization of excellence that accords with local circumstances.

Conclusion

This chapter has explored different perspectives on excellence in university teaching showing how it has been measured and evaluated. It has established that the evaluation of university teaching should give rise to reflection and guide improvements in students' learning opportunities. However, standard measures of teaching outcomes on which many universities report to governments, and consequent international rankings, have narrowed and distorted analyses of teaching. Potentially, this denies teachers and students around the world of meaningful participation in the cycle of quality improvement. Three case studies of universities in Timor-Leste, China and Vietnam showed the realities of teaching and learning in universities that do not make the cut in international rankings. They draw into question current codifications of university teaching excellence which risk narrowing the image of teaching and learning to a single, possibly simplistic, pinnacle of excellence to which all should aspire. As a consequence, this chapter has argued for measures of teaching excellence that are culturally relevant and broadly applicable because most tertiary teaching and learning takes place in institutions not classified as world class on current measures. Rather than the creation of an unsuitable and unattainable aspirational model of teaching excellence, and rather than focus resources on a small number of institutions determined to fit the world's best model, we should aim to make excellent progress towards multi-pinnacled conceptions of excellent teaching. If we do not, the consequences will be a global devaluing of the majority of higher education institutions around the world, and, for so many students, the notion that they went to an inferior institution, that even their national best is not good enough, and that anything other than best in an unfair and unbalanced world competition is not good enough.

References

Bain, K. (2004) *What the best college teachers do*, Cambridge, MA: Harvard University Press.

Chalmers, D. and Hunt, L. (2016) 'Evaluation of teaching', *HERDSA Review of Higher Education*, 3: 25–55. Online. Available at http://herdsa.org.au/herdsa-review-higher-education-vol-3/25-55 (accessed 24 March 2017).

Chalmers, D., Cummings, R., Elliott, S., Stony, S., Tucker, B., Wicking, R. and Jorre de St Jorre, T. (2014) *Australian University Teaching Criteria and Standards Project: Final Report*, Sydney, NSW: Office for Learning and Teaching.

Hicks, O. (2016) 'The very long tail that doesn't wag the dog', *HERDSA News*, 38(1): 4–5.

Hunt, L. and Chalmers, D. (2017) 'Change leadership, management and strategies to promote quality university teaching and learning', in S. Mukerji and P. Tripathi (eds) *Handbook of research on administration, policy, and leadership in higher education*, 377–403, Hershey, PA: IGI Global.

Hunt, L. (2006) 'A community development model of change: the role of teaching and learning centres', in L. Hunt, A. Bromage and B. Tomkinson (eds) *The realities of change in higher education: interventions to promote learning and teaching*, 64–77, Abingdon: Routledge.

International Association of Universities (2017) 'List of IAU members'. Online. Available at www.iau-aiu.net/content/members (accessed 24 March 2017).

Marginson, S. (2010) 'The global knowledge economy and the culture of comparison in higher education', in S. Kaur, M. Sirat and W. G. Tierney (eds) *Quality assurance and university rankings in higher education in the Asia Pacific: challenges for universities and nations*, 23–55, Penang, Malaysia: Penerbit Universiti Sains.

Maslen, G. (2012) 'Worldwide student numbers forecast to double by 2025', *University World News*, 209, 19 February 2012. Online. Available at www.universityworldnews.com/publications/archives.php?mode=archive&pub=1&issueno=209&format=html (accessed 24 March 2017).

McInnes, C., Ramsden, P. and Maconachie, D. (2012) *A handbook for executive leadership of learning and teaching in higher education*, Sydney: Office for Learning and Teaching.

Musselin, C. (2011) 'Convergences and divergences in steering higher education systems', in R. King, S. Marginson and R. Naidoo (eds) *Handbook on globalization and higher education*, 454–468, Cheltenham: Edward Elgar.

Newton, J. (2002) 'Views from below: academics coping with quality', *Quality in Higher Education*, 8(1): 39–61.

Organisation for Economic Co-operation and Development (2012) *Education at a glance 2012. Highlights*, Paris: OECD.

QILT Quality Indicators for Teaching and Learning (2017) Online. Available at https://www.qilt.edu.au/ (accessed 24 March 2017).

Ranking Web of Universities (2017) Online. Available at www.webometrics.info/en (accessed 24 March 2017).

Scott, G. (2005) *Accessing the student voice*, Final Report, Higher Education Innovation Program and the Collaboration and Structural Reform Fund, Department of Education, Science and Training, Canberra: Commonwealth of Australia.

Smith, C. (2008) 'Building effectiveness in teaching through targeted evaluation and response: connecting evaluation to teaching improvement in higher education', *Assessment & Evaluation in Higher Education*, 33(5): 517–533.

Times Higher Education (THE) (2016) *2016–17 World University Rankings*. Online. Available at www.timeshighereducation.com/world-university-rankings/2017/world-ranking#!/ (accessed 24 March 2017).

United Nations Educational, Scientific and Cultural Organization (2014) Higher education, UNESCO Institute for Statistics. Online. Available at http://uis.unesco.org/en/topic/higher-education (accessed 24 March 2017).

Universities Worldwide (2017). Online. Available at www.univ.cc/index.html (accessed 24 March 2017).

Wals, A. E. J., Walker, K. E. and Blaze Corcoran, P. (2004) 'The practice of sustainability in higher education: a synthesis', in P. Blaze Corcoran and A. E. J. Wals (eds) *Higher education and the challenge of sustainability: problematics, promise and practice*, 347–348, Dordrecht: Kluwer Academic Publishers.

Critical friend commentary

Suki Ekaratne

In bringing out that divergent views are held on teaching excellence, the chapter prods us to ask which views would be valid in different settings, since teaching is excellent when linked to effective student learning. This in turn is 'situated' and reliant on the teacher recognizing interactions across a range of situations and factors (such as the 3P model – Ramsden 1992), and acting thereon. While the proposal for a multi-pinnacled construct to teaching excellence is therefore timely, the chapter makes us think of alternative approaches in contrast to what is now the Western-orientated norm embodied in teaching excellence: for example, teaching excellence being aligned along the materially-dominated, resource-consuming 'development' paradigms. Noting, in this chapter, that teaching excellence has been achieved even in resource poor settings, it initiates us to think along these fresh directions. Some of us also know from our experiences that resource rich settings do not always, or necessarily, generate teaching excellence. Indeed, smartphones within classes of the resource rich countries are often looked at as a hindrance to student learning by many teachers, unless teachers are aware, and can harness, aspects of teaching excellence such as how to mobilize smartphones to become learning resources.

While this chapter reports that the teaching excellence construct of early university days were different from what is current, it may have induced a unidirectional flow, eventually to result in the tensions seen presently in higher education. Could it be that alternative constructs may have prevented this result? Such alternatives, that kept some societies intact and 'whole', may lie hidden to the Western gaze unless reported in chapters like this. Quite apart from the ill effects of international ranking pointed out in the chapter, another aspect that emerges is whether schemes of recognition at national level could similarly produce a negative outcome? What effects would national recognition schemes play if these are allowed to last too long? A National Teaching Fellowship scheme can start off with recognizing genuine exponents of teaching excellence, but can thereafter lead institutions to start scraping the barrel simply to rack up 'excellent teacher' numbers.

Then, should we consider as part of teaching excellence the residual time, or longevity, of the changes that teaching excellence induce in learners? While teaching excellence does bring about a change in the learner, if the transformation is transitory, is it skin deep teaching excellence? Should those who receive the 'excellent teaching' stamp develop the resilience to withstand being pressurized to regress, as does happen in various ways, for example, through social pressures of one's own department? Such questions can go on and teaching excellence should indeed make us ask these questions – and many more!

References

Ramsden, P. (1992) *Learning to teach in higher education*, London and New York: Routledge.

4

TEACHING EXCELLENCE AND TRANSNATIONAL EDUCATION: ENHANCEMENT THROUGH A FOCUS ON STUDENT DIVERSITY AND CONTEXT

Glenda Crosling

Introduction

In today's world, higher education institutions not only aspire to, but expect, excellence in teaching in their academic programmes. A significant impetus for this focus is the highly competitive and globalized environment of the knowledge society where many higher education institutions operate internationally, and transnational education is part of their operations (Waterval et al. 2017). In such a competitive setting, the higher education institution needs to pro-actively ensure that the quality of its students' educational experiences and outcomes maintain and enhance its reputation (Land and Gordon 2014), so that local and international students continue to be attracted to study there.

Excellence in teaching is an important element in the quality of students' experience, outcomes and satisfaction, but the transnational nature of many education programmes in operation today adds a further layer of complexity. The provision of academic programmes in countries other than the higher education institution's home means that the setting and the offshore student cohort differ from those in the home country; for the latter in terms of educational and cultural backgrounds and expectations. There is strong potential for such diversity to impact on the perception of the quality of the teaching in the offshore setting. This chapter explores the notion of teaching excellence in transnational education. The perspective presented is that academic programmes may be designed, delivered, and reflect teaching excellence in the home country, but it cannot be assumed that the same evaluation of excellence will be realized for students taking the programme offshore. For teaching to be excellent in the offshore setting, it needs to reflect and respond to the needs of the offshore setting and of the student cohort, impacting positively on students' satisfaction with their studies.

Excellence in teaching in higher education

Concern for the quality of teaching in higher education has come to the fore in more recent times in the context of the large-scale expansion of the higher education system that has occurred over the past few decades (Trow 1973). The outcome of the participation of large numbers of students from previously under-represented societal groups is that these students bring to their studies cultural and educational backgrounds that differ from those seen as traditional students (Chalmers et al. 2014). In Australia, Chalmers et al. (2014) classify traditional students as those drawn from the highest academic achievement levels in secondary schools, bringing with them to their studies high levels of social and cultural capital.

At the same time, in the process of globalization, higher education institutions have internationalized, and large numbers of students now study transnationally; they undertake their studies in their own countries, but the academic programmes are developed and designed in the home country of the degree-awarding institution. Accompanying these changes, governments have been concerned with the quality of higher education institutions and their academic programmes and have implemented robust quality assurance systems (Crosling et al. 2008). Thus, the huge growth in numbers of participating students has led to a focus on indicators of quality, such as rates of student attrition and retention in their studies, and by implication, student diversity. Concurrently, there is awareness of the need to retain students in their studies (Thomas and Quinn 2003).

Furthermore, and pressingly, higher education institutions need to strive for excellence in teaching, as it is a factor in their sustainability and ability to continue to attract students (Chalmers et al. 2014). While teaching excellence can be seen as distinct from *teacher* excellence and *learner* excellence (Gunn and Fisk 2013), teaching excellence refers to a broader, system-wide excellence (ibid.), but remains a contested term (Land and Gordon 2014). However, all three aspects cited above are related as they are bound in their contribution to the quality of the student experience and student outcomes, and for the purposes of this chapter, a more pragmatic understanding is taken that encompasses all three dimensions. As such, excellence in teaching impacts directly on the quality of educational experiences and outcomes for participating students, including their decision of whether to continue or leave their studies before completion and by implication on their study satisfaction. In offshore/transnational education settings, however, students' perception of the quality of their education, their educational outcomes, and their satisfaction is strongly coloured by their situation and their outlook, and this may differ markedly from that of the higher education institution's home country setting. Successful academic programmes in offshore settings, including the teaching approach implemented, need to factor in the offshore setting and the student cohort.

While a definition of teaching excellence in today's world may be elusive, evolving and multi-dimensional (Land and Gordon 2014), there are some general principles to be drawn on, and these act as a springboard in discussions of transnational education teaching excellence. Educational researchers have pointed out that a vital aspect for students' continuation in their studies, rather than dropping out, is their experience of university as reflected in social and academic engagement in their studies (Tinto 1975), and their productive learning (Scott 2005); thus, satisfaction with their studies. The curriculum, including teaching approaches, is experienced by all students regardless of their backgrounds, and thus presents a major tool to assist students' academic engagement (Crosling et al. 2008). Teaching is integral to the notion of curriculum.

Contemporary views of best practice in teaching emphasize that teaching needs to facilitate students' development as active and interactive learners, with interaction taking place not only between students, but also between student and teacher. The active nature of learning facilitated by teaching and assessment positions students to be critical, creative problem solvers as required by today's knowledge world (Crosling et al. 2015) rather than rote learners. There is also awareness that the teaching approach implemented is related to the quality of students' learning (Prosser and Trigwell 2002; Lindblom-Ylanne et al. 2006). Furthermore, as Lindblom-Ylanne et al. point out, teachers' approaches are not fixed, and thus can vary according to the situations in which they find themselves.

In the context of evolving definitions, what then are some general notions of teaching excellence? Researchers such as Chalmers (2008) explain that statistics and figures as performance indicators of, for example, retention and progression rates and students' average grades, facilitate comparison across fields and time. There is also general agreement in the field on the types of indicators, which include the areas of educational input, process, output and outcomes (ibid.), with process indicators referring to qualitative aspects that include under the process category: teaching and learning (Chalmers et al. 2014). Researchers such as Gunn and Fisk (2013) also include the dimensions of planning and delivery, such as active and group learning, critical and scholarly approaches. However, the key points of the wider discussion of teaching excellence appear to be encapsulated in the criteria used by a number of higher education institutions to determine higher education teaching excellence awards. Interestingly, these criteria in one form or another acknowledge the key characteristics of transnational education settings that impact on teaching quality; that is, diversity in students' backgrounds, experiences and expectations, and recognition of the local context/offshore setting in which the study programme takes place.

More specifically, Gunn and Fisk (ibid.) summarize the constituents of excellence award criteria used in higher education institutions in a number of countries. For instance, the criterion of curriculum design includes, among other indicators, rendering learning outcomes suitable for the discipline *as well as to the needs of students* undertaking the discipline. The latter is highly relevant to the transnational education context and its student diversity. The criterion of subject knowledge includes rendering knowledge as relevant *outside* as well as within the discipline, thus pointing to the local setting as a means to create that sense of the relevance of their studies for students and thus stimulate their interest and motivation. The criterion of inspiring and motivating refers to the teacher's classroom enthusiasm and presence, and *meaningful learning for students* in the present and the future, again implying the power of the local setting as a motivator. The criterion of respect and care for students as individuals includes: recognizing *diverse learning needs* and subsequently personalizing the teaching environment; respect for equality and diversity; addressing learners' prior knowledge and experiences. These points all indicate awareness of diverse students and context. The criterion of active and group learning includes using methods which *promote interaction*, and in this way focusing the teacher's attention on the students and their diversity, rather than solely on the subject matter. The criterion of critical and scholarly approaches captures the need to foster critical thinking and research skills in a *wider social sense*, again emphasizing context. The final criterion of engagement in assessment refers to offering students *a range of assessments* to assess their mastery, recognizing the diversity of students' preferences as seen in their response to different types of assessment.

Importantly, national quality assurance requirements also capture the essence of quality learning and teaching, mandating that higher education institutions are responsible for the quality of their education in all settings in which their pro-grammes operate, including offshore. For instance, the Tertiary Education Quality and Standards Agency of Australia (TEQSA) (2013) through Provider Registration 4.5 requires that if the higher education institution has an arrangement with another entity to deliver some or all of a course of study on its behalf, the higher education institution must manage and quality assure all aspects of the arrangement, including delivery of the course of study. Teaching and learning quality is further referred to in this code. The Quality Assurance Agency (QAA) Quality Code for Higher Education in the United Kingdom covers students across all academic levels irre-spective of their location or mode of study, and the expectation is that every student will be enabled to develop, among other attributes, as an individual learner.

Teaching quality and transnational education

Transnational education, a trend that has developed rapidly in recent times and is participated in by a large number of higher education institutions globally (McBurnie and Ziguras 2007; Crosling 2012), refers principally to the expansion of higher education beyond national boundaries; students are located physically in a country different from the country of the award-conferring institution (Edwards et al. 2010; Crosling 2012).

Transnational education can take a number of forms. These include international branch campuses where the teachers are members of the home university but located in the country of the branch campus, and the curriculum to be taught generally emanating and co-ordinated from the home higher education institution. Franchising and twinning arrangements are where the curriculum is generally designed at the home institution and the teaching outsourced from the home institution to a company in the offshore setting (Edwards et al. 2014). Alternatively, or complementary to this approach, teaching staff from the home institution may visit the offshore setting to undertake the teaching, which may be implemented in block mode form. This may be supported by electronic communication. Articulation arrangements are where students are taught in the offshore setting via one of the above teaching approaches before travelling to the home institution to continue/complete their studies (Crosling 2011). International branch campuses are increasingly popular, and while franchise programmes are the focus of this chapter, the discussion of teaching quality also applies to international branch campuses.

The quality of the education in transnational contexts, including teaching quality, has been reported as a major challenge (Tharapos 2014). The higher education institution's reputation can be damaged (Edwards et al. 2010; Crosling 2012) by outsourcing or transferring to another country some educational processes, including teaching, if they are not of a sufficient quality through not being aligned to the educational context. For instance, offshore private provider staff delivering the programme may continue to use a teacher-centred approach because of limited understanding of student-centred teaching and learning, the teacher-centred focus in their country, and their own previous educational experiences. Current day students may thus experience the teaching as uninspiring and it may not be aligned with the skills and understandings students are expected to demonstrate in assessment.

These factors impact on students' enthusiasm for the subject, the approach they take to their studies, the amount of effort they put in, and probably their achievements. Staff in the offshore setting may deliver the programme rigidly according to the teaching materials provided to them, without integrating informal feedback for students on their work and progress. Students may interpret this as an aloof approach that does not incorporate the interpersonal element in teaching, and so have less opportunity to be engaged in their studies. Significantly, given that teachers who are engaged in their work are more likely to be enthusiastic about their teaching and so engage their students, teachers who have limited, or are excluded from, involvement in curriculum development including the design of assessment and curriculum renewal may be disengaged themselves, impacting on their teaching and relations with their students. These approaches limit students' engagement in their studies and the ability for them to enhance their work. Tharapos (2014) explains that students who are dissatisfied have a significant impact on a higher education institution's reputation. Furthermore, studies have found significant differences in the students' educational experience in the home country, compared with the offshore setting.

As Edwards et al. (2010) point out, the distance in time and space and the need for communication, which are part and parcel of transnational education, can impact on the effectiveness of operations, and be exacerbated by the diversity of students and staff when compared with the home country setting for which the programme has been principally designed. O'Mahony (2014) points out that transnational/international education offers higher education institutions many opportunities, but also with the possibility of failure and consequent risk to their core mission and reputation. O'Mahony (ibid.) reports that in transnational education attrition rates are high and teaching and learning excellence must accompany sound regulation, good governance and quality control. According to Gunn and Fisk (2013), this involves the development of pedagogical knowledge and the lived experience of the classroom.

More specifically, studies of transnational education teaching quality emphasize the challenges for both teachers and students (see, for example, O'Mahony 2014), such as variance in communication styles, in learning and teaching styles, and governance (quality control and local regulatory systems). But most significantly, a major challenge is the need to shape the education to meet the needs of students who live, and will most likely work, offshore (ibid.) with the students' needs likely to diverge from those of the home institution students. A frequent response to challenges and problems is to transplant the home country approach to the transnational education setting (ibid.), but this may not be the most effective response. Transplantation of an approach implies a lack of flexibility in ability to respond more appropriately to a transnational education teaching challenge, and as O'Mahony reports, it is indicative of some degree of immaturity in transnational education as a research field into teaching and learning.

Furthermore, O'Mahony notes that collaborative authorship or activity between the host higher education institution and the offshore provider is not evident, and increased transnational education teaching and learning research would contribute to transnational education teaching quality. O'Mahony cites relevant research areas as students' learning styles, their origins and their reproduction, contextualized quality education based on understanding the socio-cultural factors that fashion knowledge communication, and the needs of students in the transnational education classroom. A better way of dealing with challenging situations is to enable intercultural and transnational comparisons in the classroom, rather than imposing solutions that are appropriate in the home institution setting (Hoare 2012).

Strategies for enhancing transnational education teaching quality and excellence

The key factors identified in this chapter that impact on teaching in transnational education, and require responses for quality teaching, are the diversity of the students when compared with the home institution, and the offshore setting for the educational programme, with the latter also implying diversity of teachers. The previous discussion has pointed to some particular dimensions for transnational education teaching enhancement, and O'Mahony (2014: 37–38) presents these succinctly as follows: first is the need to recognize that both visiting and locally-based offshore staff face challenges that are related to the transnational education context; second, it is important to support staff on offshore programmes so that they can be aware of cultural and social adjustments required of themselves as teachers and of their students for successful study outcomes; third, and significantly, teaching in offshore programmes needs to be tailored to the offshore context.

Student diversity has impact in a number of ways, including aspects such as their educational backgrounds, experiences and expectations, ways of interacting, approaches to knowledge, and post-study expectations. The peculiarities of the offshore setting include varying cultural modes of interaction, educational expectations, and desired outcomes based on national, economic and employment situations; that is, the needs of students who live and will most likely work in the offshore setting. As identified earlier in this chapter, the criteria used for teaching excellence awards in higher education institutions are aligned with the characteristics of transnational education, and thus can be used as a guide in discussions and strategies for enhancing transnational education teaching excellence. To reiterate, these criteria and the relevant indicators that specifically relate to transnational education within the criteria are: curriculum – for learning outcomes to be suitable for the needs of the students; subject knowledge, with knowledge relevant outside the discipline as well as within; inspiring and motivating students, with learning being meaningful for students; respect and care, with recognition of diverse learning needs, personalized learning, and addressing students' prior knowledge and experiences; active and group learning with interactive teaching methods; critical and scholarly approaches as in critical thinking and research skills in a wider social sense; engagement in assessment in recognizing the diversity in students' preferences.

Following from these points it is evident that a key factor to promote transnational education teaching excellence is to provide professional development for teaching staff, whether they are located offshore or are home country teachers who visit the offshore setting for teaching purposes. While there will be commonalities in academic staff professional development regardless of the setting, such as in curriculum design principles, the offshore staff will need to be alerted to the influence of the offshore setting. It may reflect assumptions that are counter to those embedded in the academic programme. For instance, the onshore-developed programme may assume that students expect to exercise independence in their learning, and so class time is devolved to students for group projects. However, offshore students may perceive with this approach their teachers neglecting their duties, and as inappropriate given that they may pay high fees for their studies and expect face-to-face teacher time. A further example concerns student group/team work. Students from more communally-orientated cultures may not initially appreciate the line between collaborative learning and collusion, and the teaching and learning approach may need to be adjusted accordingly.

Developing transnational education teaching competencies involves understanding transnational education students' learning needs and addresses a risk factor in international education (O'Mahony 2014). Furthermore, O'Mahony cites the European Commission in pointing out that such professional development should focus on developing the teachers' intercultural understandings, particularly in terms of the students. Professional development with a focus explained previously should ideally take place interactively between teachers from the home institution and offshore settings so that expectations, understandings and ideas can be shared. While implementing face-to-face interaction may be problematic, electronic communication means can be utilized. The advantage of a collaborative approach is that offshore staff can learn about the higher education institution's educational directions and preferred teaching approaches, and the perspectives of home country teaching staff can be broadened as they learn about current ways of operating in the offshore setting, the characteristics of the students, societal and cultural values, and directions in the offshore setting. These understandings underpin teachers' ability to address the teaching excellence award criteria of treating students with respect and care through recognizing students' diverse learning needs.

Such knowledge can be used in curriculum review including review of assessment modes and tasks, and thus enhance the quality of the curriculum and educational approach, and its relevance to the needs of all students, including those in the offshore setting. Increasing the relevance of studies and the subject content for students in the offshore setting encourages students' engagement, consequent interest and enthusiasm for their studies, and so addresses the teaching excellence award criterion of students' active and group learning, as well as that of engaging students in assessment. Regarding developing teacher flexibility, the professional development agenda should include understanding of different interests and ways of thinking, as well as the ability to reconcile differing perspectives, including the ability to compromise. Recognition that different situations may call for different teaching approaches from those normally implemented (Lindblom-Ylanne et al. 2006) underpins the ability for teachers to be flexible and recognize that problems/issues may arise and new and effective teaching solutions need to be devised.

A focus for staff professional development about student-centred teaching approaches enables teachers to not only focus on the diversity of their students, but also on facilitating active, interactive and problem-based learning with their students. This point aligns with the earlier-mentioned teaching excellence award criterion of curriculum, where understanding the learning outcomes in relation to the students' needs as well as in the disciplinary context is required. Staff offshore may not initially appreciate the notion of active and interactive learning and the reasons why it is important in today's knowledge-based world. The sharing of perspectives from teachers in both settings enriches the discussion and development. However, a diplomatic approach is important in introducing it and should widen the repertoire of offshore teachers and home institution teachers in terms of teaching approaches, rather than replacing current practices. There are times when different teaching and learning approaches are called for, such as with disciplinary threshold concepts where a more structured, teacher-focused approach may initially be effective. Building into the professional development programme an understanding of the need for curriculum alignment across learning outcomes, assessment and teaching and learning approaches, would provide a framework for teachers to appreciate when particular teaching and learning approaches are suitable.

Some higher education institutions recognize the importance of professional development for offshore settings, and the guide from Griffith University in Australia (Barker and Hibbins 2011) includes foci questions to develop an appreciation of student diversity and prior learning. Following are the type of questions that should drive professional development regarding students and their needs: Why have these students chosen this programme? What is the academic background of the students and the assumptions that can be made about their prior learning? Where does the subject fit within the programme they are enrolled in? Which subjects have preceded this one and which will follow? What ideas, concepts, skills in these earlier courses can be built on? What has already been done? (Barker and Hibbins 2011).

In terms of addressing the teaching excellence criterion of developing students' critical and scholarly approaches, the following questions set the scene for teachers to relate to students in ways that will facilitate their critical, creative thinking and scholarly approaches, and in addition, encourage the integration of theory with practice and the application of knowledge outside the disciplinary context as well as within. What are the learning experiences and backgrounds of the student cohort? Given the student cohort, what is the best way to connect and access key points, concepts and ideas? How is knowledge constructed and assessed in this course or discipline in this country? Is it different from your own; if so, in what ways? How do student expectations match with your expectations of the course elements (including course roles and responsibilities of teachers and of students; teaching styles and methods; learning outcomes; style of teaching and use of technology)? How familiar are students with academic conventions, and how can I support/what resources can I draw on to help students understand and apply these in their academic work? How is it best to deliver and structure assessment in this subject in a student-centred rather than teacher-focused way? How can I ensure my students appreciate the teaching approach and its rationale and engage with it? (ibid.).

The teaching excellence award criteria of inspiring and motivating students, and the relevance of subject knowledge outside the discipline, can be addressed through the following types of questions. What is it that I do in my teaching currently that engages, motivates and intellectually stimulates my students? How can I enhance my teaching environment to increasingly engage, motivate and intellectually stimulate my students in their learning? How do I use research in my teaching currently, and how can I enhance this to emphasize the importance, relevance, and integration of theory and knowledge with professional practice? How can I shape my teaching and assessment practices so students need to develop solutions to real world issues? What learning experiences can I use to develop my students as interculturally capable graduates who can operate effectively in the global setting? What content do I use in my teaching that assists students to value and respect all students? (Barker and Hibbins 2011).

Furthermore, in maintaining the integrity of the local offshore context and at the same time develop students' cross cultural perspectives, classroom discussions should focus on intercultural and transnational comparison rather than replacing the local with the home institution approach (Hoare 2012). This approach provides the opportunity for 'meaningful and reconstructive cross cultural dialogue' (Leask 2004: 2). A reality of transnational education is the distance geographically and temporally between the higher education institution home and the offshore settings. Collaboration of teachers in an academic programme across teaching contexts is important in maintaining and extending teaching quality (Smith 2009). Such collaboration provides the opportunity for teachers in both settings to develop superior modes of teaching that integrate effective features of both settings, leading to enhanced student outcomes for all. If communication and interaction do not take place, or are limited, non-inclusive modes of operation may occur, where, for instance, directions are imposed on teachers from the home to the offshore setting. Such a hierarchical approach can work against the motivation and enthusiasm of offshore teachers for their teaching. Since inspired and motivating teaching is a criterion of teaching excellence awards, it is important to create a climate of inclusion, sharing and ownership rather than dominance and control. Communication is vital for collaboration.

Inclusion, collaboration and communication can be fostered by collaborative curriculum development and assessment approaches. For instance, curriculum development groups of relevant teaching staff across the offshore and the home institution settings can be established and subsequently used for collaborative subject review on conclusion of the subject delivery. The input from all geographic settings is valuable in the review of learning outcomes, modes of assessment and tasks, and subject content, so that the curriculum is current and relevant to students in all settings (Crosling 2011). A cross-setting bank of teaching examples related to disciplinary principles can be developed, with offshore and home institution teachers contributing their local examples. Electronic filing of the materials means that teachers in both settings can draw on them enriching the teaching programme and simultaneously authenticating the offshore setting. The same approach can be taken for programme review to update and ensure the currency and relevance for all settings of the overall academic programme.

Conclusion

Teaching excellence is a requirement, not a 'wished for' luxury in higher education globally. As higher education has broadened and internationalized in its reach, transnational education operations have become increasingly common. But transnational education is not without risks and the brand and reputation of the home institution offering the programme offshore can be damaged if educational processes are not of a high standard. The quality of the teaching and the degree of students' satisfaction are strongly implicated in transnational educational quality, and excellence needs to be striven for so as to enhance the sustainability of the higher education institution and its programmes. Educational approaches, including teaching, need to address the situation whereby the offshore location of the programme brings with it different needs and requirements, and strongly take account of the student profile being diverse from the home country setting. These are areas on which research could focus to deepen understandings in the field of transnational education and teaching excellence. Research could also examine the nature of student diversity *within* offshore student cohorts and its impact on the educational programme, the student experience and satisfaction, and, importantly, students' academic achievements and outcomes.

The transnational form of the international branch campus is positioned well to customize the educational programme to the offshore context. The branch campus is integral to the higher education institution overall and therefore provides the opportunity for trust and confidence to be developed as staff across settings interact. This provides a climate for more inclusive educational approaches, allowing recognition of the characteristics of the offshore setting in educational processes. While such a climate is more difficult to achieve in a twinning/franchise transnational education arrangement, with staff delivering the academic programme belonging to a separate organization, it is incumbent on the home institution to ensure that educational equivalence occurs across the educational settings, including in staff professional development and offshore staff's inclusion in curriculum development and renewal.

Responses to the offshore characteristics in the curriculum, including teaching, result in enhanced educational programmes and teaching offshore. But there are also other spin-offs. The perspectives of the home institution's teachers can be developed and broadened if there is collaboration and communication in professional development and in curriculum development and renewal between the home institution and the offshore teaching staff. This can result in enhanced curriculum, teaching and educational experiences for all students, regardless of their geographic location, if used effectively. The challenge is for home institutions in all forms of transnational education to ensure that they appreciate and act on what constitutes teaching and educational excellence in offshore settings. This is based increasingly on recognizing not only the educational needs, but also the strengths of the education as it is played out offshore and perceiving teaching excellence in a way that brings the best of both home and transnational education settings to the higher education institution's overall educational scenario.

References

Barker, M. and Hibbins, R. (2011) *Preparation for teaching offshore: a guide*, Griffith University, Australia. Online. Available at www.griffith.edu.au/_data/assets/pdf_file/0010/391375/GU8484-Offshore-Booklet-reprint_20111124.pdf (accessed 14 June 2017).

Chalmers, D. (2008) *Teaching and learning quality indicators in Australian universities*, Paris: Organisation for Economic Co-operation and Development (OECD).

Chalmers, D., Cummings, R., Elliot, S., Stoney, S., Tucker, B., Wicking, R. and Jorre de St Jorre, T. (2014) *Australian University Teaching Criteria and Standards Project*, Department for Education, Sydney, Australia. Online. Available at http://uniteachingcriteria.edu.au/wp-content/uploads/2013/11/SP12_2335_Cummings_report_2015.pdf (accessed 14 June 2017).

Crosling, G. (2011) 'Defining identity, engaging teachers and engaging students: "education strengths" in a foreign branch campus', in L. Thomas and M. Tight (eds) *Institutional transformation to engage a diverse student body*, 245–252, Bingley: Emerald Books.

Crosling, G. (2012) 'Issues and strategies for student engagement through assessment in transnational higher education', in L. Clouder, C. Broughan, S. Jewell and G. Steventon (eds) *Improving student engagement and development through assessment: theory and practice in higher education*, Abingdon: Routledge.

Crosling, G., Thomas, L. and Heagney, M. (2008) *Improving student retention in higher education: the role of teaching and learning*, London: Routledge.

Crosling, G., Nair, M. and Vaithilingam, S. (2015) 'A creative learning ecosystem, quality of education and innovative capacity: a perspective from higher education', *Studies in Higher Education*, 40(7): 1147–1163.

Edwards, J., Crosling, G. and Edwards, R. (2010) 'Outsourcing university degrees: implications for quality control', *Journal of Higher Education Policy and Management*, 32(3): 303–315.

Edwards, R., Crosling, G. and Lim, N. C. (2014) 'Organizational structures for international universities: implications for campus autonomy, academic freedom, collegiality, and conflict', *Journal of Studies in International Education*, 18(2): 180–194.

Gunn, V. and Fisk, A. (2013) *Considering teaching excellence in higher education: 2007–2013: a literature review since the CHERI Report 2007*, Project Report, York: Higher Education Academy.

Hoare, L. (2012) 'Transnational student voices: reflections on a second chance', *Journal of Studies in International Education*, 16(3): 271–286.

Land, R. and Gordon, G. (2014) *Teaching excellence initiatives: modalities and operational factors*, York: The Higher Education Academy.

Leask, B. (2004) 'Transnational education and intercultural learning: reconstructing the offshore teaching team to enhance internationalisation', *Proceedings of the Australian Universities Quality Forum 2004*. Online. Available at http://citeseerx.ist.psu.edu/viewdoc/download?doi=10.1.1.114.9090&rep=rep1&type=pdf (accessed 14 June 2017).

Lindblom-Ylanne, S., Trigwell, K., Nevgi, A. and Ashwin, P. (2006) 'How approaches to teaching are affected by discipline and teaching context', *Studies in Higher Education*, 31(3): 285–298.

McBurnie, G. and Ziguras, C. (2007) *Transnational education: issues and trends in offshore education*, London: Routledge.

O' Mahony, J. (2014) *Enhancing student learning and teacher development in transnational education*, York: Higher Education Academy.

Prosser, M. and Trigwell, K. (2002) *Understanding learning and teaching: the experience of higher education*, Buckingham: The Society for Research into Higher Education.

Scott, G. (2005) *Accessing the student voice*, Final Report, Higher Education Innovation Program and the Collaboration and Structural Reform Fund, Department of Education, Science and Training, Canberra: Commonwealth of Australia.

Smith, L. (2009) 'Sinking in the sand? Academic work in an offshore setting of an Australian university', *Higher Education Research and Development*, 28(5): 467–479.

Tertiary Education Quality and Standards Agency (TEQSA) (2013) *Information paper: TEQSA's approach to regulating the offshore provision of regulated HE awards*. Australian Government. Online. Available at www.teqsa.gov.au/sites/default/files/Regulating OffshoreProvisionOfRegulatedHEAwardsInfoSheet.pdf (accessed 14 June 2017).

Tharapos, M. (2014) *Cultural intelligence in the transnational education classroom: the case of Australian accounting academics*, doctoral thesis submitted to the Royal Melbourne Institute of Technology, Melbourne.

Thomas, L. and Quinn, J. (2003) *International insights into widening participation: supporting the success of under-represented groups in tertiary education*, Stoke-on-Trent: Trentham Books.

Tinto, V. (1975) 'Dropout from higher education: a theoretical synthesis of recent research', *Review of Educational Research*, 45(10): 89–125.

Trow, M. (1973) *Problems in the transition from elite to mass higher education*, New York: Carnegie Commission on Higher Education.

Waterval, D., Tinnemans-Adriaanse, M., Meziani, M., Driessen, E., Scherpbier, A., Mazrou, A. and Frambach, J. (2017) 'Exporting a student–centered curriculum: a home institution's perspective', *Journal of Studies in International Education*, 1–13.

Critical friend commentary

Ron Edwards

Managing higher education student diversity for teaching excellence may be relatively easy in single site university contexts. Teachers can leverage the diverse student backgrounds to enrich the experience for the whole class; for example, by placing different background students in the same project group. However, multi-country contexts can be much more challenging in achieving teaching excellence. The priority is to provide partners in other countries with material to get them started: a curriculum, learning objectives, PowerPoint slides, tutorial questions, reading material and so on. This may occur when there is concern to protect the university's intellectual property, the supplying academic's autonomy, and both parties' financial interests. Ensuring recognition and accommodation of the interests of students of different backgrounds may be a low priority. Accordingly, Crosling's focus on this topic is timely.

As international education is primarily an exercise in sharing 'advanced', Western educational philosophies and practices with developing countries primarily, student diversity can take many forms. An important form is students' learning background. Commonly, especially in Asia, this features heavy rote learning. Students who progress to university will have used this model successfully and may persist with it in their new environment, no matter what the teacher says. Training the lecturers to address this element of classroom diversity in striving for teaching excellence requires more than the standard 'package' described above.

Differing home and host partner students' income standards is another form of diversity that might be expected. Capacity to purchase text books, a laptop computer and software will differ between the home university and the offshore partner, and within the offshore partner's classroom. In one case with which I am familiar, a lecturer prescribed a sophisticated, expensive piece of software as their subject's primary learning and teaching platform, which was to be offered in several countries. Two problems were soon apparent. First, the developing country students at that time did not have credit cards essential for the online software purchase. Second, locals around the campus were poor and sometimes supplemented their income by digging up the cable supporting the campus internet service, thereby impairing the software's operation. In these circumstances, despite wishing to ensure an equivalent learning experience and teaching excellence, the university had to abandon the software in the offshore campus.

In addition to cultural background, learning style and economic status, student diversity reflects diverse life experience. Students at the offshore setting may have never studied in English previously, lived in a city away from family, or been responsible for themselves. They often look to their lecturers for guidance and feel remote from classmates for whom university study is a smooth transition from a high quality, academic secondary school.

By presenting this issue for discussion, Crosling is assisting the international education community to take its discipline and teaching excellence to a higher level.

Having reached a stage of maturity, with so many students experiencing an international education, attention needs to move beyond student outcomes equivalence to managing student diversity. Her chapter represents a substantive contribution to that objective.

5

EXCELLENCE FOR WHAT? POLICY DEVELOPMENT AND THE DISCOURSE ON THE PURPOSE OF HIGHER EDUCATION

Mary Runté and Robert Runté

Introduction

Any discourse on teaching excellence must be placed within the larger discourse on the purpose of higher education. How one defines teaching excellence is entirely dependent on what one wishes to achieve, so it is important to understand how expectations for higher education have changed over time. Four competing discourses on the purpose of higher education are identified, each in turn leading to (or emerging out of) fundamental shifts in the institutional structures of higher education. These ideological and structural shifts necessarily call forth corresponding shifts in pedagogy, and in the metrics of teaching success. Understanding these fundamental historical shifts allows for a more penetrating analysis of any proposed framework of teaching excellence. Comparing the current UK White Paper, *Success as a knowledge economy: teaching excellence, social mobility and student choice* (Department for Business, Innovation and Skills 2016) with the North American experience raises questions about both the viability of some of the UK government's underlying assumptions and the long-term implications of the direction chosen.

Four discourses on the purpose of higher education

There has long been tension between the conflicting discourses of the university as a liberal arts institution and its role as a centre for professional training (Newman 1852: 171). For the purposes of the current analysis, however, four competing discourses can be laid out chronologically in terms of when each emerged or became dominant, drawing on examples from North America and the United Kingdom.

The discourse of enlightenment

The initially dominant view of the purpose of education can be labelled as a discourse of 'enlightenment'. For example, Cardinal Newman (1852: 130), founder of Dublin University, argued that 'the end of university education, and of the liberal or philosophical knowledge which I conceive it to impart . . . is that any kind of knowledge, if it really be such, is its own reward'. Proponents of this view argue that the purpose of education – as opposed to mere training – was to develop the 'cultured gentleman'. In addition to a cultivated intellect, a disciplined and logical mind, the graduate was expected to possess 'a discerning taste, a noble and courteous bearing in the conduct of his life, and a sense of responsibility to his society and civilization' (Newman 1852: 144). This discourse of enlightenment formed the ideological context of universities as elite institutions. The university's role was to educate the nation's social, cultural, and ruling elite(s) and, even given provision for scholarships and sponsored mobility, reproduced the social order by recruiting for the limited available seats primarily from the sons of the upper class.

Higher education was therefore a form of conspicuous consumption: one partook because it was expected of gentlemen, not because it was required for economic advantage or determined one's status in society. To the extent that governments provided funding, the benefits accruing from the establishment of universities were thought to be of a cultural, rather than economic, nature. Universities, like museums and the theatre, were the outcome of economic growth and prosperity, not the cause.

Consequently, universities were traditionally autonomous institutions; the guardians of high culture passed on through a liberal education and such professions as law and the clergy. As such, teaching was necessarily curriculum-centred: students were told what they needed to learn and held to standards set by the academy, with recitation and rote learning held in high regard as a necessary prerequisite to a disciplined and logical intellect. Teaching excellence was assessed by the university's administration and largely defined by the instructor's insistence on high standards, discipline and social correctness.

The discourse of human capital

By the 1960s the view of higher education as personal consumption was almost completely displaced by a discourse of human capital, which held that expenditures on education were an investment in the nation's economic progress. To quote human capital proponent, and subsequent Nobel laureate, Theodore Schultz (1961: 1):

> . . . skills and knowledge are a form of capital, that this capital is in substantial part a product of deliberate investment, that it has grown in Western societies at a much faster rate than conventional (nonhuman) capital, and that this growth may well be the most distinctive feature of the economic system . . .

Much of what we call consumption constitutes investment in human capital. Direct expenditures on education, health, and internal migration to take advantage of better job opportunities are clear examples. Earnings foregone by mature students attending school and by workers acquiring on-the-job training are equally clear examples (Schultz 1961).

In the post-war period, then, economists moved higher education from the 'consumption' to the 'investment' column, arguing that a broad range of skilled workers was required for the transition to a post-industrial, knowledge economy. Furthermore, investment in human capital promised to solve a broad range of social problems. The premise of the American War on Poverty of the 1960s and 1970s, for example, was that economically depressed populations lacked the basic education and employable skills that opened the door to opportunity (Karabel and Halsey 1977). Pointing to the correlation between salary and years of education, all North Americans were directed to invest in their own and their children's further education as the primary route to upward social mobility (ibid.). Faced with both the resulting escalation in the educational aspirations of the public, and the demographic bulge of the baby boom, economists encouraged policy-makers to accommodate this explosive increase in demand (Bladen Commission 1965; Economic Council of Canada 1966). Told that human skill development was fundamental to future economic development, and assured that increased revenue accruing from income taxes on the higher paid employment undertaken by post-secondary graduates would offset the heavy investment in human capital infrastructure, policy-makers gladly funded the rapid expansion of higher education from a few elite institutions into a system of mass education.

Initially embraced by American and Canadian policy-makers – in part because human capital economic theory resonated so well with the North American ideals of meritocracy, progress, and capitalism (Karabel and Halsey 1977) – a discourse of human capital was quickly exported throughout the capitalist world. Private American agencies, such as the Ford Foundation, funded publications, international conferences and consultations with leading policy-makers, while American influence over international agencies, such as the World Bank, the International Monetary Fund, and the Organisation for Economic Co-operation and Development (OECD), ensured that a discourse of human capital became the basis of development strategies throughout Asia, Africa, and Latin America (ibid.).

Although economists shifted the discourse from 'learning for its own sake' to 'education as investment', early formulations emphasized the rationality of the consumer to make sensible investment decisions, such that the needs of individuals were seen as congruent with those of the state (Worth 1972). The system of post-secondary technical institutes was similarly expanded and competed directly with universities for the students, as individuals chose between programmes that promised the best return on their investment in tuition and foregone earnings.

This discourse of the individual as rational investor resonates with the North American ideology of meritocracy, but necessarily raises issues of accessibility and equality of opportunity. As student-investors increasingly defined their own learning needs, and governments rushed to meet voter demand for post-secondary places, university teaching inevitably shifted towards more student-centred instruction (Sheffield 1970: 434). Teaching excellence came to be increasingly defined and evaluated, not by senior administration, but by student course evaluations (Murray 2005). Relevance, student engagement, and authentic assessments therefore replaced the emphasis on high standards, discipline, and the reproduction (regurgitation) of curriculum as the defining elements of teaching excellence (Sheffield 1970: 434).

The discourse of manpower

A second fundamental shift occurred when critics called into question whether *all* higher education contributed directly to economic development (Lockhart 1971; Fortier 1975). Instead of insulating the economy from recession by contributing to sustained economic growth, human–capital inspired policies had resulted in the overproduction of, and consequently un- or under-employment of, knowledge workers (Lockhart 1971). Instead of raising mean incomes by ensuring everyone had the skills required for high-paying employment, the growing reserve army of un- and under-employed knowledge workers threatened to bring wages down (Spring 1984).

Nor had investment in higher education delivered the predicted social dividends. The war on poverty, for example, had incorrectly blamed the victims of unemploy- ment for their lack of skills, whereas it became increasingly clear that their failure to find jobs that paid a living wage was because of racism, sexism, economic depres- sion, and uneven development of industries and regions. Compared with some workers who had found steady employment in high-wage industries, these workers had, in many cases, even more human capital, but happened to be the wrong colour or sex . . . or to live on the wrong side of town or in the wrong part of the country. The inadequacy of the economic system is a more important cause of poverty than the inadequacy of people (Bluestone 1977: 338). In Alberta, for example, policy-makers responded to the failure of human capital theory to deliver on prom- ised economic and social returns by adopting a more tightly targeted 'manpower' orientation, focused on meeting the specific – immediate and projected – labour needs of the provincial (or national) economy. The manpower discourse rejected funding every individual aspiring to become a nurse or teacher, for example, if the numbers entering these faculties was known to exceed the demand for graduates; which demand was easily calculated, since it was the government itself that determined how many teaching and nursing positions would be funded in the province in four years' time. Consequently, the shift from human capital to manpower discourse necessarily represents a shift from prioritizing the needs of individuals (under the human capital theory of the individual as rational investor) to prioritizing the identifiable needs of the economy.

This tighter monitoring of the economic return on investment produces two trends relevant to our understanding of teaching excellence. Programmes that could not demonstrate an immediate economic return, such as many liberal arts, were given a lower funding priority than professional and business faculties (Runté and Runté 2016). Lower funding necessarily implies less funding for growth in those disciplines, and therefore capped admissions. The most politically expedient means to restrict admissions within a meritocracy is by raising admission standards, which in turn inevitably leads to a renewed emphasis on competitive grades and 'objective' testing (McEwen 1995). Testing necessarily refocuses attention on curriculum-centric instruction, because it is easier to objectively measure mastery of curriculum-determined standards than to assess the degree of an individual's self-actualization.

For technical and professional preparation programmes that benefited from this shift in funding priorities, accountability demands quickly drilled down to the classroom level. As 'learning for its own sake' is replaced by an explicit 'vocationalization' of higher education, individual courses, and ultimately specific learning objectives within each course, are minutely examined for a demonstrable vocational relevance. In such a context, teaching excellence is evaluated primarily on the instructor's ability to prepare future workers for their specific workplace. There is, therefore, a shift back towards curriculum-centric instruction as 'relevance' is redefined to refer to the needs of the contemporary workplace rather than to 'the learning needs of students'.

As public funding has been increasingly prioritized on the basis of economic rather than individual needs, there has been a corresponding increase in the demand for greater accountability with regard to teaching outcomes. The emphasis on accountability, high standards, 'relevant' curricula, and so on, are attempts by external audiences to ensure the ongoing investment (by governments, parents, and the students themselves) in higher education delivers the promised dividends.

The discourse of consumerism

As policy-makers transitioned to a discourse of manpower planning and sought to assign a lower priority to non-vocational programmes, they had to contend with the frustrated aspirations of parent voters who, under the influence of decades of human capital logic, still pressed for an expansion of university places for their children. One response was the emergence of a new discourse of further education as a purely consumer activity.

In Alberta, for example, the shift from human capital to manpower discourse can be pinpointed to the 1971 election of the Progressive Conservative (PC) party on a platform of cutbacks to expenditures on education, health care and other human capital investments. Whereas the previous government had funded nearly unlimited expansion of higher education, establishing three new universities, the PCs were appalled at projected capital expenses of $100,000,000 for a second campus for the provincial capital, and immediately cancelled the project.

Instead of disappearing, however, the campus-less Athabasca University (AU) repositioned itself to become Canada's first open access correspondence university (on the model of the Open University in England). AU had no entrance requirements, no restrictions on admissions, delivered courses to anyone anywhere, and was the first university to accept payment by credit card. It is, therefore, one model of higher education as a consumer commodity. The government's limited funding falls into the consumption category, rather than investment, because the majority of AU students are already fully employed and work on courses in their leisure time. AU, like live theatre and museums, is deemed worthy of support as a cultural institution, but not as an engine of the economy. Although some students may successfully upgrade their credentials through AU, just as some individuals may make a living as actors or museum staff, it is a by-product of keeping these cultural institutions going, not the primary purpose.

The real dividend for policy-makers of funding the emergence of consumer-oriented higher education, however, is that it diffuses the issues of accessibility and equality of opportunity that became prominent in the human capital era. Voter discontent over limiting university places is addressed by the dual strategy of significantly raising admission standards (for example, blaming the victim for not having achieved better grades) and by offering open admission to AU as an alternative route. This is even more clearly the case with the subsequent emergence of online courses offered by both traditional institutions and private for-profit vendors, which provide universal and equal access to higher education for everyone, though at the student's own expense, as one would expect of a consumer product in a capitalist society.

The discourse of consumerism, then, defines higher education as a mass market commodity largely outside the formal, government-funded, post-secondary system, even if some public institutions (such as AU) compete with private providers. Some consumers may choose to pursue a degree, but most shop by the course, with course offerings extending far beyond traditional curricula to every conceivable topic (the reader is challenged to find a subject for which an online course is not readily available). As with any consumer product in a competitive market, the many online course vendors are necessarily student-orientated. Their offerings are entirely determined by consumer wants, and instructional assessment is predominantly through customer ratings. The criteria for teaching excellence are therefore relevant to the student's personal interests, clarity, ease, and above all, entertainment value.

Student expectations within distinct discourses

Discussions of teaching excellence sometimes overlook that teaching and learning take place within the context of student expectations. Although student attitudes are a product of individual personality, upbringing and current family pressures, previous learning experiences, cultural practices, and so on, one should not discount the influence of the dominant discourse (for example, hegemonic ideology) in shaping student expectations of higher education.

University students during the dominance of the discourse of enlightenment can best be characterized as *entitled*. Whether born into the privileged classes, selected for scholarships and sponsorship on the basis of their superior intellect and character, or earning their way through college by dint of hard work and being self-made, students of elite universities know themselves to be destined for leadership.

This necessarily influences the culture of the classroom as students predominantly come from, and are destined for, higher-status positions than their instructors currently occupy. Authority flows, therefore, from the curriculum, senior administration, the discipline of house rules, and peer pressure to conform. In such structures, students can have no expectation of teaching excellence; by definition, curriculum-centred programmes insist the instructor knows better than the student what the student's real learning needs are, and can therefore disregard student interests or engagement. Students correspondingly place few demands on their instructors, because the liberal arts curriculum may bear little apparent relevance to their specific career aspirations, and because, for those from wealthy backgrounds at least, their university standing may have little relevance to future social standing.

As elite universities expanded into post-secondary systems, students could be described as *optimistic*, reflective both of the growing prosperity of the baby-boom generation, and the promise inherent in the human capital discourse of future advancement in social economic status in return for delayed gratification. In this meritocratic context, teaching excellence can be demanded because instructor status (like all status) needs to be earned to be respected. Through the provision of student course evaluations, pressure is put on instructors to become more relevant, engaging, and to allow for student input and expression (for example, switching from rote learning, and the regurgitation of instructor opinion, to more authentic assessments).

The increasing vocationalization of education at every level inculcates in post-secondary students the discourse of higher education as job training. Instead of knowledge for its own sake, students are orientated to see learning as entirely *instrumental*, and are therefore inclined to demand of their instructors a precise accounting of the monetary value of every fact and skill learned. 'Why do we have to learn this?' is a question that frequently disrupts any attempt to enrich teaching beyond the base curriculum. Class discussion is often dismissed by these students as irrelevant because in a curriculum-centred classroom the opinions of others are not seen as directly relevant to acquiring job-related knowledge and skills. Engagement with the material is an unexpected bonus, but cannot be allowed to distract from the key purpose of obtaining high scores and crucial certification for a good résumé. Motivated primarily by the externals of grades and certificates, course requirements become mere hoops through which to jump, and instructors are viewed as hostile gatekeepers whom one must strive to placate through (often insincere) expressions of agreement. In this context, teaching excellence may require engaging students in spite of their nearly complete lack of motivation to learn anything not on the test.

This is not to suggest that such students are inherently anti-intellectual or lack curiosity, only that they do not expect to express their own interests and learning needs within the post-secondary classroom. Rather, the discourse of consumerism directs them to seek self-expression and self-actualization – learning for its own sake – as a leisure-time activity. Today, one can Google any fact or learn any skill through free content providers such as Wikipedia or Videojug, sign up for any course in which one has a personal interest, and even complete a certificate programme online should one desire to package these disparate elements into a coherent whole. In this self-directed commercial context, teaching excellence is expected as a given and enforced by market forces, but defined by the personal preferences of the consumer. Here the barrier to true teaching excellence is students' sometimes waning motivation, short attention span, and such an extreme emphasis on a student-centred approach, that curriculum and standards may get short shrift.

Excellence for what?

Table 5.1 identifies the four discourses of the purpose of higher education and summarizes their implications for post-secondary structures, student expectations, and teaching excellence.

Of course, the argument contained in Table 5.1 is painted in very broad strokes, and the reality is much more complex and nuanced. For the purposes of the current brief analysis, however, these four columns may be taken to represent 'ideal types', even though likely never found in pure form. Most North American universities, for example, have become 'multiversities', delivering a wide variety of programmes, such that different components might easily fall within different columns on the table; particular courses may serve different purposes for individual students; or the same course may fulfil multiple purposes for the same student. Indeed, it is often difficult to disentangle the underlying assumptions of particular policies and frameworks, as policy-makers and university administrators confabulate contradictory elements of these distinct discourses to better pitch their case to particular audiences (Runté and Runté 2016). To that extent, all four discourses remain current, though the manpower discourse tends to dominate national and state policies (ibid.).

The 2016 UK White Paper, *Success as a knowledge economy: teaching excellence, social mobility and student choice* (Department for Business, Innovation and Skills 2016: 7), begins within a discourse of human capital: 'Higher education is no longer limited to the academic elite within a small and primarily Government-funded set of institutions . . . (it) continues to be a sound financial and personal investment with a wide range of societal benefits'. The proposed policy is premised on the assumption that expenditures on higher education are a necessary and sufficient investment to increase Gross Domestic Product (GDP):

> a 1% increase in the share of the workforce with a university degree raises long-run productivity by between 0.2% and 0.5%; and around 20% of UK economic growth between 1982 and 2005 came as a direct result of increased graduate skills accumulation. Recent research at the London School of Economics demonstrates the strong correlation between opening universities and significantly increased economic growth. Doubling the number of universities per capita is associated with over 4% higher future GDP per capita (ibid.: 8–9).

Ignoring for the moment the logical flaw in projecting the precise return on the investment in universities, while simultaneously changing the definition of

TABLE 5.1 Implications of the four discourses on higher education

Dimension	Enlightenment discourse	Human capital discourse	Manpower discourse	Consumerism discourse
Institutional structure/ governance	Universities autonomous	Universities autonomous within provincial or state system	Universities and state secondary system directed by government priorities	Public institutions compete (outside central mandate) with private providers for consumer dollars
Institutional scale	Universities elite institutions	Universities become mass institutions; technical schools and colleges expanded	Multiversities part of universal post-secondary system	Mass market largely outside formal government-funded post-secondary system
Scope	Liberal education and traditional professions only	Liberal education & broadly expanded vocational preparation	Vocational preparation – prioritized by current & projected manpower needs	(Online) offerings of every conceivable topic
Consumption vs investment	Costs borne by the individual (consumption)	Costs borne by public purse and individual (investment)	Cost borne by individual and public subsidy (investment)	Cost borne by the individual (consumption)
Individual needs vs societal needs	Needs of university-graduated elite equated with needs of society	Needs of individual seem as converging with needs of society	Societal needs given priority over needs of individual	Wants of the individual given priority
Curriculum-centred vs student-centred	Curriculum-centred	Student-centred	Curriculum-centred	Student-centred (student-directed)
Ideological watchwords	Standards, learning for its own sake, cultured	Relevance; accessibility; equality of opportunity	Vocational relevance; employability of graduates	Choice; self-actualization; learning for its own sake; lifelong learning

Dimension	Enlightenment discourse	Human capital discourse	Manpower discourse	Consumerism discourse
Predominant criteria for teaching excellence	Intellectual rigour; (rote) reproduction of cultural knowledge; socialization into appropriate elite as cultured graduate; etc.	Relevance to student learning needs; student engagement; authentic assessment	Vocational relevance; demonstrable dollar value of skills and knowledge acquired; a renewed emphasis on standards in liberal arts	Relevance to student personal wants; entertainment; clarity and ease
Predominant form of teaching evaluation	Administration's assessment of instructional rigour and instructor's personal conduct (role modelling)	Student course evaluations	Outcomes-based programme accountability by stakeholders (government and business) external to institution	Consumer ratings of instructor and course programme
Student attitude	Entitlement	Optimism	Instrumentality	Self-directed

Note: The above represent 'ideal types' and may not exist in pure form; speakers frequently confabulate discourses 'university' ('a range of reforms to the way in which providers can award their own degrees . . . or call themselves a University' (ibid.: 10)), the policy addresses itself to developing a tertiary system of higher education that more fully integrates technical and academic education, and which now attracts forty per cent of the population (ibid.: 7–10).

We nevertheless find evidence of a shift towards a manpower discourse in the statements such as 'employers are suffering skills shortages, especially in high skilled STEM areas; at the same time, around 20% of employed graduates are in non-professional roles three and a half years after graduating' (ibid.: 8). The report acknowledges that although universities provide a context for deeper and wider learning, allowing for the development of skills such as analytical and creative thinking, objective inquiry and primary research, most students' see a priority in higher education in helping them find employment. The central thrust of the White Paper is to evoke student choice (for example, the student as rational investor), to apply pressure (for example, erode institutional autonomy through the application of market forces), to force institutions to 'raise their game' (ibid.: 8). The discourse represented by the White Paper is one of a narrow vocationalization; for example:

> . . . we will link higher education and tax data together to chart the transition of graduates from higher education into the workplace better. This rich new data source will give students the information about the rewards that could be available at the end of their learning, alongside the costs. This innovation is at the heart of delivering our reform agenda ambitions: improving choice, competition and outcomes for students, the taxpayer and the economy (ibid.: 14).

This discourse of the 'rewards' of higher education is here clearly reduced to the value of employment, and student choice is reduced to making sound career choices rather than, say, following one's passions or seeking generalized (and generalizable) skills and knowledge. Although there is obviously nothing inherently wrong with providing data for informed decision-making, identifying this as 'the heart' of the White Paper proposals strongly suggests a manpower orientation with all the associated implications for teaching: the needs of the economy given priority over the needs of individuals, a curriculum-centred classroom, students motivated only by grades and certificates and focused entirely on the immediate utility of the knowledge and skills presented.

Similarly, the White Paper's observation that one in three students believe their course represents poor value (ibid.: 11) begs the question of how students assessed 'value'. The correlations with such technocratic considerations as 'class size' or 'satisfaction with instructor support', provided within the Student Academic Experience Survey itself, entirely fail to address the larger question of what students consider as *the purpose* of their courses. Is it unrealistic to suggest that the steady decline in student perceptions of course value represents not an inexplicable decline in actual value, but rather a shift in the student definition of what constitutes 'value'?

Students raised within the discourse of human capital are more likely to value learning and personal growth, in the belief that any and all education improves one's life chances, whereas the shift towards a manpower discourse inculcates in students a much narrower and more instrumental assessment of course outcomes based solely on the criteria of relevance to employability. Revealingly, the White Paper itself acknowledges that students are already becoming 'instrumentalist', which it says characterizes the American higher education system (ibid.: 12); in other words, movement towards an American-style discourse of higher education as manpower management may encourage an instrumentalist, hoop-jumping orientation among students, that may actually work against teaching excellence.

Similarly, the metrics adopted for the *Teaching Excellence Framework* (Department of Education 2016) are the metrics of a manpower discourse: student *employment* outcomes; the learning environment measured by manpower-orientated criteria such as the dropout rate; and teaching and assessment measured by criteria such contract hours, course design, and (presumably) student feedback. The difficulty is that the criteria for course design or student engagement and so on are not specified within these documents, and necessarily vary depending upon the larger (but largely implicit) discourse of the purpose of education. Evaluating course objectives against the larger goal of vocational preparation gives a very different result than when assessed for personal growth. A manpower discourse gives rise to curriculum-centred course design, based on the skills and knowledge identified as crucial by employers. In contrast, a human capital discourse likely accommodates a more student-centred approach, with broader and more flexible course objectives to allow space for student needs and interests. 'Rigour' and 'stretch' therefore imply entirely different things, depending on one's understanding of the purpose of higher education.

The White Paper also asserts that teaching excellence is key to social mobility, 'since we will not truly begin to reduce inequality unless more students fulfil their aspirations and progress on into their chosen careers' (Department for Business, Innovation and Skills 2016: 13). Although the latter statement is unquestionably true, it is at most a necessary, but not necessarily sufficient, factor. Just as the American War on Poverty blamed the poor for not having requisite skills, the White Paper shifts blame for social inequality to institutions of higher education. Institutions can certainly do a better job of admitting minorities and the disadvantaged, but it remains for businesses to hire their graduates; no amount of excellent skill training can create jobs or overcome the barriers of class, race, gender or regional disparity. The White Paper's explicit confabulation of teaching excellence, student choice, and social mobility lays the entire weight of social and economic development on the shoulders of instructors, as if teaching excellence were a universal panacea. The suggestion that everyone could prosper if only everyone had an excellent education is as much a logical fallacy in the UK today as in North America in the 1980s: the economy does not magically produce jobs just because there are graduates to take them. On the contrary, the overproduction of knowledge workers can only lead to declining wages and greater opportunities for discrimination, to the disadvantage of the working class and minorities when labour supply outstrips demand.

More inclusive student recruitment and increased priority given to teaching are both admirable goals. The devil is in the details, however, and the failure to explicitly define the purpose of higher education leads to ambiguity in subsequent attempts to define 'teaching excellence'. The proxy metrics chosen reflect the discourse of manpower; the lack of specificity for qualities such as 'rigour' and 'stretch' similarly encourage further drift towards vocationalization, without necessarily being recognized as such.

To truly develop teaching excellence, one must first articulate a vision of what excellence would mean within the context of a particular discourse of purpose. Professional faculties, for example, must distinguish between 'education', which endows graduates with professional judgement; and 'training', which focuses on more specific skills, geared to the immediate needs of particular workplaces. Liberal arts institutions need to make the case for the purpose of liberal arts as distinct from mere vocational preparation, and then define teaching excellence within *that* context. And so on. Instead of passively accepting the external imposition of implicit definitions that run counter to their institution's vision, instructors need to explicitly argue the case for both the purpose of their programme, and the character of instruction that would best serve that purpose. Moreover, having defined teaching excellence on their own terms, institutions and disciplines need to establish their own metrics to encourage and document progress towards that goal. This is not to argue for impractical boycotts or rejection of nationally established metrics, but rather to balance these imposed metrics with one's own to provide a more complete description of teaching at one's institution. Understanding the competing discourses that underlie our definitions of teaching excellence both exposes the unwarranted assumptions of the current UK framework, and helps guide the process of developing alternative and supplementary measures. Ultimately, there can be no one universally applicable definition of teaching excellence, because the definition always depends on one's answer to 'excellence for what?'

References

Bladen Commission (1965) 'Association of Universities and Colleges of Canada Commission on financing higher education in Canada', *University Affairs*, 8: 2.
Bluestone, B. (1977) 'Economic theory and the fate of the poor', in J. Karabel and A. H. Halsey (eds) *Power and ideology in education*, 335–340, New York: Oxford University Press.
Department for Business Innovation and Skills (2016) *Success as a knowledge economy: teaching excellence, social mobility and student choice*, May 2016, London: Department for Business Innovation and Skills. Online. Available at www.gov.uk/government/uploads/system/uploads/attachment_data/file/523546/bis-16-265-success-as-a-knowledge-economy-web.pdf (accessed 27 March 2017).
Department of Education (2016) *Teaching Excellence Framework: year two specification*. Online. Available at www.gov.uk/government/uploads/system/uploads/attachment_data/file/556355/TEF_Year_2_specification.pdf (accessed 27 March 2017).
Economic Council of Canada (1966) *Annual report*, Ottawa: Economic Council of Canada.
Fortier, A. (1975) 'Economy cannot support too many artists', *University Affairs*, 16: 19.

Karabel, J. and Halsey, A. H. (1977) *Power and ideology in education*, New York: Oxford University Press.

Lockhart, A. (1971) 'Graduate unemployment and the myth of human capital', in D. Davies and K. Herman (eds) *Social space: Canadian perspectives*, 251–254, Toronto: New Press.

McEwen, N. (1995) 'Educational accountability in Alberta', *Canadian Journal of Education*, 20(1): 27–44.

Murray, H. (2005) *Student evaluation of teaching: has it made a difference?* paper presented at the Annual Meeting of the Society for Teaching and Learning in Higher Education, Charlottetown, Prince Edward Island, June 2005. Online. Available at www.stlhe.ca/wp-content/uploads/2011/07/Student-Evaluation-of-Teaching1.pdf (accessed 27 March 2017).

Newman, Cardinal J. H. (1852) *The idea of a university*. Reprinted in 1959 with an introduction by G. Shuster, New York: Image Books.

Runté, M. and Runté, R. (2016) 'The evolving discourse of the purpose of higher education: the rhetoric of higher education reform', in S. Mukerji and P. Tripathi (eds) *Handbook of research on administration, policy, and leadership in higher education*, 532–548, Hershey, PA: IDI Global.

Schultz, T. (1961) 'Investment in human capital', *The American Economic Review*, 51(1): 1–17.

Sheffield, E. (1970) 'The post-war surge in post-secondary education: 1945–1969', in D. Wilson, R. Stamp and L-P. Audet (eds) *Canadian education: a history*, 416–443, Scarborough, Ontario: Prentice-Hall.

Spring, J. (1984) 'Education and the Sony War', *Phi Delta Kappan*, 65(8): 534–537.

Worth, W. H. (1972) *A choice of futures: a future of choices*, report of the Commission on Educational Planning, Edmonton, Alberta: Queen's Printer.

Critical friend commentary

Pedro Teixeira

The discourses presented focus on individual empowerment or on social responsiveness. In the first group, we can identify two strands, one emphasizing a tradition of intellectual empowerment of individuals, and another emphasizing the economic and social empowerment of individuals. In the second group, we also have two streams, one focusing on responding to social needs as defined by the State, such as supplying qualified labour, and the other more recent, focusing on social responsiveness as signalled by the market system.

The emergence and relevance of each discourse varies geographically. The shift from personal development to economic and social empowerment has expanded in many parts of the world, nurtured by human capital theorists and international agencies, though initially facing resistance as debasing the noble purposes of education (Teixeira 2007). In European higher education, the discourse on external demands has been traditionally dominated by supplying State needs (Neave 2012), and a reluctance to expose institutions to market and private demands; though either from necessity or ideological shifts, this has been eroding with the growing influence of market stimuli (Teixeira et al. 2004). Given limitations on public expenditure, the latter has been enhanced by the pressures to develop mass access, which in many parts of the world has led to a greater role for private supply and a greater exposure to market demands (Teixeira et al. 2017).

The overlap of these various discourses raises tensions between short and long-term priorities (Bok 2003) and difficulty finding commonality between various stakeholders. The overlap is also a reflection that higher education now includes a greater variety of students and institutions (Burrage 2010). Though some values and concerns are shared, there are differences across systems, institutions, disciplines, regions, or students. Differences also exist in issues like the importance awarded to research (and the types of research), the degree of vocationalism, or in the engagement with external stakeholders. Europe presents differences vis-à-vis the United States, as the former has been more reluctant to embrace the realities of mass higher education and the diversities associated with it (see Burrage 2010). The balance between these discourses reflects the embeddedness of higher education systems in specific cultural, social, and political contexts. Higher education faces multiple challenges, not the least in justifying its relevance in a cacophony of multiple discourses.

References

Bok, D. (2003) *Universities in the market place: the commercialization of higher education*, Princeton, NJ: Princeton University Press.

Burrage, M. (ed) (2010) *Martin Trow – Twentieth-century higher education: elite to mass to universal*, Baltimore, MD: John Hopkins Press.

Neave, G. (2012) *The evaluative state, institutional autonomy and re-engineering higher education in Western Europe*, London and New York: Palgrave Macmillan.

Teixeira, P. (2007) *Jacob Mincer: the founding father of modern labor economics*, Oxford: Oxford University Press.

Teixeira, P., Jongbloed, B., Dill, D. and Amaral, A. (eds) (2004) *Markets in higher education: rhetoric or reality?*, Dordrecht: Kluwer Academic Publishers.

Teixeira, P., Kim, S., Gilani, Z. and Landoni, P. (2017) *Re-thinking the public-private mix in higher education: global trends and national policy challenges*, Rotterdam: Sense.

6

THE IMPACT OF GOVERNANCE ON TEACHING EXCELLENCE IN ACADEMIC MICROCULTURES

Torgny Roxå and Katarina Mårtensson

Introduction

Aside from conceptualizing what teaching excellence is per se, this chapter more explicitly explores what signifies academic contexts where teaching excellence thrives. First, we address what norms, values and habits are developed in so-called microcultures, the collegial contexts of teaching excellence, and are foremost in the way in which such microcultures are governed. Second, we consider how different types of governance might influence teaching excellence in academic microcultures.

Referring to Gunn and Fisk (2013) and to our previous research (Roxå and Mårtensson 2009; 2011/13; 2014; 2015; Olsson and Roxå 2013), we start with the point that excellence in teaching results in excellent learning among students. Such learning incorporates depth and breadth in theoretical and practical knowledge – what Biggs and Tang (1999) refer to as *functioning, professional knowledge*. On the one hand, excellent learning includes a deep approach to learning (Marton and Booth 1997), a continuous strive towards membership in professional communities (Wenger 1999), and an overall sense of personal meaning in the learning situation (Entwistle and Entwistle 2003). On the other, excellent teaching is about going that extra mile in planning, performing, assessing, evaluating and developing the teaching in order to move students towards that deep approach to learning, and to inspire them to gradually become members of various professional communities. We have previously shown that in academic microcultures, which are strong in both teaching and research as assessed by external audits, this principle is institutionalized to an extent where new members experience it as an imperative. You are not allowed to become a member unless you live by the credo that student learning and a constant striving for excellent teaching is important. Or, as one senior teacher said: 'How can we have the best research unless we have the best teaching'.

There is obviously a variation among academic microcultures (Roxå and Mårtensson 2015). Not all academic microcultures are signified by a collegial strive for teaching excellence, but by studying those that are strong we can inspire those who seek to enhance higher education organizations towards excellence. In this chapter, we briefly discuss the governance of a number of excellent (strong) micro-cultures in order to explore the issue of what impact different governance principles have on teaching excellence. The aim is to contribute to a discussion on governance in higher education in general and, in particular, suggest a potential link between governance and teaching excellence. Governance here is seen as a combination of institutionalized norms, developed over time, thereby embedded in everyday practice, and deliberate and explicit decisions made through leadership.

The empirical material presented here originates in Roxå and Mårtensson (2011/13), where a small number of excellent, so-called strong microcultures were studied through ethnographically inspired methods of interviews and observations. They were chosen because: they had a strong reputation within and outside their institution based on documented evidence of teaching involving a deep approach to learning; because the teaching there was assessed by external audits; colleagues and students were regarded as excellent, and because the researchers, after decades within the institution, knew them as contexts of extremely high standards in teaching. We will in this chapter return to some of that material in order to shed light upon the issue of governance in relation to teaching excellence.

The question here is whether there are any common features across the micro-cultures in how they were governed internally. We argue that research which explores governance of existing excellence can fuel a constructive critique and understanding of how to promote excellence in higher education organizations. The need for further discussions on how to promote teaching excellence in higher educa-tion through governance is important, especially since excellence can be distorted through malpractice in governance. This chapter contributes to such a discussion.

As a starting point the chapter refers to a current debate about governance in academia in Sweden on the assumption that this debate is recognizable in other national contexts too. The chapter then discusses the differences between three general principles for governance: collegiality, managerialism and bureaucracy. Thereafter, five academic microcultures that are considered to be excellent in teaching are described. The chapter ends with a discussion on the following questions: what are the dominant principles of governance in existing microcultures seen as excellent in teaching (and research)? What therefore is the impact of governance on teaching excellence?

Background

In Sweden there is an ongoing debate about how to best organize and manage higher education, its institutions and its main activities. The main tensions in the debate centre on two areas of governance, one being the system of new public management (managerial and bureaucratic) and the other collegial. Some of the main traits of this debate are highlighted in what follows.

One recent critical voice came from six senior managers from the Confederation of Swedish Enterprise, claiming to speak for 60,000 companies and 1.5 million people in the corporate sector. Leadership in the academic sector is vague and weak, they said, suggesting that the students and the staff should no longer be able to influence who would become Rector (Vice-Chancellor), that the appointment processes should be made transparent, and that weak rectors should be easier to remove (Mogren et al. 2016, our translation). This can be seen as an argument towards increased managerialism, inspired by experiences from the private sector.

A rector at one of the most prestigious institutions in Sweden, the Karolinska Institute, portrays the sector as a bureaucratic system where she, as Rector, is a civil servant. In a way, she depicts higher education as a bureaucratic system where different individuals have to act according to their roles (Hellmark Knutsson 2016). Another voice in the debate, a well-reputed researcher of academic organizations, claimed that too much power is assigned to the top of the organization (Bennich-Björkman 2016) and this power demands and achieves loyalty among subordinates. She argued for a collegial university, governed by peers with a solid base in scientific knowledge.

The voices in the debate illustrate three main lines in a more global discourse on governance in academia. In short, the debate concerns whether academic organizations should be led and managed through *collegial*, *managerial*, or *bureaucratic* principles. These principles are explored in a recent Swedish book: *Kollegialitet. En modern styrform* [Collegiality. A modern form of governance], by Sahlin and Eriksson-Zetterquist (2016). We will introduce and use this framework in the following sections of the chapter.

A general observation is that this public governance discussion only concerns teaching or education to a limited extent. Rather, the debate illustrates the belief that governance in academic settings is more linked to performance, arguably applied to teaching, although such discussions are rarely made public (Quinlan 2014). Recently, however, studies have shown that academics do appreciate good leadership provided it is sensitive to the specific collegial context in which the academic practice takes place (Mårtensson and Roxå 2015; Bolander Laksov and Tomson 2016).

The perspective taken is consistent with international research looking at organizations as being in a state of 'dynamic equilibrium' (Smith and Lewis 2011). Organizations persist over time due to many, sometimes contradictory, forces balancing one another (ibid.) and Gosling, Bolden and Petrov (2009: 300) support such a perspective noting that in academia we have seen 'a steady transition from collegial to more managerial models of administration'. The process is masked by a discourse about distributed leadership allowing for managerial strategies of economic accountability to gain influence. This perception, that managerial forces have gained ground, echoes throughout the literature (for example: Naidoo et al. 2014; Quinlan 2014). In terms of excellence in research, this development has been evaluated in a Finnish study including 966 academics and showed negative effects from managerial governance on creative performance (Kallio and Kallio 2012). However, it is harder to find similar studies focusing on education (Quinlan 2014).

In what follows, therefore, we complement this discussion by investigating the aforementioned three principles for governance in relation to teaching in excellent academic microcultures. In this exploration, we focus on the organizational meso-level (Mårtensson 2014; Roxå 2014). The questions we raise are: what signifies governance in existing microcultures that are excellent in teaching and research, within a higher education organization? In what proportions are they governed through *collegial, managerial,* or *bureaucratic* principles?

Broadly, these three principles can be used to briefly contextualize and offer a historic overview of the Swedish higher education system. Traditionally, it is a Germanic system with strong professors governing a discipline through Humboldtian principles. In 1977 a national reform emphasized what looked more like an industrial production model, where planned progress through well-defined programmes became the backbone of the education system. Later, new public management influenced more of the system and introduced quality discourses, budgeting models, and added more weight to management in the system. A traditional collegial system is influenced by a bureaucratic system for production and then later by a managerial system emphasizing decisive decision-making by managers.

Collegiality, managerialism and bureaucracy

This section relies on the previously mentioned book, *Kollegialitet. En modern styrform* [Collegiality. A modern form of governance] by Sahlin and Eriksson-Zetterquist (2016). Since the book was published in Swedish it is especially relevant for this discussion, but it also deserves an introduction. Sahlin and Eriksson-Zetterquist are both professors in business administration. For five years (2006–2011) Sahlin acted as Pro-Rector (Pro-Vice-Chancellor) at Uppsala University, one of Sweden's oldest and largest universities. Eriksson-Zetterquist is currently the director for the Gothenburg Research Institute at University of Gothenburg School of Business, Economics, and Law. The authors contrast the three principles for governance as ideal-types, and apply these not only to academia, but also many other forms of organizations. Their views on the three main principles of governance – collegial, managerial, and bureaucratic – are summarized below.

In order to function well, *collegial governance*, the authors argue, demands a shared knowledge base and colleagues who continuously discuss together how to advance the practice they are engaged in. A critical conversation based on mutual trust is essential. Colleagues share a responsibility and they challenge one another. Leaders are often elected because they are trusted as experts in the field. Through trust individuals can engage in practice flexibly, allowing them to use necessary knowledge and skills as the demands of practice change. Therefore, collegiality appears to be particularly suitable for knowledge-intensive organizations where the members use a well-integrated knowledge base.

Collegiality bears resemblance to culture, as it forms patterns of embedded behaviours that over time become tacit for the members. However, the main risk with collegiality arises when these necessary critical conversations run out of steam. If no critical discussion pushes the practice forward, collegiality is a good place for allowing things to remain as they are in an atmosphere of mutual non-interference.

Or, since collegiality is dependent on the conversations that lead to informed decisions, powerful individuals can deadlock the conversation, or assemble a number of loyal subordinates, and thereby push the agenda towards decisions that are not best for the majority, but benefit the few. Nepotism and other forms of corruption are constant companions to those collegial organizations that do not manage to sustain the critical conversation. For an organization to be successfully collegial, it is not enough that colleagues lead; it is the ongoing critical conversation that is key.

In *managerial governance* power is assigned to one person (or a small group of people) at the formally structured, hierarchical top of the organization. Hence, decisive decision-making can strategically move resources, information, or personnel around according to need. This is possible because the coordination is in the hands of one, or a few individuals, but it is also easier for external stakeholders to hold decision-makers accountable if something goes wrong.

Managerial principles excel in situations of risk and threat, as in times of conflict or in a competitive market. The manager can formulate a strategy for how to best use resources in order to achieve an objective and implement this strategy thanks to his or her power to control others within the organization, and the organization responds swiftly in a coordinated way. The importance of decisiveness in management over time tends to become a skill and a profession in its own right.

The risks with decisiveness in managerialist, knowledge-intensive contexts where outcomes cannot easily be evaluated, or when complexity is integral to everyday practice, are frequent. Managers often make decisions from a distance, not being directly involved in specific practices that generate core value for the organization, therefore swift decisions run the risk of destroying functioning practices. If the feedback to managers is complex, and perhaps contradictory, or members of the organization fail to provide authentic information to the manager due to deteriorating trust, the result might be an organization where every new, managerial decision adds to an already distorted view of what is going on with potentially disastrous outcomes.

Thus, if collegial governance runs the risk of becoming deadlocked because of an absent critical conversation, management governance runs the risk of making rushed decisions thereby destroying practices essential for the organization. This risk is multiplied in circumstances with unclear complexity, and even contradiction, in combination with knowledge intensive practice.

In its purest form, *bureaucratic governance* can be described as a machine where rules guide roles rather than individuals. Personal judgement is secondary to instructions, protocols, and policies. Individuals can be replaced without affecting the organization. The outcomes of decisions are the same, regardless of who is involved. Relationships between members of the organization become clear since they are regulated by instructions and rules. Information travels swiftly from one end of the organization to the other since it does not have to pass through individuals' personal judgements. The organization is also easy to restructure since it is built on rules and these can be rewritten.

A potential drawback, however, is that rules are not necessarily adapted to unique situations but rather on what is normal. Hence, in knowledge-intensive practices it is normal for practitioners to have to adapt to unique situations in order to maximize outcomes (Schön 1983). An emphasis on rules instead of the specific conditions at hand pinions the practitioner and forces them to either deviate from the rules or impose rules upon situations to which they are not adapted. In both alternatives, the practice suffers.

Sahlin and Eriksson-Zetterquist emphasize that the three principles are ideal-types and that in most organizations they co-exist. It is rather the balance between them that forms the unique setting for an organization. Furthermore, they conceive any organization as dynamic and unstable, therefore the balance between the three principles for governance is in itself an object for analysis, based on how the balance plays out in a specific organization and how it changes over time.

Governing teaching excellence in strong academic microcultures

This section revisits a previous investigation of strong academic microcultures within a research-intensive university and investigates how principles of collegial, managerial and bureaucratic governance influence excellence in education. For a fuller account of each microculture, readers are invited to read the original report (Roxå and Mårtensson 2011/13; 2014; 2015; or Mårtensson and Roxå 2016).

Research process

The five microcultures studied were selected from three different faculties within a research-intensive Swedish university comprising a small department, a unit/division within a department and a team of staff working together on one educational programme. Group size varied between ten and sixty people. The aim was to identify and explore local organizational contexts known for, and documented as, being excellent in teaching as well as in research. They were identified through interviews with student unions, deans, heads of departments, and through the researchers' knowledge of the organization. Research quality was assessed through an international research audit (Lund University 2008).

Between four and five semi-structured interviews of about forty-five to sixty minutes were conducted in Swedish in each microculture, individually with leaders, senior and junior academics, and in groups with students. Altogether seventeen academics and twenty-eight students were interviewed with staff interviews in each microculture being completed before interviewing the students. Interview questions concerned internal issues such as group values and teaching practices, decision-making processes, group history, improvements and developments, as well as collaborations outside the microculture, such as relations to formal, organizational structures and so on.

Findings

In all interviews a strong engagement with teaching and student learning came across, as testified both by academics and students. Students were typically challenged and subjected to high demands, but combined with a high level of support and clear guidance. Teaching methods varied across the five microcultures, including lecture-and-seminar or lecture-and-labs-based to problem-based learning. However, whichever teaching method was preferred, members of the microcultures displayed a constant desire to improve their practice, to share and critically reflect upon it with colleagues, and to deal with problems that arose (for instance, critical issues raised in students' course evaluations). Students were valued, for example: known by names; actively encouraged to engage with their learning through projects and collaboration; their work put on display; and they were often described as 'future colleagues', or 'our most important assets'.

The inner organization of the five microcultures was characterized by a high degree of interactions, communication and collaboration. One interviewee expressed this as: 'It is we, not me'. In many instances, members of the microculture would sit in on one another's lectures; plan, enact, evaluate and develop teaching collaboratively; or take a collegial approach to addressing criticism from students or general problems in teaching. Within each microculture there were established and effective routines for sharing information (such as shared dossiers, internal websites, and public spreadsheets), and arenas for collaboration and interaction (such as joint coffee breaks every day, a shared lunchroom, and formal and informal meetings with conversations about teaching quality).

The principle of *collegial governance* is evident in the fact that all microcultures were permeated by trust, both in the collective ability of the unit itself, but also in every member's capacity to engage in practice according to the locally developed standards: dealing with education as if it really mattered. Several examples were given about how support was offered to those who for some reason did not meet the standards; for instance, it was acceptable to approach a colleague who had received somewhat negative student evaluations. Furthermore, all microcultures had elaborated strategies to secure functioning internal communications, albeit in different ways. All respondents could formulate a personal account of what the microculture was trying to achieve and how this was linked to teaching students and the importance of teaching quality. Student learning and perception of teaching appeared seamlessly linked to other practices, which, taken together, earned the microculture a strong academic reputation.

We argue that these signs of intense internal communication in combination with high levels of trust and the sense of a shared responsibility are strong and significant signs of collegiality (in accordance with the description offered above). With a lower level of internal trust or a weaker sense of shared responsibility, the microculture would not be considered as strong (Roxå and Mårtensson 2015). The engagement for teaching was built into the norms holding the microculture together and was not only related to personal interest, but also embedded and institutionalized such that in order to be a full member, a teacher had to be engaged (Mårtensson and Roxå 2016).

The principle of *managerial governance* manifested itself in the fact that all five microcultures were hierarchical. Important decisions were made by one leader or by a few leaders who spoke for the group on behalf of all members. This hierarchy was fully accepted internally, as expressed in interviews. Externally, the microcultures engaged selectively with the larger organization (department, faculty or institution); for example, in processes of policy-making or policy implementation. These managers kept track of what was going on, and engaged actively when deemed important. They constantly maintained their agency and made choices about how to engage in processes initiated by the Dean or by the Rector. If they found a policy useful in relation to their own enterprise, they engaged fully. If not, they engaged more superficially or not at all (Mårtensson et al. 2014).

Finally, the principle of *bureaucratic governance* was also visible in all microcultures. The roles internally were clear and accepted by everybody as far as our results show. But again, external bureaucratic governance, rules formulated elsewhere in the organization, had a different meaning and were carefully interpreted and acted upon. The microcultures all performed as expected in relation to external rules, regulations and policies, but they did it differently depending on how meaningful the rules appeared for the members as a group. If the rules applied constructively to the internal enterprise, they engaged fully; otherwise not or again superficially (Mårtensson et al. 2014).

Discussion

The aim in this chapter has been to briefly discuss the governance in a number of microcultures that are considered excellent (strong) in teaching and research. In relation to excellent teaching this is important since it says something about how managers, local-level leaders, and academic developers can pay attention to, and support, emergent organizational context towards excellence in teaching.

The brief analysis shows that all three principles for governance – collegial, managerial and bureaucratic – are present in the strong microcultures. This is in line with the literature claiming that the three principles always exist in combination with one another. For instance, from organizational research focusing on dynamic equilibrium, Sundarämurthy (2003: 407) stated:

> A control approach helps curb human limitations through vigilance and discipline, while a collaborative approach taps individuals' aspirations via cooperation and empowerment. Yet if one approach becomes overemphasized, perils of groupthink or distrust can fuel reinforcing cycles. From a paradox perspective, however, embracing and balancing both approaches facilitates learning and adaptation.

Since the balance between the three principles for governance is one defining aspect of the organization, if shifted this balance not only changes the face of the organization, but also impacts on the practice itself. However, even though all three principles existed together there appears to be a hierarchy among them inside all microcultures. The intense internal communication, as well as the trust and the natural engagement in colleagues' teaching, indicate that collegiality is strong in these contexts; perhaps the strongest principle. But the use of written and unwritten rules and the distinct hierarchy among the members indicate that elements of both managerial and bureaucratic governance are in play. Furthermore, the fact that rules and managerial actions outside the microcultures were always interpreted in relation to the internal enterprise, indicates a complex relationship between how hierarchies and bureaucratic rules were perceived internally and externally. It was the aims and directions of the microculture itself as interpreted by the members that was the leading principle. Everything else was evaluated against this.

Conclusion

After this brief discussion, we conclude that in this small number of organizational contexts where teaching is taken seriously, collegial governance is the dominating principle. Managerial and bureaucratic principles do exist, but when priorities have to be made, the collegial principle dominates over the other two. These results have implications both for how higher education organizations try to foster excellence in general, and excellence in teaching in particular. For example, one should be very careful about pushing for managerial or bureaucratic governance. Such moves might harm existing excellence and will fail to support emerging excellence in teaching. In other words, excellence is something that can be achieved with the right sort of governance; that is, with a constructive mix of the three principles. Competing interests in governance seem potentially to jeopardize teaching excellence. Having said this, it is important to note that this chapter relies on a study with a small sample. Even so, it is rare in the literature that governance in academia is discussed particularly in relation to teaching. More studies are needed to develop our understanding of how various principles for governance can foster or potentially harm teaching excellence.

References

Bennich-Björkman, L. (2016) 'När lojalitet blir det största sveket' [When loyalty becomes the worst betrayal], *Svenska Dagbladet*. Online. Available at www.svd.se/nar-lojalitet-blir-det-storsta-sveket (accessed 15 June 2017).

Biggs, J. and Tang, C. (1999) *Teaching for quality learning at university*, 4th edn, Maidenhead: Open University Press/McGraw Hill Education.

Bolander Laksov, K. and Tomson, T. (2016) 'Becoming an educational leader – exploring leadership in medical education', *International Journal of Leadership in Education*, 20(4): 506–516.

Entwistle, N. and Entwistle, D. (2003) 'Preparing for examinations: the interplay of memorising and understanding, and the development of knowledge objects', *Higher Education Research & Development*, 22(1): 19–41.

Gosling, J., Bolden, R. and Petrov, G. (2009) 'Distributed leadership in higher education: what does it accomplish?', *Leadership*, 5(3): 299–310.

Gunn, V. and Fisk, A. (2013) *Considering teaching excellence in higher education: 2007–2013*, York: The Higher Education Academy.

Hellmark Knutsson, H. (2016) 'Heckschers rapport är missvisande och undermålig', [Heckscher's report is misleading and deficient], *Dagens Nyheter*. Online. Available at www.dn.se/debatt/heckschers-rapport-ar-missvisande-och-undermalig/ (accessed 15 June 2017).

Kallio, K-M. and Kallio, T. (2012) 'Management-by-results and performance measurement in universities – implications for work motivation', *Studies in Higher Education*, 39(4): 574–589.

Lund University (2008) *RQ08 A qualitative review of research at Lund University 2007/08*. Online. Available at http://staff.lunduniversity.lu.se/sites/lunduniversity.prodwebb.lu.se/files/rq08-summary-lund-university.pdf (accessed 15 June 2017).

Marton, F. and Booth, S. (1997) *Learning and awareness*, Mahwah, NJ: Lawrence Erlbaum.

Mårtensson, K. (2014) *Influencing teaching and learning microcultures: academic development in a research-intensive university*, Published PhD thesis, Lund University, Sweden.

Mårtensson, K. and Roxå, T. (2015) 'Leadership at a local level – enhancing educational development', *Educational Management Administration & Leadership*, 1–16.

Mårtensson, K. and Roxå, T. (2016) 'Peer engagement for teaching and learning: competence, autonomy and social solidarity in academic microcultures', *Uniped*, 39(2): 131–143.

Mårtensson, K., Roxå, T. and Stensaker, B. (2014) 'From quality assurance to quality practices: an investigation of strong microcultures in teaching and learning', *Studies in Higher Education*, 39(4): 543–545.

Mogren, H., Jacke, J.-O., Markides, K., Olving, L., Strømme, M. and Söderström, J. (2016) 'Minska anställdas inflytande över rektorstillsättningar' [Decrease the employees' influence on who should become rector], *Dagens Nyheter*. Online. Available at www.dn.se/debatt/minska-anstalldas-inflytande-over-rektorstillsattningar (accessed 15 June 2017).

Naidoo, R., Gosling, J., Bolden, R., O'Brian, A. and Beverley, H. (2014) 'Leadership and branding in business schools: a Bourdieusian analysis', *Higher Education Research & Development*, 33(1): 144–156.

Olsson, T. and Roxå, T. (2013) 'Assessing and rewarding excellent academic teachers for the benefit of an organization', *European Journal of Higher Education*, 3(1): 40–61.

Quinlan, K. (2014) 'Leadership *of* teaching *for* student learning in higher education: what is needed?', *Higher Education Research & Development*, 33(1): 32–45.

Roxå, T. (2014) *Microcultures in the meso level of higher education organizations – the Commons, the Club, the Market and the Square*, Published PhD thesis, Lund University, Sweden.

Roxå, T. and Mårtensson, K. (2009) 'Significant conversations and significant networks – exploring the backstage of the teaching arena', *Studies in Higher Education*, 34(5): 547–559.

Roxå, T. and Mårtensson, K. (2011/13) *Understanding strong academic microcultures – an exploratory study*, Lund: Lund University Centre for Educational Development.

Roxå, T. and Mårtensson, K. (2014) 'Higher education commons – a framework for comparison of midlevel units in higher education organizations', *European Journal of Higher Education*, 4(4): 303–316.

Roxå, T. and Mårtensson, K. (2015) 'Microcultures and informal learning: a heuristic guiding analysis of conditions for informal learning in local higher education workplaces', *International Journal for Academic Development*, 20(2): 193–205.

Sahlin, K. and Erikson-Zetterquist, U. (2016) *Kollegialitet. En modern styrform* [Collegiality. A modern way of governance], Lund: Studentlitteratur.

Schön, D. (1983) *The reflective practitioner: how professionals think in action*, Aldershot: Ashgate.

Smith, W. and Lewis, M. (2011) 'Towards a theory of paradox: a dynamic equilibrium model of organizing', *Academy of Management Review*, 36(2): 381–403.

Sundarämurthy, C. and Lewis, M. (2003) 'Control and collaboration: paradoxes of governance', *Academy of Management Review*, 28(3): 397–415.

Wenger, E. (1999) *Communities of practice: learning, meaning, and identity*, Cambridge: Cambridge University Press.

Critical friend commentary

Marianne Merkt

Roxå and Mårtensson conclude with collegiality being the leading principle in excellent academic microcultures. These show how high levels of trust, long-term orientation and intense internal conversation influence important decisions. Managerialism on the other hand risks damaging excellent practices instead of developing new ones. My question here is: why is collegiality a good process for academic microcultures that provide excellent teaching?

I presuppose that academic formation in the sense of 'Bildung' is a social transfer mechanism that has the potential to spread new knowledge generated in universities into society by offering students an excellent academic formation. This transfer process consists of educational development which identifies research findings for specific societal contexts and transfers them into subjects of learning embedded in curricula and learning environments. In short, we are talking about a complex process carried out by mixed teams of researchers, teachers and administration staff with different expertise and different logics of action. On one hand this work process will end in new practices of learning and teaching within institutions, and on the other, the results of the developed education may have an impact on societal change. Innovation and social responsibility are inherent aspects of this kind of cooperative work.

How can this kind of cooperative responsible work be conceptualized? My suggestion is to refer to a theoretical model that focuses on the knowledge of mindfulness as a cooperative competence of teams in complex work processes (Langemeyer 2015). The concept of mindfulness derives from empirical research on teamwork in high technological plants with high complexity and high risk for accidents, such as nuclear power plants. In this context, mindfulness is generated by the behaviour of all participants of the organization. Teams in such organizations develop strategies to learn from all incidents occurring, not only to solve emerging problems, but to gain a deeper understanding of them. They generate a cooperative knowledge-in-practice.

By analysing the technical disasters of the nuclear reactor at Fukushima in 2011, and of the oil platform 'Deepwater Horizon' in the Gulf of Mexico in 2010, Langemeyer asserts that one reason for the disaster in both cases was the gap between intensive research done beforehand and the striking lack of this knowledge within the working team. Langemeyer points out that in such contexts it is fundamental that the team itself develops a cooperative competence that integrates dimensions of knowledge and of ability in shared practices. It enables work teams to make reasonable and responsible decisions in challenging situations and to act in a way that cannot rely on routines, standards or the knowledge of individuals. This kind of cooperative competence can only be acquired in cooperative actions and appreciative work relations among team members. It presupposes that the team members are able to pursue collective aims and that they develop an attitude of mindfulness in relation to their work processes.

Mindfulness includes the ability to learn from one's own errors, to be eager in relation to the quality of the work products, to appreciate and learn from the expertise of team members, and to reflect critically on one's own practice. This kind of mindfulness cannot be mandated; it relies on belief and motivation. The principle of collegiality with its high level of trust, long-term orientation, and intense internal conversation influencing important decisions may well be a process that supports the development of cooperative competence in academic microcultures when aiming for educational excellence.

References

Langemeyer, I. (2015) *Das wissen der achtsamkeit. Kooperative kompetenz in komplexen arbeitsprozessen*, Waxmann: Münster.

7

A NATIONAL STRATEGY FOR TEACHING EXCELLENCE – ONE UNIVERSITY AT A TIME

Denise Chalmers and Beatrice Tucker

Introduction

This chapter outlines a case study on the development of a national strategy for teaching excellence and its implementation in over two thirds of Australian universities. This has resulted in a growing consensus on teaching criteria and performance expectations for higher education teachers at different promotional levels. The strategy began as a national strategic priority project, funded by the Office for Learning and Teaching, a department of the Australian Federal Government. An outcome of the project was a fully trialled and functional teaching excellence framework designed as an exemplar, or illustrative model, for universities to use to develop their own explicit teaching excellence criteria and standards. Nationally, the conversation about teaching excellence was supported through the engagement of organizations and institutions in a collaborative process of defining and clarifying expectations and standards. Individual institutions engaged in a facilitated process to review their policy, processes, criteria and expectations of teaching, and developed their individual responses in the context of their values and priorities. This nationally orchestrated strategy of supporting institutions with the provision of a framework, supported by processes and resources, has resulted in building a consensus on teaching excellence that is embedded in institutional policy and its outcomes. The impact has been both national and international as institutions chose to utilize the framework and processes.

This case study demonstrates the need for teaching excellence to be defined according to the values and context of the university, for it is in the universities that teaching excellence is recognized and rewarded in order to enhance the quality of teaching and the student learning experience. However, while there was an explicit desire by leaders in universities to do this better, the lack of an exemplar framework and associated processes has contributed to ad hoc approaches to such recognition and reward of teaching excellence. Our national project was designed to support universities' desires to have their distinct missions reflected in their definition of teaching excellence through a facilitated, systematic, peer-supported approach to teaching criteria and standards.

To date, the teaching excellence framework and resources developed by the project team have been used in over two thirds of Australian universities. They have also been used internationally by universities in Thailand, Canada, Chile and South Africa, which demonstrates their utility and flexibility. Examples of the ways different universities have implemented their teaching excellence frameworks and processes illustrate how teaching excellence has been imbedded in institutional policy, processes, governance structures and role statements. These universities have revised their policies and processes, related to appointment, probation, performance review, promotion and professional development, in a comprehensive and wide-ranging review that recognizes the complexity of better acknowledging and rewarding teaching excellence by undertaking a whole-university approach. As a consequence, a number of institutions have developed new academic and professional roles to support teaching and learning, with professional development and peer review of teaching strategies established to support academics in career progression. While the approach has been to support individual universities to define excellence in their own context, the national framework and supported process has resulted in a growing consensus on teaching excellence expectations for different levels of academic appointment across Australia.

The impetus for the development of the Australian framework for teaching excellence in higher education was in response to changes in the higher education sector in the last decade that were occurring globally. Many Australian universities recognized that quality teaching was a key feature in attracting and retaining students, and therefore maintaining standards of excellence in learning and teaching was critical to securing a competitive edge. The Australian federal government, through the Office for Learning and Teaching (OLT) and its predecessor bodies, had invested in higher education via grants and teaching awards aimed at the enhancement of teaching and the student learning experience. The OLT commissioned two strategic priority projects on the *Professionalization of the Academic Workforce* (Chalmers et al. 2014; Chalmers et al. 2015; James et al. 2015) and a discussion paper on teaching-focused academic appointments (Probert 2013). Concurrently, a Fellowship project entitled 'Transforming Practice Programme (TPP) – Reward and Recognition: Promotion Process and Policy' was led by Crookes (2014). This chapter reports on the Australian University Teaching Criteria and Standards project and its ongoing implementation (Chalmers et al. 2014; Chalmers et al. 2015; Chalmers 2016).

Background

There have been numerous changes that have impacted on the Australian higher education sector over the past decade. Student numbers rose sharply in response to the Australian Government's ambitious target to significantly increase the number of twenty-five to thirty-four year olds with at least bachelor-level qualifications to forty per cent by 2025 (Department of Education and Training 2015). The context for academic work followed international trends, including a greater culture of compliance, accountability, regulation and expectations for a positive student experience across a diverse student cohort able to meet labour force needs (Universities Australia 2014). The digital revolution impacted on learning and teaching practices with new pedagogies shaping the approaches to student engagement and learning (Ramsden 2008; Kukulska-Hulme 2012; Little 2016). Global mobility provided a greater diversity of the student population and the academic workforce (Bhandari and Laughlin 2009). Many Australian universities set targets to reposition their institution in the global market, and in pursuit of increasing their international ranking, by focusing on the intensity of their research outputs and impacts. These factors directly affected the academic workforce who primarily concentrated on teaching, many of whom reported workload pressures, a lack of clarity of their role in university teaching, and their perceived limited career opportunities (Kimber 2003; Bexley et al. 2011; Locke 2014).

Over this same period the academic teaching workforce was facing increasing casualization and the growing perception that teaching was an activity for employment rather than a profession (Kimber 2003; Percy et al. 2008; May et al. 2013; Ryan et al. 2013). Academics enter the workforce via numerous pathways from research, occupational and professional practice, from other teaching paths and direct from higher education studies (Coates et al. 2009; Bexley et al. 2011). This results in an academic population diverse in terms of their teaching capabilities and expectations. In response to the changes in workforce demands, there has been a trend amongst Australian universities to establish teaching-focused, or teaching only, academic appointments, signalling a major departure from the traditional teaching and research academic (Probert 2013).

Further workforce challenges include an ageing academic workforce and increased international mobility. Coates and colleagues (2009) identified a need for policy development, planning and research on Australia's academic workforce to increase the attractiveness of the academic profession. Most notably, they argued for the need to recognize the diverse roles of the academic and to establish a set of calibrated industry-wide professional standards for university teaching that could be used for assessing performance and for providing a harmonized approach to professional learning. James et al. (2015: 1) have argued for new ways for recognizing and supporting professional practice of university teaching with professionalization defined as the 'knowledge and skills in designing curricula, planning and implementing teaching and learning experiences, supporting students and assessing student progress and outcomes – in other words, knowledge and skills in teaching and learning'.

The Australian University Teaching Criteria and Standards framework project

The Australian University Teaching Criteria and Standards (AUTCAS) project was designed as a national strategy for creating a teaching excellence framework that drew on good practice principles and evidence-based measures of teaching performance (Chalmers et al. 2014) that could be utilized and contextualized institutionally. The AUTCAS framework was designed to provide institutions with a multi-dimensional resource for recruitment, probation, promotions, professional development and policy development related to quality teaching. The framework was also designed to provide individual academics with clarity on expected levels of teaching performance for the purpose of career planning, preparation for performance development reviews, and preparation for applying for promotion.

The framework was informed by a set of principles of quality teaching identified as contributing to student learning. These were drawn from the international empirical and research literature, OLT project reports and university documents. An initial list of twenty-seven principles were generated, and refined to a list of ten principles which underpin quality teaching across universities and disciplines. These were widely interrogated through a process of consultation, seeking feedback from academic and professional colleagues, educational development leaders from the Council of Australian Directors of Academic Development (CADAD) and Australasian Council on Open, Distance and e-Learning (ACODE), and leaders in higher education.

The AUTCAS framework comprises seven indicative criteria that apply across all five academic levels of appointment typical in Australia (associate lecturer to professorial levels). The seven teaching criteria are:

1. Design and planning of learning activities
2. Teaching and supporting student learning
3. Assessment and giving feedback to students on their learning
4. Developing effective learning environments, student support and guidance
5. Integration of scholarship, research and professional activities with teaching and in support of student learning
6. Evaluation of practice and continuing professional development
7. Professional and personal effectiveness.

For each level of appointment, indicative examples of performance and achievements are provided under each of the seven criteria. Descriptors identified within each criterion as 'minimum standard' are highlighted.

Trialling the framework and process

Testing of the framework began in 2013 with the five universities that led the national project mapping their existing teaching criteria against the AUTCAS and seeking feedback from their senior leadership and human resources units. Feedback from each university informed the subsequent version of the framework, published on the AUTCAS website along with examples of teaching practice and project planning documents. Twenty-three Australian and two international universities reviewed the framework and resources and provided feedback to the project team which informed the final iteration of the framework and resources.

In 2014, all thirty-nine Australian universities were invited to consider participating in the AUTCAS project by establishing an institutional team nominated by the Deputy-Vice Chancellor (Education/Academic) (DVCA), comprising senior staff from areas of human resources, policy, academic promotions and teaching and learning centres. The institutional team membership of senior leaders from different areas of the university, under the patronage of the DVCA, was considered critical as it provided executive level endorsement and brought together senior staff with authority and oversight of policy, processes and implementation related to rewarding and recognizing teaching excellence. Twenty-one universities agreed to participate, with several additional universities becoming involved as the project progressed. The universities involved were fully representative of the range and type of Australian universities: for example, research intensive, comprehensive, innovative, regional, and technical.

The involvement of the university teams centred around two workshops with each university undertaking specific work before and between the workshops. Each workshop was scheduled for a day and held approximately four months apart. The workshops were held in each state to maximize the involvement of all members of the university teams as well as to facilitate regional networks of the universities engaged in the process, and to minimize the costs for the universities in terms of time and money.

The focus of the first workshop was on facilitating each university team to identify their current policies and processes related to academic appointment, performance review and promotion, and review the clarity of criteria and expectations for teaching through responding to planning documents developed by the project team. While the compilation of policies and documents was carried out before the first workshop by one or more members of the university team, the facilitated process in the first workshop brought all members and the documents to the same table. The institutional teams were then able to review the extent to which there was alignment and clarity in documents and process for these important career performance and development stages.

Not surprisingly, just as the project team members found when carrying out their initial institutional reviews, there was little if any alignment between appointment, performance review and promotions descriptions, policies and expectations. Typically, within each institution their teaching criteria were different, or differently described in appointment, performance review and promotion documents. Expectations of performance were typically vague or absent, as were the evidence requirements to inform performance review and promotion. Multiple versions and oversight control was also identified as an issue, for example, different documents or websites advised on performance review and promotion on the human resources, teaching and learning centre, and faculty websites. It was only when these team members came together at the workshop and considered their own university documents and processes that the extent of the misalignment and variation in descriptions of criteria and expectations became evident. The teams were then able to consider their institutional priorities and plan for their next steps, utilizing the AUTCAS framework and resources. The state-based workshops brought several institutional teams together where they found they had common issues, or they shared experiences and responses where they had been addressed. Some university teams found this so useful that they scheduled their own additional state-based meeting to continue working and sharing their experiences and solutions.

In the interim period between the two workshops the project team members regularly contacted the institutional teams to provide support and resources. The second workshop, held four months later, repeated the process of bringing institutional teams together to share their experiences and challenges. The focus was on strategies for implementing and embedding their institutionally developed framework into practice. University team participants shared their key challenges, outcomes (anticipated and unanticipated), and the strategies that had worked best for their institution. With the help of the project team and participants from other universities, they also identified gaps and additional steps needed to embed their versions of the quality teaching criteria and standards at their institution going forward.

Each university utilized the AUTCAS framework differently, demonstrating its intended flexibility and reflecting the diversity of the institutions involved. They were eager to engage with, and customize, the process to suit their individual values, criteria and context. For example, some universities chose to adopt the full set of AUTCAS criteria and indicative evidence, and instituted an institutional wide discussion of the standards that would apply in their university for the different levels. Other universities chose to keep their original criteria, but adopted the framework structure to make explicit the performance expectations for each career level. Another university mapped its criteria and expectations against the AUTCAS framework as part of a benchmarking process to inform the development of a continuing professional development programme for staff (Thomas et al. 2016). Others used the framework and resources for framing their professional development programme and directing their staff to the resources to assist them in building and reporting their evidence of teaching excellence.

While very few of the universities were able to fully implement their planned strategies in the six-month period of the project, all had identified strategies for maintaining the momentum into the future. Over the following two years, many of the universities progressed the development of their teaching criteria and expectations via consultation and formal endorsement, and ratification through their university governance approval processes. The timeline for changes of this magnitude involving review, consultation, policy development and approval through governance was typically over two years, with the development of supporting documents and implementation of professional development for academics, supervisors and members of promotion committees taking a further year.

It must be emphasized that the AUTCAS framework was not designed to apply only to teaching focused or teaching only roles. The framework was designed to be applied to any role that involves teaching, including the traditional research and teaching academic role. Indeed, the framework highlighted the need to provide more explicit criteria and performance expectations for the research and service aspects of academic work. The University of Western Australia project team devised a comparable research and service framework to demonstrate the feasibility of applying the AUTCAS model to all dimensions of academic work. This has been made available to a number of universities and utilized by them to develop a comprehensive set of criteria and expectations for all aspects of the academic roles. It is important to note that research intensive universities were just as interested in clarifying their teaching criteria and expectations in order to ensure that academics could progress through a teaching excellence pathway as those in the other university models, including regional, technical and modern universities.

Several universities wrote case studies of their experience of their involvement in the project and utilization of the AUTCAS framework. The drivers for change for many of the universities that participated were similar. There was recognition that professionalization of the university workforce in Australia was critical in order for universities to be agile and competitive in future environments (PricewaterhouseCoopers 2016). Many universities established teaching academic roles, research academic, and teaching and research roles, which provided a need to establish a career pathway, including promotions process, that defined and rewarded teaching excellence. Numerous universities were also in the process of renewing their Strategic Plans focusing on the student experience, student outcomes and teaching quality. At the same time, universities were reforming their promotions policies, establishing teaching loads and expectations for teaching excellence for the new teaching academic roles. Human Resource departments across Australia had also identified the need to redesign existing roles, create new roles, and redesign performance management and reward processes to support and advance their academic and professional workforce (ibid.). Where universities adopted the AUTCAS framework and worked with policy, university and committee leaders, and Human Resources personnel, the criteria were incorporated into probation, promotion and work performance processes.

Drawing from the case studies, the experiences of the universities who worked with us, and confirmed by the participants and the project evaluation, four key factors were identified as contributing to the successful implementation of institutional defined teaching excellence criteria and expectations:

1. Consultation and communication between academics, schools, faculties, university units (such as: Human Resources recruitment and promotions sections; teaching and learning) and university leadership facilitated the embedding of policies and practices across the institution.
2. Leadership and timely endorsement from leaders within institutions provided momentum and university-wide implementation. At some institutions,

implementation was hindered where the project did not fit into the strategic priorities identified by the leadership, or where there was instability in leadership and/or project teams.

3. Alignment between processes and consistency in terminology and processes ensured an institutionally shared common understanding in policies and practices such as recruitment, probation, performance review and promotion.

4. Evidence of impact through the adoption of institutionally developed and endorsed criteria and standards, and subsequent promotion and recognition of excellent teachers at the different performance levels.

Building on the outcomes of the AUTCAS project, a National Senior Teaching Fellowship was funded by the OLT to continue supporting institutions to utilize the AUTCAS framework and resources, and to contribute toward the national strategy to better recognize and reward excellent teaching (Chalmers 2016).

As a consequence, over two thirds of Australian universities and a growing number of private tertiary institutions have engaged in the process of reviewing their criteria and the expectations of their academic and teaching staff, and revised their policies and procedures. Many more have used the framework and resources to define and clarify their institutions' understanding and expectations of teaching excellence for performance and career development. Through this bottom-up process, consensus is building towards a shared understanding of teaching excellence; for while it is critically important to recognize and reward excellent teaching within institutions, it is just as important to move towards consensus on teaching excellence across the university sector so that academic teachers can plan their career development and advancement and move across the Australian and international tertiary sector with their teaching achievements noted. As Ramsden (2008: 2.23) suggests: 'We should recognize that the academic workforce is part of a wider workforce; increased fluidity and transferability between sectors is desirable, not only for research purposes but also to ensure high quality teaching'. The AUTCAS framework through its provision of explicit criteria and indicative standards of performance have generated a national conversation on what might be minimum or threshold levels of performance, and what might represent excellent levels of performance, as well as ways in which excellence can be recognized and rewarded.

Building a national strategy from the bottom-up

Several factors are considered to be critical to the large scale, successful utilisation of the AUTCAS framework across Australia. First, the AUTCAS framework was designed as an institutional *indicative* framework which fostered institutional and national conversations of teaching criteria and excellence standards. The indicative framework enabled universities to see that teaching criteria and performance expectations could be meaningfully described and evidenced. They could choose to utilize the framework to suit their context to develop clarity of expectations for teaching excellence. This contributed to a greater acceptance and rapid uptake of reviewing policy and processes for establishing institutional standards and criteria within universities by both the leadership and the individual academics who welcomed the clarity.

Second, the workshops and mentoring provided by the project team, and resultant networking and collaboration between universities by those charged with utilizing the framework within their university, provided a momentum as well as a timeline for the universities collectively to work towards their respective goals. In two years, the majority of Australian universities had considered, to a greater or lesser degree, their criteria and expectations for teaching excellence and the policies and processes by which they would be recognized.

Third, the composition of the university teams, sponsored by a senior member of the university executive, typically the Deputy Vice Chancellor (Academic), and delegated to senior university staff in leadership roles that included: oversight of policy, governance, human resources and teaching and learning, professional development, promotions and performance management, and often involved the unions, ensured that a whole of university discussion and approach was enacted.

Fourth, the engagement of national and sector organizations was also part of the project strategy for engagement and dissemination These included CADAD, ACODE, Higher Education and Research and Development Society of Australasia, OLT forums and the Deputy Vice Chancellor (Academic) group of Universities Australia, all of which have an interest in promoting teaching excellence. These have well-established networks of members and as representatives across the Australian higher education sector. Presentations were made and reports were circulated throughout the project implementation, and still continue through the ongoing involvement of the project members and the current Fellowship programme. This facilitated the linking of the institutional approaches and activities to the national conversation about recognizing and rewarding excellent teaching.

The successful development and utilization of the AUTCAS framework has now resulted in further dissemination and interest by vocational and private tertiary education providers to develop teaching criteria in this sector. International interest in the framework has extended beyond Australia, demonstrating its utility and applicability in different cultures and contexts. Universities in Canada, Iceland, Sweden, South Africa, Malaysia, Thailand and Chile have drawn on the AUTCAS framework and resources. Despite the different cultures and contexts in these countries, the very different universities have found that the resources, criteria and standards have relevance and comparability for defining teaching excellence in their institutions.

The further development of the AUTCAS framework and its implementation has been incorporated into the National Senior Teaching Fellowship funded by the Federal Government's OLT (Chalmers 2016).

Our national project has been designed to support the recognition and reward of excellence in teaching through the bottom-up engagement with universities. Their involvement has been driven by the goal of providing their students with an excellent learning experience. The universities have recognized that by supporting their teachers to achieve their shared understanding of teaching excellence, which is in part identified by the quality of student learning and engagement (Chalmers and Hunt 2016), they can work towards their goal of providing their students an excellent learning experience.

Conclusion

In this chapter we have argued for teaching excellence to be defined according to the values and context of the university, for it is in the universities that teaching excellence is recognized and rewarded. The purpose of this is not for a self-serving goal of simply achieving the career advancement of university teachers. It is a critical strategy if institutions are to enhance the quality of teaching and the student learning experience, for teaching excellence is only able to be demonstrated through quality teaching practices and student learning and achievements. This can only be achieved by each university considering its goals and values and making these clear in criteria, expectations and processes that are transparent, and their achievement supported through all levels of the institution. The national AUTCAS project, through the provision of an exemplar framework and processes, supported universities in their desire to have their distinct missions reflected in their definition of teaching excellence through a facilitated, systematic, peer-supported approach to defining teaching criteria and standards.

The AUTCAS framework and processes, with its clearly defined standards for teaching excellence has assisted institutions to review their policies for appointment, performance review and promotion, and the provision of support such as professional development for academics to achieve their desired criteria and standards. The resources have been freely shared on the AUTCAS website for sector-wide use. Engagement with sector and national organizations has further extended the reach of the project. In combination, these have resulted in a national strategy for building a shared understanding of criteria for teaching excellence, and expectations for different academic levels across Australia that is embedded in university policies and practices.

Acknowledgements

The AUTCAS project team members were Denise Chalmers (University of Western Australia), Rick Cummings (Murdoch University), Sofia Elliott (University of Notre Dame, Australia), Sue Stoney, (Edith Cowan University), Beatrice Tucker (Curtin University), Rachel Wicking and Trina Jorre de St Jorre (UWA). Funding for the project was provided by the Australian Government Office for Learning and Teaching.

References

Bexley, E., James, R. and Arkoudis, S. (2011) *The Australian academic profession in transition: addressing the challenge of reconceptualising academic work and regenerating the academic workforce*, Melbourne: Centre for the Study of Higher Education.

Bhandari, R. and Laughlin, S. (2009) *Higher education on the move: new developments in global mobility*, New York: Institute of International Education.

Chalmers, D. (2016) *Recognising and rewarding teaching: Australian teaching criteria and standards and peer review*, National Senior Teaching Fellowship. Online. Available at www.oltconference2016.com.au/cms/uploads/denise%20chalmers.pdf (accessed 3 April 2017).

Chalmers, D. and Hunt, L. (2016) 'Evaluating teaching', *HERSDA Review of Higher Education*, 3: 25–55.

Chalmers, D., Cummings, R., Elliott, S., Stoney, S., Tucker, B., Wicking, R. and Jorre de St Jorre, T. (2014) *Australian University Teaching Criteria and Standards Project: Final Report*. Online. Available at www.olt.gov.au/project-professionalisation-academic-workforce-project-2012 (accessed 3 April 2017).

Chalmers D., Cummings, R., Elliott, S., Stoney, S., Tucker, B., Wicking, R. and Jorre de St Jorre, T. (2015) *Australian University Teaching Criteria and Standards Project Extension*. Online. Available at http://uniteachingcriteria.edu.au/wp-content/uploads/2013/11/SP12_2335_Cummings_report_2015.pdf (accessed 3 April 2017).

Coates, H., Dobson, I., Edwards, D., Friedman, T., Goedegebuure, L. and Meek, L. (2009) *The attractiveness of the Australian academic profession: a comparative analysis*, Research briefing October 2009. Online. Available at http://research.acer.edu.au/cgi/viewcontent.cgi?article=1010&context=higher_education (accessed 3 April 2017).

Crookes P. (2014) *Transforming Practice Programme (TPP) – reward and recognition: promotion process and policy*. Online. Available at www.olt.gov.au/secondment-crookes (accessed 3 April 2017).

Department of Education and Training (2015) *Higher education in Australia: a review of reviews from Dawkins to today*. Canberra: Australian Government Department of Education and Training. Online. Available at https://docs.education.gov.au/system/files/doc/other/higher_education_in_australia_-_a_review_of_reviews.pdf (accessed 3 April 2017).

James, R., Baik, C., Millar, V., Naylor, R., Bexley, E., Kennedy, G., Krause, K., Hughes-Warrington, M., Sadler, D., Booth, S. and Booth, C. (2015) *Advancing the quality and status of teaching in Australian higher education: ideas for enhanced professional recognition for teaching and teachers*, Melbourne: University of Melbourne.

Kimber, M. (2003) 'The tenured "core" and the tenuous "periphery": the casualisation of academic work in Australian universities', *Journal of Higher Education Policy and Management*, 25(1): 41–50.

Kukulska-Hulme, A. (2012) 'How should the higher education workforce adapt to advancements in technology for teaching and learning?', *The Internet and Higher Education*, 15(4): 247–254.

Little, A. D. (2016) *The future of higher education: transforming the students of tomorrow*. Online. Available at www.adlittle.be/uploads/tx_extthoughtleadership/ADL_Future_of_higher_education_2016.pdf (accessed 3 April 2017).

Locke, W. (2014) *Shifting academic careers: implications for enhancing professionalism in teaching and supporting learning*, York: Higher Education Academy.

May, R., Peetz, D. and Strachan, G. (2013) 'The casual academic workforce and labour market segmentation in Australia', *Labour & Industry: a Journal of the Social and Economic Relations of Work*, 23(3): 258–275.

Percy, A., Scoufis, M., Parry, S., Goody, A., Hicks, M., Macdonald, I., Martinez, K., Szorenyi-Reischl, N., Ryan, Y., Wills, S. and Sheridan, L. (2008) *The RED report, Recognition-Enhancement-Development: the contribution of sessional teachers to higher education*, Sydney: Australian Learning and Teaching Council.

PricewaterhouseCoopers (2016) *Australian higher education workforce of the future*, Melbourne: Australian Higher Education Industrial Association. Online. Available at www.aheia.edu.

au/cms_uploads/docs/aheia-higher-education-workforce-of-the-future-report.pdf (accessed 3 April 2017).

Probert, B. (2013) *Teaching-focused academic appointments in Australian universities: recognition, specialisation, or statification?* Office for Learning and Teaching, Department of Education and Training (Australia). Online. Available at http://apo.org.au/node/35663 (accessed 3 April 2017).

Ramsden, P. (2008) *The future of higher education teaching and the student experience*, York: Higher Education Academy.

Ryan, S., Burgess, J., Connell, J. and Groen, E. (2013) 'Casual academic staff in an Australian university: marginalised and excluded', *Tertiary Education and Management*, 19(2): 161–175.

Thomas, L., Harden-Thew, K., Delahunty, J. and Dean, B. A. (2016) 'A vision of You-topia: personalising professional development of teaching in a diverse academic workforce', *Journal of University Teaching & Learning Practice*, 13(4): 5.

Universities Australia (2014) *The student experience*. Online. Available at www.universities australia.edu.au/uni-participation-quality/students/The-Student-Experience#.WOJciG_yvcs (accessed 3 April 2017).

Critical friend commentary

Erika Kustra

In common with Australia, universities in Canada are under increasing pressure to assure quality of teaching and learning, and there has been a parallel interest to improve evaluation of teaching (Wright et al. 2014). However, as Canadian universities are funded by provincial governments, there are few national initiatives to support the process. The University of Windsor (2016) in Ontario has been exploring how to enhance teaching through multiple avenues, and to determine its own interpretation of teaching excellence. Faculty members expressed interest in the Australian framework to plan career development, graduate students wondered about expectations when applying, and senior administrators expressed interest in having a more transparent framework, with greater clarity in processes.

Building on this growing interest, the Centre for Teaching and Learning co-sponsored a forum with the Office of the Provost to identify fair and effective evaluation practices that contribute to teaching improvement and to a sophisticated understanding of teaching quality. In parallel, our small grants programme prioritized evaluation of teaching projects, particularly encouraging departmental collaboration. The Office of the Provost set up an institution-wide initiative for departmental revision of renewal, tenure and promotion criteria. Through workshops and consultations, department heads and faculty members examined modified versions of the AUTCAS teaching and research frameworks, mapped their existing criteria, and modified the criteria, indicators, and standards on the assumption that each department would modify the criteria for their context. The goal of the revision did not require adoption of the frameworks, but did require: clear, well-organized criteria; illustrative practices; explanation of evidence to demonstrate an individual met a criterion (multiple sources); the standard at which individuals must meet established criteria for tenure and promotion.

While the project is still underway, the lessons learned in the Canadian context reflect the Australian context. Time for a change is substantially greater than most expect, closer to three to four years. Our experience indicates iterative communication is critical – working towards transparency to multiple groups, and consistency across the implementing team. This communication process needs extensive consultations with respect to discipline and context, as well as responsiveness to concerns that are raised. There is usually not a shared understanding of teaching excellence, or quality teaching, and consequently this process triggers important but difficult conversations. Finding champions and addressing the emotional impact associated with evaluation are both key. Finally, the importance of trust-building and sustaining trust throughout the process is essential (Hamilton et al. 2017). While we are one institution part-way through, the open sharing of resources from AUTCAS has facilitated the process and we continue to collaborate and share our own experiences with colleagues across Canada.

References

Hamilton, B., Berryman, J. and Kustra, E. (2017) *Enhancing teaching and disrupting tradition: implementing a Teaching Evaluation Framework in the Canadian context*, paper presented at the Educational Developers Caucus Conference (Re)thinking Tradition, 24 February 2017 at Guelph.

University of Windsor (2016) *Renewal, tenure and promotion research and teaching evaluation frameworks*. Online. Available at www1.uwindsor.ca/provost/renewal-promotion-and-tenure-rpt-research-and-teaching-evaluation-frameworks (accessed 3 April 2017).

Wright, W. A., Mighty, J., Muirhead, B., Scott, J. and Hamilton, B. (2014) *The Ontario universities' teaching evaluation toolkit: a feasibility study*. Online. Available at http://ctl.uwindsor.ca/ctl/system/files/Teaching_Evaluation_Toolkit.pdf (accessed 3 April 2017).

8

NATIONAL TEACHING AWARDS AND THE PURSUIT OF TEACHING EXCELLENCE

Mark Israel and Dawn Bennett

Introduction

In various parts of the world, government agencies, corporations and non-government organizations have supported award programmes that celebrate teaching excellence. As a result, the higher education sector now offers a diverse range of teaching awards that exist for a multiplicity of purposes and operate at a national level as well as within institutions and across many fields of study. However, the rationale for teaching awards is not always well articulated, consistent or understood – by the sector, institutions or individual academics. There is also limited evidence about their impact on awardees, teaching in general or student learning.

Teaching awards are most often explicitly connected with teaching excellence, sometimes celebrating past achievements, and in other instances supporting future endeavours. Arguably, these awards foster the emergence of educational leaders by motivating teachers to enhance their practice and apply for an award, and by giving recipients more authority and, hence, new opportunities to influence teaching practice. In their review of teaching excellence in higher education, Gunn and Fisk (2013: 9) note 'the inability of the sector to come to some regularised consensus about what constitutes teaching excellence, teacher excellence, excellent teaching as well as excellent student learning'. This lack of consensus persists despite efforts in many countries to create teaching equivalents of the various national research evaluation frameworks and a growing number of institutional systems for recognition and reward. Here, we consider teaching excellence in relation to national teaching awards. Drawing on the common characteristics of teaching excellence identified by Hammer et al. (2010) in their work on teaching awards, for the purposes of this chapter teaching excellence is characterized by: positive student-faculty contact, effective and active learning, achievable yet high expectations, respect for diverse talents and ways of learning, effective communication, and a commitment to teaching well.

In this chapter, we explore how and where awards have been established, and consider how they might have had an impact on the development of leaders in learning and teaching. We outline the work of national and international communities of awardees, highlighting the activities of the Association of National Teaching Fellows in the United Kingdom, the Ako Aotearoa Academy of Tertiary Teaching Excellence in New Zealand, the Canadian 3M National Teaching Fellows, and the Multinational Teaching Fellows group within and now beyond the International Society for the Scholarship of Teaching and Learning (ISSOTL).

National teaching awards

While the Canadian and United States national higher education awards processes predate those of Australia, the Australian programme was among the first to be run by a national government. As such, it has arguably provided a model for the schemes developed in several other English-speaking countries. In this section, we set the context with an overview of the awards schemes in Australia, the United Kingdom and New Zealand.

The Australian government has invested considerable resources in the Australian Awards for University Teaching (AAUT) since they were first established in 1996. Successive federal ministers promoted the scheme as a way of increasing the status of teaching in the higher education sector (Israel 2011). The awards programme has evolved over time in an effort to promote long-term change in the higher education sector and recognize the different sectoral institutional priorities and missions. As such, it includes individual and programme-based awards, citations, and lifetime achievement awards. Despite criticism that advocates for the awards had failed to demonstrate systemic impact (Probert 2015), and that awardees might do more to share their knowledge (Johns 2011), the awards were the only part of the Australian Government Office for Learning and Teaching's funding initiatives to survive the closure of that Office in 2016.

In 2000, the Higher Education Funding Council for England (HEFCE) and Department for Employment and Learning in Northern Ireland established a National Teaching Fellowship Scheme to raise the profile of teaching and learning and to reward and celebrate teaching excellence. Wales joined the scheme in 2011. Recognizing past achievement but also seeking to support future development (Skelton 2007: 216), the scheme awarded the title of National Teaching Fellow (NTF) alongside a grant that backed professional development in learning and teaching. Since their inception, the number of annual awards has increased; by 2015, fifty-five awards were available each year and over 698 National Teaching Fellows had been appointed from over forty disciplines (Rolfe 2015). In 2016, new Collaborative Awards for Teaching Excellence (CATE) were piloted, acknowledging collaborative and innovative practice that had a positive impact on the student experience. Within a research-intensive university culture, the financial component of the NTF Scheme was initially intended to signal a serious commitment to teaching and learning. However, over sixteen years, the amount awarded diminished significantly from £50,000 to £5,000.

The New Zealand government established national teaching awards in 2002 as a way of recognizing and encouraging excellence in teaching across the tertiary sector. Like Australia and the United Kingdom, the awards were intended to enable teachers to enhance their careers and teaching practice (Maharey 2002; Jesson and Smith 2007). The awards were described by the Minister for Tertiary Education as important in countering the tendency in the past of rewarding academic staff primarily on the basis of their research (Cullen 2006). Cullen explicitly identified award winners as the current and future leaders in tertiary education. To advance this aim, the expectation was that award money would be used for the awardee's professional development. There are specific awards for teachers of *Kaupapa Māori* and plans to introduce a category for Pasifika teachers. By 2016, almost 200 academics in New Zealand had received a national award.

Awardees working collaboratively

Several national groups of award-winning teachers have been established over the past three decades. These groups vary in how they were formed, membership criteria and processes, and whether they are self-administering or supported by a parent organization. However, in each case they have struggled to play a collective role as educational leaders. Three of the most established groups are those in the United Kingdom, New Zealand and Canada, and we draw on these experiences to consider the benefits and challenges of awardees working together.

In the United Kingdom, an early aim for the NTF scheme was for fellows to work together to promote effective teaching and learning. Operating as a collective, this offered the potential for what Skelton (2007: 217) described as a 'platform for the expression of "grassroots" opinion on teaching in higher education'. Reviewing the collective in its infancy, Skelton (2004: 460) was critical that '"shared identity" beyond camaraderie has failed to develop among the fellowship holders'. He argued that this was a feature 'typical of any interdisciplinary group, split, for example, by subject and experience' (ibid.: 460) and lacking a 'shared sense of purpose and common set of educational values' (ibid.: 464). Skelton (in Leon 2002) also noted that fellows could be encouraged to act as agents of change.

In line with any community of practice, however, collective agency requires a shared vision and purpose enacted through joint enterprise, mutual engagement and shared repertoire (Wenger-Trayner and Wenger-Trayner 2015). In 2005, with support from the Higher Education Academy (HEA) the NTFs furthered the idea of a community with the formation of the Association of National Teaching Fellows (ANTF), placing the leadership of the Association in the hands of the Fellows. The ANTF sought to further the impact of National Teaching Fellows in promoting excellence in teaching and learning (ANTF 2017). To support these activities, the ANTF was given a small annual grant from the HEA.

The ANTF's premise that its Fellows might have a greater impact on higher education teaching and learning as a collective has resulted in a decade of activities including facilitated networking, the promotion of innovative practices, and responses to government policy initiatives (Wakefield and France 2010). Each year, NTFs undertake work for the HEA as specialist readers, evaluators and consultants. NTFs also support the induction of new Fellows and organize a variety of opportunities for collaborative work. Another strand of the Fellows' work concerns presentations at national and international learning and teaching conferences. Notably, since 2012 the ANTF has supported the development of future Fellows with regional workshops for colleagues who wish to become an NTF, and for those whose role it is to support staff professional development and NTF nominations. The ANTF holds an annual conference, on occasion inviting colleagues from other countries to join as keynote speakers and work with Fellows. In 2014, the ANTF opened its annual conference to the sector to encourage greater promotion of the NTF Scheme and collaboration opportunities.

In 2007, focus groups convened by the New Zealand Qualifications Authority and Tertiary Education Commission suggested the sector could do more to draw on the expertise of those with already proven excellence (Cullen 2006). Charged by the government to look for further ways in which expert teachers might bring maximum advantage to the whole sector (Street 2008), Ako Aotearoa was established as New Zealand's Centre for Tertiary Teaching Excellence comprising part of a $20 million Government initiative to boost teaching quality across the post-school education sector.

In 2008, Ako Aotearoa proposed a national academy of award winners known as the Ako Aotearoa Academy of Tertiary Teaching Excellence to enhance teaching practice in New Zealand and influence the development of tertiary education policy. Operating under the umbrella of Ako Aotearoa, this Academy has since 2008 held annual symposia for past award winners, who are automatically members. The Academy's first national event focused on educational leadership and was opened by the Associate Minister for Tertiary Education who saw the Academy as providing a structure so that excellent teachers can reinvest their expertise in others (Street 2008). The Academy pursued its role by providing support and advice on tertiary education practice and policy from a practitioner's perspective, and by collaborating with Ako Aotearoa and other organizations for the benefit of educators and learners across all tertiary sectors (Academy of Tertiary Teaching Excellence 2009). The Director of Ako Aotearoa described the Academy as:

> . . . an important national resource for New Zealand's tertiary sector, being a repository of teaching expertise, wisdom and innovative practice. They are an important voice in the continuing debate about how to provide the best possible educational opportunities to all of New Zealand's tertiary learners.
>
> *(Coolbear 2010: 9)*

The Academy provided funds to enable its members to develop and disseminate teaching practice and promote the academy (Academy of Tertiary Teaching Excellence 2010). The Academy has contributed to Ako Aotearoa's professional development programme, offering mentorship and drafting and presenting position papers on aspects of tertiary teaching; it also has representation on the national awards judging panel and the Board of Ako Aotearoa.

Another long-established community of teaching award winners is found in Canada, where since 1986 the Society for Teaching and Learning in Higher Education (STLHE) and corporate sponsor 3M Canada have jointly sponsored the 3M National Teaching Fellowship. The 3M Fellowship recognizes exemplary contributions to teaching and educational leadership in Canadian universities. With an immediate focus on collaboration, new Fellows have participated in four-day retreats to discuss and share past teaching experiences and develop new ideas.

In 2003, with the aim of making a difference to the quality of teaching in all Canadian universities (Ahmad 2004), forty-two 3M Fellows met in Toronto to discuss how they might organize and share collectively. The result was the Council of 3M National Teaching Fellows for Teaching and Learning in Higher Education, which has since met annually. The Council has lobbied government, run STLHE conference sessions on best practice, undertaken collaborative projects, published collections of stories celebrating teaching and learning, and provided funding for members involved in educational leadership initiatives (Enns 2016).

Since the inception of the award schemes, individual fellows and awardees from various parts of the world have continued to build international collaborative relationships. More recently, these informal networks have coalesced into international communities and more formal international bodies. Fellows have regularly contributed to international meetings focused on the Scholarship of Teaching and Learning. This resulted in a multinational scholars' forum, which met with the Carnegie Scholars in the US in 2004, the 3M Fellows in Canada in 2005 and 2008, and the ANTF in the United Kingdom in 2006.

International collaboration has focused on shared challenges such as the low value of teaching versus research (Arimoto 2014), ways of enhancing teaching excellence (Land and Gordon 2015) and the generation of 'an international approach to learning and teaching' (Rosie et al. 2006: 1). At the 2005 Canadian meeting, attendees encouraged 'teaching and learning champions' to 'go where they are "valued and invited" to share and extend experience, visions and strategies' (Fancy 2005: 8). Following the suggestion that dialogue across borders might be best achieved through three-day international retreats – an extension of the Canadian 3M model – the Multinational Teaching Fellows Group was formed. This cohort has met as a special interest group at EuroSoTL and the International Society for the Scholarship of Teaching and Learning (ISSOTL) conferences, including those held in Sydney (2007), Indiana (2009), Liverpool (2010) and Minnesota (2011). The group has celebrated multinational perspectives on teaching excellence, considered book and article submissions, and presented panels on teaching excellence for conferences and symposia.

These formal and informal networks led eventually to the launch of an International Federation of National Teaching Fellows (IFNTF) in 2016. The IFNTF sought to advance excellence in learning and teaching in higher education globally by bringing together award-winning teachers from across the world.

Within its first year the Federation had quickly facilitated multinational, collaborative events including a world summit in 2017, to be followed by a second summit in Canada in 2018. One of the immediate benefits of such face-to-face initiatives was the identification of three common themes (high-impact pedagogies, learning gain, and excellence within the disciplines), followed by a collaborative strategy for action.

Do awards contribute to university teaching?

There is substantial interest among awardees in the development of networks and collaborative activities. Awardees share a commitment to quality and equality in higher education in the face of massification, diversification and increasing institutional accountability (Mahat and Millot 2014), and in some environments a lack of government or institutional support. In broad terms, challenges include transnational programmes, global perspectives, and tackling deep inequalities.

One of the claims of national teaching award benefits is that they elevate the status of university teaching by improving the reward structure and increasing the public profile of academics with strong track records in the practice and scholarship of teaching (Centre for the Study of Higher Education 2005). Israel's (2011) study of Australian awardees found awards helped some people enter and then move up a developmental pathway through positions such as programme director and associate dean at school and faculty levels. Awards also helped people secure positions on university-level committees, become part of the informal networks upon which senior management draw for advice, and apply for Commonwealth government-funded Learning and Teaching Council projects or Fellowships. Of course, as Israel's study also found, award winners might already be quite senior (at associate professor or above). This is perhaps not so surprising – while not being a formal precondition of an award, the criteria used to assess national awards can value applicants who already demonstrate leadership with broad influence on the profession. Indeed, some seem to have come to expect an exceptional record of educational leadership.

Recipients may be strategic assets who can play a key role in developing teaching and learning initiatives and championing change in learning and teaching policies and practices, undertaking the kinds of leadership roles identified by Hammer et al. (2010). National award winners have been employed at the institutional, national and international levels as teaching assessors, drivers of change and motivational speakers. Many awardees have become high-status role models for teaching excellence within their disciplines (Department for Education and Skills 2003; Skelton 2004; Israel 2011), and leaders of quality improvement, pivotal to policy, funding and mentorship.

However, the consequences of recognition may not always be positive. The respondents to Skelton's (2004) British study noted a lack of interest in their achievement among colleagues and managers, which the authors related to: the low value of teaching within a research-focused environment; lack of promotional or career scripts in which teaching excellence is recognized; and the perception that a Fellowship 'as a form of reward is less valued than other forms of award achievement' (ibid.: 418). This highlights the unequal treatment of teaching and research (Bexley et al. 2011), and the lack of career pathways based on teaching. Bennett et al. (2017) emphasize that this inequality will change 'only when higher education funding and policy ameliorates the historically subordinate status of teaching in relation to research and research ranking exercises'. At the institutional level, authors assert the need for institution-wide career scripts, workloads appropriate to career intentions and achievement, role models promoted to the professoriate on the basis of their teaching, and strong institutional leadership.

A further potentially negative effect is that some awardees find themselves labelled as 'just teachers'. Many respondents to Skelton's (2004) survey of NTF recipients reported the scheme had reinforced their teaching identities. Some welcomed this; others, however, felt torn between the possibilities of an educational role and the conventional demands of a discipline-based research career. In Australia, Israel (2011) reported that a few awardees were concerned their success as teachers would pigeonhole them into a teaching-only profile and they would lose the time and opportunity to focus on research. They considered this could well be detrimental to their careers. Several deliberately placed greater emphasis on their research after their awards to counter the possibility that this might happen. Similarly, within the United Kingdom, Frame et al. (2006) found that in a research-intensive institution, being identified as a teacher can create a 'career block'.

Conversely, perceptions of exclusivity present a significant challenge to national teaching groups and associations. In addition to national recognition as a 'teaching fellow', many institutions and indeed countries have alternative recognition processes in the form of academy memberships, grant-related fellowships and so on. As such, there is a need to extend memberships to colleagues who have been awarded a significant discipline or regional teaching and learning award, but to do this in a way that is equitable. This is no small challenge and requires, in an international organization, the inclusion of scholars from around the world.

Arguably, therefore, teaching awards might foster the emergence of educational leaders by incentivizing the pursuit of teaching excellence in advance of award applications and by giving award recipients greater authority to influence the teaching of others and enhance their own practice. Viewed from the perspective of Ramsden and colleagues' (2007) scales of leadership, awards might thus be seen to foster the emergence of educational leadership by providing clear goals and contingent reward, and by promoting teachers who might engage others through 'inspiration, exemplary practice, collaboration, spontaneity and trust' (ibid.: 66).

Awards and the pursuit of teaching excellence

Advocates for the awards that we discuss in this chapter have argued that their schemes would further teaching excellence. However, several critics have suggested there are a number of problems with this proposition that have yet to be tackled.

First, various government and institutional initiatives have struggled to identify the links between good teachers, teaching quality and student learning, and in some contexts, there has been some move in focus within higher education away from the language of individual teaching excellence towards quality assurance and quality improvement. For example, Probert (2015: 41) noted a shift in Australia 'from prizes and celebrations to performance management and accreditation' alongside the advantages and disadvantages of seeking accreditation from an overseas organization such as the Higher Education Academy.

Second, national awards have found it difficult to articulate a conception of teaching excellence. This leaves the criteria used to assess applicants without firm theoretical or empirical bases. Gibbs (2008) found that awards within British universities sometimes avoided the issue, but that when they did attend to excellence had vastly differing ideas of what it meant and how it might, or indeed should, be demonstrated. So, the failure of national awards to tackle the link to excellence might reflect a pragmatic decision to attract the interest of as many higher education institutions as possible and not favour the preferences of some institutions over others.

Third, reviews of various awards programmes only hint at the strategic role awards might play in cultivating a new generation of educational leadership. This is partly because many awards sit uneasily between looking backwards at people's past achievements and forward to their future contributions. However, the omission is curious given that some award recipients do appear to be drawn into teaching and learning-related leadership and administrative roles (Anderson and Johnson 2006; Israel 2011).

Fourth, despite the terminology adopted in various countries – 'university teaching' in Australia, 'teaching excellence' in New Zealand, 'teaching fellowships' in the United Kingdom and Canada – awards generally focus on the recognition of individuals and groups of *teachers* rather than the practices of *teaching*. They assume that teachers can have a significant influence on student learning independent of the various institutional and student cultures within which they work. And yet, as Gibbs (2010: 5) notes: 'Few relationships between a single dimension of quality and a single measure of either educational performance or educational gain can be interpreted with confidence because dimensions interact in complex ways with each other', and the organizational setting has a direct impact on matters such as class sizes, student effort and engagement. Finally, there is at best mixed evidence that awards have challenged the primacy of research as a driver of institutional behaviour (Bexley et al. 2013).

Reservations about the impact of national teaching awards should not be confused with the value of using the awards as a device to construct and support groups of strong teachers who engage within and across disciplines, and countries to advocate for and promote scholarship around teaching. We call on awardees to continue to inspire learning, link research and teaching, and respect and support students. We encourage them to build networks with other award-winning teachers both within and beyond their own organizations, and to consider what they can do to extend best practice, support the wider teaching community, and develop teaching-research groups. We ask their institutions to help award winners make a contribution to the sector by enabling their engagement with other institutions and with national policy formation in a way that reflects their distinctive institutional missions. Finally, we urge those bodies with sector-wide responsibilities, such as Ako Aotearoa in New Zealand and the Higher Education Academy in the United Kingdom, to empower award winners to contribute towards their institution, discipline, and the sector as a whole. After all, those with expertise in and a passion for teaching could, and should, play an important role in forming and challenging policies and practices in higher education.

Acknowledgements

Parts of this chapter draw from material originally published in Israel (2011). We acknowledge and thank colleagues from around the world who helped us ensure that we were accurate in our descriptions of national teaching fellowship schemes. In particular we wish to thank Sally Brown, Kirsten Hardie, Carol Evans, Earle Abrahamson and Selene Mize.

References

Academy of Tertiary Teaching Excellence (2009) *Academy brochure.* Online. Available at http://akoaotearoa.ac.nz/download/ng/file/group-20/n2392-the-academy-brochure.pdf (accessed 10 April 2017).

Academy of Tertiary Teaching Excellence (2010) *The academy year.* Online. Available at http://akoaotearoa.ac.nz/academy (accessed 10 April 2017).

Ahmad, A. (2004) *The 3M Teaching Fellowship – making a difference.* Online. Available at https://3mcouncil.stlhe.ca/initiative/making-a-difference-a-celebration-of-the-3m-national-teaching-fellowship/the-3m-teaching-fellowship-making-a-difference-arshad-ahmad/ (accessed 10 April 2017).

Anderson, D. and Johnson, R. (2006) *Ideas of leadership underpinning proposals to the Carrick Institute: a review of proposals from the 'Leadership for Excellence in Teaching and Learning Program'.* Online. Available at http://citeseerx.ist.psu.edu/viewdoc/download?doi=10.1.1.93.5831&rep=rep1&type=pdf (accessed 10 April 2017).

Arimoto, A. (2014) 'The teaching and research nexus in the third wave age', in J. C. Shin, A. Arimoto, W. K. Cummings and U. Teichler (eds) *Teaching and Research in Contemporary Higher Education,* 15–34, Utrecht: Springer.

Association of National Teaching Fellows (2017) *Association of National Teaching Fellows supported by the Higher Education Academy.* Online. Available at http://ntf-association.com/about/ (accessed 4 April 2017).

Bennett, D., Roberts, L., Ananthram, S. and Broughton, M. (2017) 'What is required to develop career pathways for teaching academics?', *Higher Education,* 23 March 2017, 1–16. Online. Available at https://link.springer.com/article/10.1007/s10734-017-0138-9 (accessed 4 April 2017).

Bexley, E., Arkoudis, S. and James, R. (2013) 'The motivations, values and future plans of Australian academics', *Higher Education,* 65(3): 385–400.

Bexley, E., James, R. and Arkoudis, S. (2011) *The Australian academic profession in transition,* Melbourne: Centre for the Study of Higher Education.

Centre for the Study of Higher Education (2005) *Recommendations for an expanded program of awards for university teaching*, Melbourne: Centre for the Study of Higher Education. Online. Available at http://melbourne-cshe.unimelb.edu.au/research/policy-development/recommendations-for-management (accessed 10 April 2017).

Coolbear, P. (2010) 'Director's comment', *Profiling the 2010 Recipients of the Tertiary Teaching Excellence Awards*, 9, Wellington: Ako Aotearoa.

Cullen, M. (2006) 'Tertiary teaching awards ceremony', *Scoop Independent News*, 27 June. Online. Available at http://www.scoop.co.nz/stories/PA0606/S00517.htm (accessed 10 April 2017).

Department for Education and Skills (2003) *The future of higher education*, London: Her Majesty's Stationery Office.

Enns, E. E. (2016) 2015 Report of the Council of 3M National Teaching Fellows. Online. Available at https://3mcouncil.stlhe.ca/resources/reports-list/annual-report-2015 (accessed 10 April 2017).

Fancy, A. (2005) *Towards a framework for quality enhancement in teaching and learning: an exploratory seminar*, The Charlottetown Forum on Teaching and Learning Report of the Second Multi-National Forum of Teacher Scholars. Online. Available at www.mcmaster.ca/stlhe/3M.council/Forum%20Report.pdf (accessed 10 April 2017).

Frame, P., Johnson, M. and Rosie, A. (2006) 'Reward or award? Reflections on the initial experiences of winners of a National Teaching Fellowship', *Innovations in Education and Teaching International*, 43(4): 409–419.

Gibbs, G. (2008) *Designing teaching awards schemes*, York: Higher Education Academy.

Gibbs, G. (2010) *Dimensions of quality*, York: Higher Education Academy.

Gunn, V. and Fisk, A. (2013) *Considering teaching excellence in higher education: 2007–2013*, York: Higher Education Academy.

Hammer, D., Piascik, P., Medina, M., Pittenger, A., Rose, R., Creekmore, F., Soltis, R., Bouldin, A., Schwarz, L. and Scott, S. (2010) 'Recognition of teaching excellence', *American Journal of Pharmaceutical Education*, 74(9: 164): 1–11.

Israel, M. (2011) *The key to the door? Teaching awards in Australian higher education*, Fellowship Final Report, Strawberry Hills, NSW: Australian Learning and Teaching Council. Online. Available at file:///C:/Users/hsx413/Downloads/Israel,%20M%20UWA%20Fellowship%20report%202011.pdf (accessed 10 April 2017).

Jesson, J. and Smith, R. (2007) 'Tertiary teaching matters: political economy of a New Zealand centre for tertiary teaching excellence', in A. Skelton (ed.) *International perspectives on teaching excellence in higher education*, 133–146, Abingdon: Routledge.

Johns, A. (2011) *Higher education learning and teaching review*, Canberra: Commonwealth of Australia.

Land, R. and Gordon, G. (2015) *Teaching excellence initiatives: modalities and operational factors*, York: Higher Education Academy.

Leon, P. (2002) 'Received with reservations', *Times Higher Education*, 14 June 2002. Online. Available at www.timeshighereducation.com/news/received-with-reservations/169823.article?sectioncode=26&storycode=169823 (accessed 10 April 2017).

Maharey, S. (2002) 'Showcasing tertiary teaching excellence', *Scoop Independent News*, 25 June. Online. Available at www.scoop.co.nz/stories/PA0206/S00429.htm (accessed 10 April 2017).

Mahat, M. and Millot, B. (2014) *Rankings and employability: a system and institutional perspective*, paper presented at the IREG-7 Conference: Employability and Academic Rankings – Reflections and Impacts, 14–16 May, University College London.

Probert, B. (2015) *The quality of Australia's higher education system: how it might be defined, improved and assured*, Australian Government Office for Learning and Teaching. Online.

Available at www.hes.edu.au/assets/HECQN-2015/Probert-Quality-Aust-HE-2015.pdf (accessed 24 April 2017).

Ramsden, P., Prosser, M., Trigwell, K. and Martin, E. (2007) 'University teachers' experiences of academic leadership and their approaches to teaching', *Learning and Instruction*, 178: 140–155.

Rolfe, V. (2015) *Welcome to all new fellows!* Association of National Teaching Fellows/Higher Education Academy, 11 June 2015. Online. Available at http://ntf-association.com/national-teaching-fellows/welcome-to-all-new-fellows/ (accessed 24 April 2017).

Rosie, A., Johnson, M. and Frame, P. (2006) *Measuring impact of a national award scheme: the case of the national teaching fellowship scheme*, paper presented at the Higher Education Academy Annual Conference, July 2006, York.

Skelton, A. (2004) 'Understanding "teaching excellence" in higher education: a critical evaluation of the National Teaching Fellowship Scheme', *Studies in Higher Education*, 29(4): 451–468.

Skelton, A. (2007) 'The National Teaching Fellowship Scheme 2000–2006: rest in peace?', in A. Skelton (ed.) *International perspectives on teaching excellence in higher education*, 213–225, Abingdon: Routledge.

Street, M. (2008) 'Ako Aotearoa Academy for tertiary teaching', *Scoop Independent News*, 16 October 2008. Online. Available at www.scoop.co.nz/stories/PA0810/S00353.htm (accessed 24 April 2017).

Wakefield, K. and France, D. (2010) 'Learning and teaching network of national teaching fellows: a preliminary study', *Learning Exchange*, 1(1): 12–19.

Wenger-Trayner, E. and Wenger-Trayner, B. (2015) *Communities of practice, a brief introduction*. Online. Available at http://wenger-trayner.com/introduction-to-communities-of-practice/ (accessed 24 April 2017).

Critical friend commentary

Sally Brown

The UK Association of National Teaching Fellows (ANTF) is a well-established and active network of around 750 colleagues recognized for their excellent teaching since 2000. Building on sound foundations laid by Bob Rotherham, Lesley-Jane Eales-Reynolds and Kirsten Hardie, we are working hard in the current constrained-resource environment to demonstrate the impact of our community members as leaders, change agents and activists. I was responsible for setting up the scheme when I was a Director of the Institute for Learning and Teaching in Higher Education (ILTHE), later part of the Higher Education Academy (HEA), and from the outset our aim was to build the 'Fellowship of the Fellowship-holders'. This was no small task as the group is an aggregate of diverse and often quirky individuals with often little in common other than a shared passion for teaching and enhancing the student experience. Part of the original aim of the National Teaching Fellows was to identify excellent champions who could act like so-called 'beacon schools' to demonstrate what excellence looks like in practice.

Israel and Bennett succinctly identify what needs to be done by national teaching excellence award-holders. I would add we must first demonstrate how we add value to the nations and communities to which we belong. For National Teaching

Fellows that includes working hard for communities, including the HEA for whom they work as consultants, volunteers, reviewers, authors, advisors, project leaders and crucial friends, as well as for organizations like the Staff and Educational Development Association and the Association of Learning Developers in Higher Education in which they are post holders. National Teaching Fellows also add value by leading and managing pedagogic change and contributing to strategic and policy-making activities for their higher education institutions.

Second, we need to evidence the impact our work has made. Examples of this could be publications, conference presentations and keynotes deriving from National Teaching Fellow-led projects that show evaluated outcomes in terms of practice and process. We also need to practise scholarship by using evidence-based and research-informed processes to investigate, test, analyse and evaluate new and established approaches to teaching and the support of student learning. Good practice needs to be modelled, for example, by committing to ongoing professional development and reflection in our professional lives. The ANTF symposia both for ourselves and those we open to the wider community often provide a stimulus for these activities.

We need to share expertise and resources with our fellows. One of the key benefits of ANTF, many argue, is our ability to seek help and advice from one another on practical and theoretical matters, particularly via the ANTF Jiscmail mailbase. Ask a question (particularly on a Friday afternoon) and you can practically guarantee ten good suggestions or artefacts by teatime! We also need to advocate and lobby for the causes which concern us. For example, the ANTF has been very active in lobbying to ensure that the new United Kingdom Teaching Excellence Framework includes metrics that genuinely reflect excellent teaching, rather than poor proxies which often merely demonstrate existing advantage.

Mentoring needs to be provided for the next generation of excellent teaching, certainly by supporting new applicants for national awards, but also by helping them gain accredited recognition in other ways for their teaching (for example, through Staff and Educational Development Association or HEA Fellowships). Finally, we need to engage beyond our own national communities; many teaching fellows have been working since the turn of the century to network with colleagues globally through organizations like the Multinational Teaching Fellows group, the International Society for the Scholarship of Teaching and Learning (ISSOTL) and the emergent International Federation of National Teaching Fellows. To my know-ledge, many of us make it personal too by inviting international colleagues into our universities, events and even our own homes. The British–Australian collaboration on reward and recognition for teaching (Wills et al. 2013) is a great example of this.

References

Wills, S., Cashmore, A., Sadler, D., Booth, S., McHanwell, S. and Robson, S. (2013) *Promoting teaching: international inter-university benchmarking of academic promotion*, 1–52, eCite Digital Repository, University of Tasmania. Online. Available at http://ecite.utas.edu.au/107608 (accessed 7 April 2017).

9

TRAINING AND DEVELOPMENT NEEDS FOR A 21ST CENTURY ACADEMIC

Siara Isaac, Ingrid Le Duc, Cécile Hardebolle and Roland Tormey

Introduction

As the importance of excellence in teaching is increasingly recognized across the 21st century higher education landscape (European University Association 2015), universities need to reconsider how to support the pedagogical development of faculty. Academic Development Units, also called Centres for Teaching and Learning or Teaching Support Centres, have contributed appreciably to the increased value accorded to teaching and learning over the last decades, including at research-intensive institutions (ibid.). However, the actual practice of university teaching has changed very little over this period. Traditional lectures, tutorials and laboratory work more or less still dominate students' schedules regardless of growing research evidence which questions the efficacy of these methods.

We, along with others (for example: Gosling 2009; Gibbs 2013; Loads and Campbell 2015), argue that a new approach is required to respond to the current training and development needs among academic teachers. In short, we need an approach capable of enacting a substantive change in teaching practices so that they better reflect the broad consensus on the elements which comprise excellent teaching, such as active learning and feedback (Hattie 2008; Freeman et al. 2014). Our claim is that to achieve this shift, 21st century academic development should be *teacher-led*, *data-driven*, and *evidence-informed*. In such an approach, teaching excellence becomes a process of scholarly improvement, conducted by the teacher who sets discipline and context appropriate benchmarks, and leverages teaching and learning data to select and refine teaching strategies. This process requires institutional leadership on teaching excellence which explicitly values the expertise of teachers, enabling the development of a culture of contextualized definitions of teaching excellence and hence supporting profound changes in pedagogical practices.

This chapter will first present the characteristics of such an approach. Following that, we will describe its application both at the level of an institution and at the level of a single course. In doing so, we will explore both the micro- and macro-strategies for promoting teaching excellence.

Framework for a teacher-led, data-driven and evidence-informed approach to teacher development

It has been well documented that, despite massive changes in educational systems over the last century, the basic patterns of teaching and learning have not changed significantly (Cuban 2013), and many changes that have been introduced (such as increased use of information technology, laptops, tablets, or online learning platforms) end up being grafted on to traditional, content delivery-focused teaching models rather than transforming them. It is relevant to acknowledge that a range of barriers impede changes to teaching practices, from classroom architecture to the commodification of education (Briseño-Garzón et al. 2016); however, this chapter will focus on the pedagogical development of teachers and initiatives which recognize teaching excellence.

While externally-proposed teaching reforms appear to be a simple and cost-efficient method of effecting change, teaching practices have been shown to be quite resistant to top-down approaches as they typically do not solve problems that teachers feel they have. Consequently, many teachers resist change, or engage in superficial compliance without actually adopting the evidence-informed practices underlying the policy (Mårtensson et al. 2011: 53). The support offered by academic development units is generally more collegial, but has evolved little in recent decades. Following 21st century educational reforms (European University Association 2015), academic development should become more individualized by offering flexible delivery and time paths, and more opportunities to pursue specialization. If efforts to promote teaching excellence are to be effective, they need to support teachers in identifying and addressing problems which concern them in their own context. This implies an integrated approach, where academic developers work with teachers *in situ* on their course to define what excellence means and to engage in a dialectic process with their own teaching and learning data. Academics' teaching practice is the best location for developing pedagogical competence but such development requires explicit reflection (Boud and Brew 2013). When academic developers work collegially with teachers, they can create contextualized opportunities and space for such reflection. This integrated approach can be contrasted to the more traditional methods of offering teaching development workshops, where the out-of-context nature poses challenges for transfer of concepts and practices into classroom life (Darling-Hammond 2006). We believe that a successful approach must be *teacher-led*, and anchored in the discipline, context and problematics of the teachers concerned.

It is clear that we need reform which is teacher-led, but it is also clear that this is not in itself sufficient. There is now abundant evidence that many common teaching practices in higher education could be made more effective by incorporating collaborative learning (Hattie 2008; Crouch and Mazur 2001), use of visualization technology (European University Association 2015), and use of conceptually-oriented tasks (Ruiz-Primo et al. 2011), interactive teaching approaches (Freeman et al. 2014), and concept maps (Nesbit and Adesope 2006). Again, the fact that such practices are not more widely used underlines the need to adopt a new approach to supporting pedagogical development that can stimulate disruptive, rather than iterative, evolution.

At present, while there are differences across countries (Fraser et al. 2010; Rège Colet 2010; Isaac and Sylvestre 2012; Pleschová et al. 2012; Fernández and Márquez 2014; Cosnefroy 2015), academic development units typically focus on training workshops, individual coaching, and student course appreciation questionnaires which tend to promote the incremental and iterative improvement of current practices. We propose that teachers should be supported in engaging with rigorous evidence on the effectiveness and limits of teaching practices, and thus stimulated to re-evaluate their own practices. Enacting Quinn's (2012: 1) definition of *disruptive* academic development, 'adopting a stance of questioning, challenging and critiquing taken-for-granted ways of doing things in higher education' is well suited to an *evidence-informed* challenge to current teaching practices but may require change within some academic development units.

Of course, we should be careful in interpreting such evidence – just because one teaching practice works better on average than another does not mean that it is necessarily appropriate for a given lecturer's discipline, learning goals, or students. Educational innovations need to be tested in context by academics; in other words, teaching excellence should be *data-driven*. In doing so, teachers can draw on the well-developed traditions of Scholarship of Teaching and Learning and action research (Hutchings and Shulman 1999; Trigwell et al. 2000; McKinney 2012; McNiff 2013). The recent focus on the development of learning analytics can also inform teachers' data-driven decision-making. Unfortunately, at present, the data produced in relation to teaching in higher education overwhelmingly relies on student course appreciation questionnaires (European University Association 2015; Wieman 2015), a data source which can consume considerable resources to produce yet shows a near zero correlation with measures of student learning (Clayson 2009; Wieman 2015; Uttl et al. 2016). Academic development units clearly need to move beyond the use of such low-quality data and find more effective ways of helping teachers to evaluate their practices.

As represented in Figure 9.1, we conceptualize teacher development in terms of Kurt Lewin's action-research cycle of Reviewing, Planning, Implementing, and Evaluating practices (Adelman 1993). In this model, the teacher is central to the process and is implicated in all phases. In particular, the teacher holds the disciplinary expertise and knowledge of the students, as well as the responsibility for the course essential to Planning and Teaching activities. The role of academic development units lies primarily in accompanying the teacher in the Evaluate and Review phases. We thus recommend that academic development units accompany teachers in

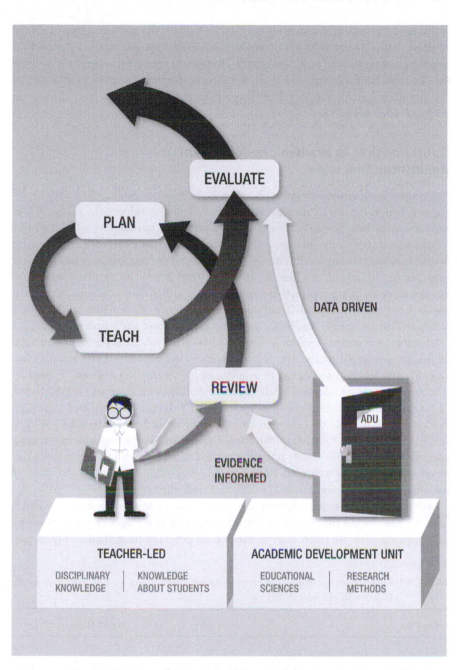

FIGURE 9.1 Teacher–led, data–driven and evidence-informed approach to academic development conceptualized in terms of Lewin's Action Research Cycle

applying the results of research on learning in higher education and in generating relevant high-quality data about student learning. For example, an academic development unit could propose research methods to support teachers in collecting data on aspects of learning which are not directly targeted by assessments, such as the development of transversal skills, performance on concept inventories, or students' study habits.

Good practices in academic development at the institutional scale

Accompanying the institutional application of the framework described above may require something of a paradigm shift for academic development units. While supporting the Scholarship of Teaching and Learning is sometimes part of the brief of an academic development unit, it appears that staff in many centres internationally do not have the training in educational research to aid the translation of this research into practice (Harland and Staniforth 2003; Patel 2014). Since many academic development units are regarded as administrative, rather than academic, they may also lack the culture of research and the lived experience of university teaching that is required to adequately undertake this function (Harland and Staniforth 2003).

Another institutional-level challenge to address is the value and prestige frequently afforded to research activities over teaching both by institutional culture and policies. Encouraging teachers to engage in a full range of scholarship activities related to their teaching can be impeded by the significantly lower citations and impact factor of teaching journals versus disciplinary journals. Taking chemistry and sociology as examples (see Table 9.1) the differences can be an order of magnitude. With a specific mandate to recognize educational publications, promotion and tenure committees will be more likely to attribute value to such work and hence foster the development of research into teaching, which could assist the realization of institutional goals around teaching innovation and improvement.

Student evaluations of teaching can also act as an institutional factor which impedes educational innovation and development. When student course appreciation questionnaires are taken as an 'evaluation' of good teaching, then incorporating

TABLE 9.1 Differences in impact of representative disciplinary and teaching journals (Thomson Reuters 2016)

Journal title	Total cites	Impact factor
Journal of the American Chemical Society	504,778	13.0
Angewandte Chemie International Edition	263,526	11.7
Journal of Chemical Education	8,556	1.2
American Sociological Review	14,620	4.0
European Sociological Review	2,190	1.8
Teaching Sociology	465	0.6

teaching strategies, which are less familiar to students and thus more likely to make students uncomfortable, may mean a teacher undermining their own career advancement (Steventon 2016). Empowering teachers to set their own indicators for teaching excellence can transform a climate of resistance by reducing the risk for teachers to innovate. Ultimately, the use of student course appreciation questionnaire data as the sole or major source of information on teaching quality in tenure and promotion decisions is incompatible with an institutional culture which seeks to challenge students' intellectual and personal development.

There are a number of examples of academic development units that have already taken a lead in one or more dimensions of the development of teacher-led, evidence-informed and data-driven practice. We present three of them below who have published on their approach.

The Eberly Centre for Teaching Excellence and Educational Innovation at Carnegie Mellon University identifies two key principles of its work as being research-based and data-driven. The Centre describes its work as follows: 'starting with what is known from learning science research and leveraging additional data for ongoing improvement'. The Centre supports faculty in undertaking educational research, with fifty-five faculty members being supported in using learning data to inform their instructional choices in 2014–15.

Harvard's *Derek Bok Centre for Teaching and Learning* aims to 'continuously improve teaching and learning at Harvard by supporting experimentation, innovation, and evidence-based practices' by collaborating with faculty. The Bok Centre also includes faculty members from Life Sciences and Mathematics Education among their team as well as a director of research.

Lund University's *Academic Development Unit* aims to develop an institutional culture of Scholarship of Teaching and Learning (Mårtensson et al. 2011). The goal is to make the use of educational research and data-driven innovation the norm within the institution. The Unit does so by supporting teachers in undertaking evidence-based reports on their own teaching, offering a platform for teachers' educational research through campus conferences on teaching and learning as well as through undertaking research on how best to support teaching and learning (Roxå et al. 2007). An independent review of faculty development and educational innovation in Swedish higher education (Gran 2006 in Roxå et al. 2007) has noted the success of the Lund model, and the team have consistently evaluated their own practice using data and subjected this to independent peer review through publication.

Other examples of notable practice exist internationally including at the Oxford Learning Institute, and at the Technical University of Denmark. These diverse examples show some common trends. First, an academic development unit needs to have staff skilled in applied educational research in order that these staff can bring the benefit of contemporary research findings to consultations with faculty (evidence-informed), and can aid them in design of appropriate research (data-driven). Second, faculty members should have a leading role in deciding which innovations to test (teacher-led) and therefore the focus of the academic development units should be to support faculty members. This includes support on accessing prior educational research findings, in research design and in dissemination.

Good practices in academic development at the scale of individual courses

We describe below the support offered by our team at the École Polytechnique Fédérale de Lausanne for the creation of an ambitious new course as an example in practice of this 21st century framework of faculty development and training. The Global Issues course is mandatory for all first-year students and seeks to introduce science and engineering students to the possibilities for their disciplines to address major international challenges (such as transport, health, or energy), while at the same time sensitizing them to the ethical and technical complexity of working with technology in human contexts. Central to the course is an interdisciplinary collaborative project, which requires students to be able to use project management and interdisciplinary teamwork skills. About 1,800 students take the course each year, organized into eleven classes, each class being taught by a pair of teachers, one from social and human sciences and the other from applied sciences. A detailed account of the course has already been published elsewhere (Holzer et al. 2014; Holzer et al. 2016).

Rather than relying solely on student appreciation questionnaires, we worked with the teachers to identify what kind of data would best enable them to evaluate the impact of the first edition of the course in 2014. While teachers were able to enumerate objectives for students' learning in their discipline, other learning goals were not readily assessable with traditional methods. These included students' ethical reasoning and their attitudes towards interdisciplinary teamwork. In addition, it was identified that what happens within student groups is often invisible to teachers, and that future developments of the course could be informed through a better understanding of student team work processes.

When the teachers confirmed their interest in having data on these topics, the academic development units team brought to bear their knowledge of relevant educational research to identify and develop appropriate research instruments. To assess student's ethical reasoning, a French-language version of the Engineering and Science Issues Test (Borenstein et al. 2010) was developed. To assess attitudes towards interdisciplinary teams, the Readiness for Inter-Professional Learning Scale (Reid et al. 2006) was adapted to the disciplinary context and also translated into French. A number of questionnaires on student group work processes were developed and integrated into the course where they could act as data collection instruments while at the same time acting as reflection tools and feed forward for students.

The data collected was presented back to teachers before the beginning of the next course cycle in order that they could use the evidence to inform future stages of the course development. In addition, some useful insights did come from student course appreciation questionnaires as this data indicated that students treated the course material on project management and group process as 'academic' content to be learned rather than as practical knowledge to be used. This led to a restructuring of this aspect of the course. The insight provided by the Engineering and Science Issues Test and Readiness for Inter-Professional Learning Scale data identified that the course did not lead to increases in students' ethical reasoning capacity, or to more positive attitudes to interdisciplinary group work. A number of teachers used this data as an opportunity to reflect upon the way in which their style of teaching could better model for students the uncertain and discursive nature of ethical, social and human dimensions of technological questions. The need to better conceptualize and clarify the benefits and challenges of interdisciplinary work was also identified and, indeed, this has now become a broader theme within developments in social and human sciences in the university more generally.

This experience of assisting teachers in applying solid, well-developed research instruments to gather data relevant for their course has also served to introduce the Scholarship of Teaching and Learning to the teaching team and to the university more widely. Teachers on the course have generated a number of publications about the course, added to those authored by the academic development unit alone or with teachers (Isaac and Tormey 2015; Tormey et al. 2015). Furthermore, this has opened a new area of work for the academic development unit as our team has been invited to assist in generating student learning data in the context of other courses. For example, specific requests from teachers have resulted in an analysis of the errors made by first year students on their physics mechanics exam (Campiche et al. 2015), and an investigation of the impact of learning culture on peer instruction in chemistry (Boullier et al. 2015).

Conclusion

The *teacher-led, data-driven* and *evidence-informed* framework presented in this chapter proposes that 21st century pedagogical development of faculty occurs by working with teachers *in situ* as they plan and reflect on their teaching, specifically by providing evidence-informed teaching approaches and research techniques to fuel data-driven analysis and improvement. We have shown how this framework applies at the level of an institution and that of a single course.

Some academic development units around the world are moving forward an approach compatible with the proposed *teacher-led, data-driven* and *evidence-informed* framework to teaching development. However, its realization can only occur with the support of the governance of an institution. In particular, recognition of the power of an individualized model of teaching excellence must be accorded space alongside existing quality management systems. Moreover, the institution must offer coherent follow-through by providing working conditions to attract the highly skilled academic development unit staff with the research skills necessary to design and accompany teachers in the *data-driven* and *evidence-informed* aspects of the mission. Criteria which could enable an academic development unit to attract staff with more academic credentials may include an academic affiliation, ability to access research funding, and a mandate to supervise theses.

Our framework for supporting teaching excellence is relevant at both the institutional level and for academic development units who seek to place themselves at the heart or operational 'centre' of their university's endeavours in teaching and learning (Holt et al. 2011). We need to redirect some of the resources invested into student course appreciation questionnaires and other legacy approaches shown to provide only incremental improvement, and promote complementary evidence-informed and data-driven methods to disrupt the current paradigm of university teaching and finally implement the massive backlog of effective teaching practices.

References

Adelman, C. (1993) 'Kurt Lewin and the origins of action research', *Educational Action Research*, 1(1): 7–24.

Borenstein, J., Drake, M. J., Kirkman, R. and Swann, J. L. (2010) 'The Engineering and Science Issues Test (ESIT): a discipline-specific approach to assessing moral judgment', *Science and Engineering Ethics*, 16(2): 387–407.

Boud, D. and Brew, A. (2013) 'Reconceptualising academic work as professional practice: implications for academic development', *International Journal for Academic Development*, 18(3): 208–221.

Boullier, J., Faucon, L., Gotteland, J. and Páez, L. (2015) *Does peer instruction enhance students' understanding in Europe?*, Unpublished project report for the course 'How People Learn' at EPFL, co-supervised by R. Tormey and C. Hardebolle. Online. Available at http://cape.epfl.ch/smart-learning-space-programme (accessed 16 June 2017).

Briseño-Garzón, A., Han, A., Birol, G., Bates, S. and Whitehead, L. (2016) 'Faculty perceptions of challenges and enablers of effective teaching in a large research-intensive university: preliminary findings', *Collected Essays on Learning and Teaching*, 9: 133–144.

Campiche, P., Chandran, O., Lombardo, D. and Trömel, A. (2015) *Identification of common errors in learning classical mechanics*. Unpublished project report for the course 'How People Learn' at EPFL, supervised by Roland Tormey. Online. Available at http://cape.epfl.ch/smart-learning-space-programme (accessed 16 June 2017).

Clayson, D. (2009) 'Student evaluations of teaching: are they related to what students learn? A meta-analysis and review of the literature', *Journal of Marketing Education*, 31(1): 16–29.

Cosnefroy, L. (2015) *État des lieux de la formation et de l'accompagnement des enseignants du supérieur*, Report for ENS Lyon/IFE, Lyon: Institut Français de L'Éducation.

Crouch, C. H. and Mazur, E. (2001) 'Peer instruction: ten years of experience and results', *American Journal of Physics*, 69(9): 970–977.

Cuban, L. (2013) 'Why so many structural changes in schools and so little reform in teaching practice?' *Journal of Educational Administration*, 51(2): 109–125.

Darling-Hammond, L. (2006) *Powerful teacher education: lessons from exemplary programmes*, San Francisco, CA: Jossey-Bass.

European University Association (2015) *Trends 2015: learning and teaching in European universities*. Online. Available at www.eua.be/publications/ (accessed 16 June 2017).

Fernández, I. and Márquez, M. D. (2014) 'Capítulo 9: Formación docente o desarrollo educacional? Situación actual y tendencias emergentes en las universidades del Estado español', in Carlos Monereo (coord) *Enseñando a enseñar en la Universidad: la formación del profesorado basada en incidentes críticos*, 251–292, Barcelona: Octaedro.

Fraser, K., Gosling, D. and Sorcinelli, M. D. (2010) 'Conceptualizing evolving models of educational development', *New Directions for Teaching and Learning*, 2010(122): 49–58.

Freeman, S., Eddy, S. L., McDonough, M., Smith, M. K., Okoroafor, N., Jordt, H. and Wenderoth, M. P. (2014) 'Active learning increases student performance in science, engineering, and mathematics', *Proceedings of the National Academy of Sciences*, 111: 8410–8415.

Gibbs, G. (2013) 'Reflections on the changing nature of educational development', *International Journal for Academic Development*, 18(1): 4–14.

Gosling, D. (2009) 'Educational development in the UK: a complex and contradictory reality', *International Journal for Academic Development*, 14(1): 5–18.

Gran, B. (2006) *Pedagogisk utbildning för högskolans lärare – utvärdering av ett pilotprojekt* [Pedagogical training for university teachers: evaluation of a pilot project]. Lund: Lund University.

Harland, T. and Staniforth, D. (2003) 'Academic development as academic work', *International Journal for Academic Development*, 8(1–2): 25–35.

Hattie, J. (2008) *Visible learning: a synthesis of over 800 meta-analyses relating to achievement*, Abingdon: Routledge.

Holt, D., Palmer, S. and Challis, D. (2011) 'Changing perspectives: teaching and learning centres' strategic contributions to academic development in Australian higher education', *International Journal for Academic Development*, 16(1): 5–17.

Holzer, A., Bendahan, S., Vonèche Cardia, I. and Gillet, D. (2014) *Early awareness of global issues and development of soft skills in engineering education: an interdisciplinary approach to communication*, paper presented at the 13th International Conference on Information Technology Based Higher Education and Training (ITHET), 11–13 September 2014, University of York.

Holzer, A., Vonèche Cardia, I., Bendahan, S., Berne, A., Bragazza, L., Danalet, A., Fasoli, A., Feige, J., Gillet, D., Isaac, S., Le Duc, I., Preissmann, D. and Tormey, R. (2016) 'Increasing the perspectives of engineering undergraduates on societal issues through an interdisciplinary program', *International Journal of Engineering Education*, 32(2A): 614–624.

Hutchings, P. and Shulman, L. S. (1999) 'The Scholarship of Teaching: new elaborations, new developments', *Change: The Magazine of Higher Learning*, 31(5): 10–15.

Isaac, S. and Sylvestre, E. (2012) 'Pedagogical support services and academic developers at French universities', *Higher Education Research Network Journal*, 5: 19–28.

Isaac, S. and Tormey, R. (2015) 'Undergraduate group projects: challenges and learning experiences', *QScience Proceedings (Engineering Leaders Conference 2014)*, 2015: 19.

Loads, D. and Campbell, F. (2015) 'Fresh thinking about academic development: authentic, transformative, disruptive?', *International Journal for Academic Development*, 20(4): 355–369.

Mårtensson, K., Roxå, T. and Olsson, T. (2011) 'Developing a quality culture through the Scholarship of Teaching and Learning', *Higher Education Research & Development*, 30(1): 51–62.

McKinney, K. (2012) 'Increasing the impact of SoTL: two sometimes neglected opportunities', *International Journal for the Scholarship of Teaching and Learning*, 6(1): Article 3.

McNiff, J. (2013) *Action research: principles and practice*, London: Routledge.

Nesbit, J. C. and Adesope, O. O. (2006) 'Learning with concept and knowledge maps: a meta-analysis', *Review of Educational Research*, 76(3): 413–448.

Patel, F. (2014) 'Promoting a culture of scholarship among educational developers: exploring institutional opportunities', *International Journal for Academic Development*, 19: 242–254.

Pleschová, G., Simon, E., Quinlan, K., Murphy, J., Roxå, T. and Szabó, M. (2012) *The professionalisation of academics as teachers in higher education*, Science Position Paper, Brussels: European Science Foundation.

Quinn, L. (ed.) (2012) *Re-imagining academic staff development: spaces for disruption*, Stellenbosch, SA: African Sun MeDIA.

Rège Colet, N. (2010) 'Faculty development in Switzerland', in A. Saroyan and M. Frenay (eds) *Building teaching capacities in higher education: a comprehensive international model*, 43–60, Sterling, YA: Stylus.

Reid, R., Bruce, D., Allstaff, K. and McLernon, D. (2006) 'Validating the readiness for interprofessional learning scale (RIPLS) in the postgraduate context: are health care professionals ready for IPL?', *Medical Education*, 40: 415–422.

Roxå, T., Olsson, T. and Mårtensson, K. (2007) 'Scholarship of Teaching and Learning as a strategy for institutional change', *Proceedings of the HERDSA (Higher Education Research and Development Society of Australia) Annual Conference*, 8–11 July 2007, Adelaide, Australia.

Ruiz-Primo, M. A., Briggs, D., Iverson, H., Talbot, R. and Shepard, L. A. (2011) 'Impact of undergraduate science course innovations on learning', *Science*, 331(6022): 1269–1270.

Tormey, R., Le Duc, I., Isaac, S., Hardebolle, C. and Vonèche Cardia, I. (2015) *The formal and hidden curricula of ethics in engineering education*, paper presented at the 43rd Annual SEFI Conference, 29 June – 2 July 2015, Orléans, France.

Trigwell, K., Martin, E., Benjamin, J. and Prosser, M. (2000) 'Scholarship of Teaching: a model', *Higher Education Research & Development*, 19(2): 155–168.

Steventon, G. (2016) 'Authentic learning: a route to student attainment?', in G. Steventon, D. Cureton and L. Clouder (eds) *Student attainment in higher education: issues, controversies and debates*, 98–110, Abingdon: Routledge.

Uttl, B., White, C. A. and Gonzalez, D. W. (2016) 'Meta-analysis of faculty's teaching effectiveness: student evaluation of teaching ratings and student learning are not related', *Studies in Educational Evaluation*, 54: 22–42.

Wieman, C. (2015) 'A better way to evaluate undergraduate teaching', *Change: The Magazine of Higher Learning*, 47(1): 6–15.

Critical friend commentary

Aline Germain-Rutherford

As our world is changing, so is higher education, pressured by new societal needs from an expanding number of traditional and non-traditional students in our knowledge-based economy. Digital technologies have removed space and time constraints for people to access education in a diversity of ways (Bokor 2012; Educause 2015), and are transforming modes of learning and collaborating. Competency-based educational credentialing is adding levels of flexibility that will soon replace the instruction-time model based on credit hours. Learner-centred approaches, active learning strategies, inclusive pedagogies, experiential learning and blended learning are the expected norms in a growing number of institutions. At the same time, rising costs and competing demands for funds have increased the public's expectations for quality assurance and higher education accountability.

These transformations are prompting institutions to question and revisit the way they develop and deliver programmes, as well as how they support faculty development to enhance the quality of learning experiences. The 'teacher-led, data-driven and evidence-informed' faculty development strategies described by the authors to address this shift in higher education are important and timely in today's academic world where measurable learning outcomes and student performance indicators are increasingly predominant in universities' key performance indicators. Current technology advances in learning analytics (Ecar-Analytics Working Group 2015), as well as the growing recognition of the Scholarship of Teaching and Learning (SOTL) in academia (Chalmers 2011), align with and strengthen this approach of supporting faculty to question and adapt their pedagogical strategies based on data collected within their teaching contexts. However, the authors accurately note that such a change in academic development strategy involves institutional leadership and a cultural shift in the definition of teaching excellence.

To be successful, a systemic approach involving all levels of leadership and stakeholders in the institution is needed. Distributed leadership models implemented in school settings have consistently shown a positive impact on organizational performance and student achievement (Heck and Hallinger 2010; Bierly et al. 2016). For post-secondary institutions, they might be a promising direction to explore further. Reporting on 'embedded educational leadership initiatives' in their university, Wright and Hamilton (2014: 6) describe how Canadian higher education institutions can build strong educational distributed leadership capacity by pursuing six core objectives:

> fostering individual and system capacity for change; addressing structural barriers to educational leadership and innovation; improving communication, knowledge exchange, and circulation; fostering horizontal networks and encouraging egalitarian collaboration; advocating for and supporting improved decision-making; and coordinating and improving data collection.

The integrated and contextual faculty development approach proposed by the authors is an important first step towards a more comprehensive model of distributed leadership in higher education.

References

Bierly, C., Doyle, B. and Smith, A. (2016) *Transforming schools: how distributed leadership can create more high-performing schools*. Online. Available at www.bain.com/publications/articles/transforming-schools.aspx (accessed 16 June 2017).

Bokor, J. 2012. *University of the future: a thousand-year-old industry on the cusp of profound change.* Online. Available at www.ey.com/Publication/vwLUAssets/University_of_the_future/%24FILE/University_of_the_future_2012.pdf (accessed 16 June 2017).

Chalmers, D. (2011) 'Progress and challenges to the recognition and reward of the Scholarship of Teaching in higher education', *Higher Education Research & Development*, 30(1): 25–38.

Ecar-Analytics Working Group (2015) *The predictive learning analytics revolution: leveraging learning data for student success*, ECAR working group paper. Online. Available at http://net.educause.edu/ir/library/pdf/ewg1510.pdf (accessed 16 June 2017).

Educause (2015) *Technology in higher education: defining the strategic leader*. Online. Available at www.jisc.ac.uk/sites/default/files/educause-jisc-report-technology-in-higher-education-march-2015.pdf (accessed 16 June 2017).

Heck, R. and Hallinger, P. (2010) 'Testing a longitudinal model of distributed leadership effects on school improvement', *The Leadership Quarterly*, 21: 867–885.

Wright, A. and Hamilton, B. (2014) *Leading the leaders: embedded educational leadership initiatives at the University of Windsor*, Windsor: University of Windsor.

10

TEACHING EXCELLENCE AND THE RISE OF EDUCATION-FOCUSED EMPLOYMENT TRACKS

Johan Geertsema, Chng Huang Hoon,
Mark Gan and Alan Soong

Introduction

The starting point of this chapter concerns two separate but potentially correlated phenomena. Recent years have seen much attention paid to quality in higher education, including the outcomes-oriented Bologna reforms and the introduction in the UK of the new Teaching Excellence Framework. Initiatives to foster teaching excellence are often accompanied by increasing emphasis on the Scholarship of Teaching and Learning (SoTL) as an instrument of quality assurance in the domain of teaching and learning (Chalmers 2011; Vardi 2011).

At the same time, academic practice in contemporary higher education is marked by ever-increasing fragmentation, perhaps most apparent in the sharp increase in the number of non-tenure track academics, including adjuncts or sessional staff, in the UK, US and elsewhere (Cross and Goldenberg 2009). There is even talk of a 'Third Paradigm' in higher education characterized by: 'faculty appointments . . . being ever more radically redistributed away from traditional tenure and tenure-track appointments'; 'functional specialization' in faculty roles; and a 'polarization or restratification in the hierarchy of faculty appointment types' (Finkelstein et al. 2016: 35). Many, if not most, non-tenure-track academics are appointed to focus on one aspect of academic work – teaching (O'Meara et al. 2009: 60). One marker of the recent growth in the number as well as prominence of such appointments is the fact that, as of early 2016, twenty of the twenty-four Russell Group universities in the UK had introduced a full professorial grade for education-focused staff (Fung and Gordon 2016). Staff members on education-focused tracks are defined as academics that predominantly focus on teaching and other ways of supporting student learning, though they are often expected to be also active in other domains.

Our main goal in this chapter is to examine the relationship between these two phenomena – teaching excellence, and teaching-only or education-focused pathways or tracks. While much has been written about the increasingly disaggregated and fragmented world of academe on the one hand, and also about how teaching excellence might be fostered on the other, the relationship between these phenomena is under-explored. If a key rationale for increasing specialization, and the concomitant fragmentation of academic work, relates to the aim of fostering quality and to providing alternative, 'strength-based' pathways for academics (Fung and Gordon 2016), then it is important to understand just how teaching-only or education-focused employment tracks may actually foster such excellence, and also to ask whether they in fact have the potential to do so. This question is especially important because the scholarly literature raises serious questions about such tracks and their potential to improve academic practice, despite the good intentions behind them of categorizing exceptional teachers with reference to their contribution to the scholarship of teaching and learning (Roxå et al. 2008; Ryegård et al. 2010; Macfarlane 2011). Moreover, there is little, if any, evidence that individual academics on teaching-only contracts actually produce better educational outcomes than those on regular appointments (Cross and Goldenberg 2009), a situation that is mirrored in the case of teaching awards (Chalmers 2011).

Our method in this chapter is mainly conceptual, though we end by considering a case. Consequently, our approach is to provide an overview of the literature in order to relate teaching excellence and education-focused tracks, identify principles that may inform such tracks, and consider our own case in light of what the literature suggests. We start by exploring the changing nature of academic work, including the increasing fragmentation of this work as evidenced by, among other things, the rising number of non-tenure track academics with functionally specialized roles. We then turn to the matter of teaching excellence in order to relate excellence to expertise. We do so by considering arguments that suggest the importance of an integrated view of academic practice. Such an integrated view is based on the idea that good – and at higher levels excellent – teaching requires both expertise in disciplinary content, and the ability to teach the discipline. This leads to a number of key principles that we believe need to inform this kind of track, and that we attempt to illustrate with reference to our case: a leading research-intensive university in Asia, which established an education-focused employment track for academics more than a decade ago and is now in the process of reforming it with the goal of fostering evidence-based teaching excellence. We document the history of the institution's 'educator track', identify triggers that led to the decision to reform it, and consider potential solutions to the institutional and conceptual challenges that are concomitant upon an education-focused employment track. We end by delineating ways in which the institution is planning to translate key principles into practice in order to meet its goal of fostering teaching excellence through an education-focused employment pathway while mitigating the dangers attendant upon it.

Teaching excellence and the changing nature of academic work

In this chapter, we focus less on what 'teaching excellence' is and how it may be fostered than on what the literature suggests its relationship might be to education-focused employment pathways. We do so in order to establish good principles that might inform the conceptual underpinnings of such a pathway or track. We pay special attention to the connection between, and integration of, different but related areas of expertise: the *content* or subject being taught (broadly, disciplinary expertise), and *the way* in which it is taught (broadly, pedagogical competence).

Debates on what constitutes teaching excellence in higher education have been fuelled by the growing complexity in academics' roles; the challenges of globalization; technological changes in increasingly knowledge-based economies; the impact of rewards, recognition and promotion; and the constant need to improve as an institution and as a professional (Skelton 2007; Gunn and Fisk 2013). Much of the discussion of teaching excellence in higher education has focused on documenting good practices and identifying characteristics of excellent teachers (Kember 1997; Elton 1998; Kane et al. 2004). More recently, studies have sought to identify the difference between the excellent, high-impact practices of expert teachers on the one hand, and the lower-impact practices of experienced teachers on the other (Hattie 2012). There has further been a concerted effort to highlight the scholarly approaches employed by the best teachers to enhance student learning (Gibbs 2008; Kreber 2013), as well as to develop criteria to guide institutional/national reward and recognition systems (Chalmers 2011; Hénard and Roseveare 2012).

Finally, there has also been work that considers the normative aspect of high-quality teaching and argues that it is not sufficient to think of good teaching only in terms of whether it is *effective*, but that it needs to have *desirable* results and thus requires judgement as to balancing the key purposes of education, namely those relating to qualification, socialization, and subjectification (Biesta 2015). While we do not focus on this important issue, we do take the view that good, and at higher levels excellent, teaching is not reducible just to effectiveness or 'evidence-based best practices' as measured in attainment on outcomes. Instead, we understand excellent teaching with reference to the integration of different educational dimensions that seek to attain a complex set of goals.

Though teaching excellence and ways to foster it take on different meanings in different contexts, Brockerhoff et al. (2014: 238) identify three approaches: the individual, which focuses on behaviour; the cultural, which is more indirect but among other things involves 'symbolic or concrete initiatives to reward or recognize teaching as a key activity'; and the structural, which involves 'direct and functional changes in the organization of teaching and learning'. Brockerhoff et al. (ibid.: 250) go on to argue that teaching excellence requires an organizational strategy since it is necessary for the university leadership to create the conditions for high-quality teaching, and doing so requires a combination of structural and cultural changes, not just a focus on individuals. In this light, education-focused pathways for individual academics are hybrid constructs since they function on the cultural level by having the potential to foster teaching quality through structural means that affect the way the teaching and learning environment is organized (through, for example, workload allocation) and thereby have the potential not only to reward and recognize excellence, but also to foster it in the case of individual academics.

Given, however, that 'the intra-individual *coherence* in academics' experiences of research, teaching, learning and knowledge is a key to what makes higher education distinctive, and what makes academic work both satisfying and compelling' (Robertson 2007: 551), why is it that universities institute teaching-only or education-focused tracks that disrupt such coherence? The answer is complex. On the one hand, this phenomenon is closely connected with the well-documented unbundling of academic labour and increasing differentiation within the profession: the separation of teaching and research, the disaggregation within each of these categories, and increased casualization. These tendencies relate to the decline of academic tenure, rapid advances in technology across campuses, and other phenomena connected with the increased marketization of higher education (Cross and Goldenberg 2009; Finkelstein et al. 2016; Locke 2016). Approached more positively, the rise in education-focused employment pathways speaks to an institutional desire to provide more flexibility to employees by seeking to provide scope for specialization in their areas of strength, in this case teaching, given that not all faculty are likely to excel in all areas of academic work. Such specialization would then allow faculty with strength in teaching and learning to focus on it, which would thereby allow teaching and learning to flourish. The rise to prominence of such tracks would thus mark a renewed emphasis on teaching or, perhaps rather, the student learning experience (Locke 2016), and a shift from an emphasis on teaching to one on learning, or 'learnification' (Biesta 2009).

The literature suggests that education-focused pathways are often instituted with noble intentions: 'Like teaching awards and funding for learning and teaching research, teaching professorships are designed to raise the status of teaching' (Macfarlane 2011: 128–129). A pathway for individual teachers, one founded increasingly on the scholarship of teaching and learning (Chalmers 2011; Vardi 2011) may seem to have the potential of providing 'legitimacy for deeper engagement with student learning, as well as opportunity for professional advancement in a culture previously dominated by traditional research' (Roxå et al. 2008: 277). By the scholarship of teaching and learning, we refer to SoTL as the systematic reflection on, and investigation of, student learning. Being a literature-informed, evidence-based analysis of learning, SoTL is made public in appropriate ways and thus subjected to peer review (Mårtensson et al. 2011: 52). As rigorous reflection on practice shared in appropriate ways, SoTL can help develop teaching quality by shifting the culture of an institution on condition that it respects academic teachers' identity, which is vested in their discipline – not the discipline of education – as well as in the notion of academic freedom (ibid.: 60).

There are problems attached to using SoTL as a means of developing teaching excellence, however, particularly when it is used to underpin education-focused employment pathways. Macfarlane (2011: 129) argues that despite their noble intention of enhancing the status of teaching, such pathways 'do directly the opposite . . . the unfortunate effect is only to further undermine efforts to raise the status of teaching and reinforce the divide with "research"'. In a similar vein, Roxå et al. (2008: 277) warn that:

> However tempting [a view of SoTL that focuses on] its promise to reward
> exceptional teachers, this view of the scholarship of teaching and learning
> involves several problematic issues . . . [By] opening a pathway for institutions
> to reward excellent teachers who are not engaged in traditional research, the
> scholarship of teaching and learning may support a further division between
> teaching and research.

Such pathways form part of a larger set of developments in higher education, which
include a huge increase in the diversity and numbers of students, the exponential
growth in the use of information technology in education, increased governmental
demands for accountability and productivity, and thus the imposition of a
managerialism marked by the corporatization of universities and the use of key
performance indicators (Vardi 2011: 2–3). Because of these changes, some would
argue that the faculty's role is being shrunk to the extent that as a body it has 'lost
potency in its capacity to affect – and indeed, shape – postsecondary education',
leading to a so-called 'Third Paradigm' that marks the transformation of the way
in which higher education is practised (Finkelstein et al. 2016: 33). Against this
backdrop, the rise of education-focused employment pathways that draw on SoTL
to improve quality can be seen as a function of much larger forces, which may have
as much to do with larger trends that relate to the changing nature of academic
work as with the potential of such pathways to foster teaching excellence. Indeed,
these kinds of education-focused pathways may be counterproductive in increasing
the fragmentation of academic work.

Why would such fragmentation matter? If it is problematic, then it follows that
any institution that seeks to go down this path would need, as far as possible, to
mitigate potential problems. First, fragmentation can have a negative impact on
teaching. The segmentation of academic roles is often couched in language that
justifies it on the basis of the need to 'free up' the time of researchers by allocating
more teaching to non-research staff (Chalmers 2011: 33). In this way, a separate
pathway for education-focused staff signals that teaching is the concern of only a
small percentage of faculty – those on an educator track – with 'the very clear and
consistent message [being] that successful academics do disciplinary research and less
successful academics teach' (ibid.). It thereby threatens to undermine a key idea of
scholarship relating to teaching and learning, namely that it is community property
(Shulman 2004). For this reason, it will be important that the distance between the
regular tenure and educator tracks be minimized as much as possible, and that
expectations relating to performance on each be commensurate with those on the
other. An implication is that an education-*focused* pathway is preferable to a teaching-
only track: there should be space for faculty on both pathways, regular tenure and
education-focused, to engage in activities that apply to both. Ideally, for example,
an education-focused pathway would be closer to the regular tenure track if faculty
on it had the freedom to be rewarded for research so that it not be seen as the
preserve of those on the tenure track, while measures for evaluating teaching
achievement in the case of the education-focused pathway might also – with

appropriate adjustments given different workloads – apply to those on the regular track. Through this kind of harmonization between pathways, the distance between them would be reduced.

A second and related point is that the fragmentation of academic work has the strong potential to undermine collegiality by leading to the kind of 'polarization or restratification in the hierarchy of faculty appointment types' to which Finkelstein et al. (2016) allude. Yet collegiality is important if an institution is to enhance quality; limiting it to individuals constrains its reach. Impact not only on student learning but institutionally and on colleagues is therefore necessary, though this aspect is often overlooked in the literature on teaching achievement (Graham 2016: 15). An emphasis on collegiality that can develop into educational leadership, premised on an integrated (or less fragmented) view of academic work, is a further important component of SoTL as a means of improving practice through sharing and mutual support, or 'going public' (Kreber 2002; Shulman 2004). Such contributions to disseminating educational practice can have as much, or even more, impact than contributions to education scholarship in fostering institutional culture change, given that 'a true academic community of practice should comprise a group of staff and students brought together because of a focus on a subject or discipline rather than a focus on a function such as teaching or research or learning' (Smith and Rust 2011: 121). For this reason, an understanding of teaching achievement cannot refer solely to classroom performance, but needs to cover all activity relating to teaching, including impact on the environment through collegiality and educational leadership, and also, where applicable, education scholarship and research in the disciplines.

A third reason why an integrated view of academic work is important relates to teaching excellence itself. In brief, the entwinement of expertise in both disciplinary content and how to teach the discipline, strongly suggests that teaching excellence is dependent on such integration. Teaching effectiveness, and at higher levels excellence, depends to a significant extent on the content expertise of the teacher (Gunn and Fisk 2013: 20), and hence requires appropriate levels of expertise in the discipline, for which it is a necessary if not sufficient condition. The reason is that 'the processes of thinking are intertwined with the content of thought (that is, domain knowledge)' (Willingham 2008: 21). Teaching is always teaching of *something*, and consequently a crucial component is the content of domain knowledge. As studies have shown, the transfer of 'generic' skills, such as critical thinking, either does not take place or is severely limited given the distinction between 'the pedagogic content of the learning experience [and] the methods and processes (i.e. the epistemology) of the discipline being studied' (Kirschner et al. 2006: 78). This distinction goes back to Shulman's (1986) discussion of the integration of content and pedagogical expertise, or what he calls pedagogical content knowledge: an integration of the two is essential if teaching excellence is to be achieved. Expertise in the discipline is peer evaluated by the scholarly community with reference to the quality of research in that discipline; the challenge is to develop scholarly expertise in teaching and learning that can complement scholarly expertise in the discipline, thereby weaving academic research and teaching practice together. Thus, the precondition for high levels of teaching quality, and concomitantly of student learning, relates to *both* expertise in teaching and to expertise in the discipline.

Teachers can be excellent, however, without reaching the highest levels of expertise in teaching (Kreber 2002), which is one reason that expertise that equates with the ability to conduct research in education need not be expected as a requirement for teaching excellence (Gunn and Fisk 2013: 9). Another reason is that there is no necessary correlation between research excellence and teaching excellence (Hattie and Marsh 1996; Marsh and Hattie 2002). Publication about teaching does not necessarily lead to better student learning (Fung and Gordon 2016) and pressures on academics to publish SoTL work 'can shift the focus and methods of SoTL, aligning them more with the requirements of educational research as identified in existing research excellence frameworks' (Gunn and Fisk 2013: 9). It is therefore useful to draw a distinction between SoTL and educational research, and to emphasize that the point of engaging in SoTL is to help develop expertise in teaching and learning: not necessarily to advance knowledge of education, but to integrate relevant knowledge of teaching and learning into practice so as to improve practice (Geertsema 2016). SoTL then involves 'going public' with teaching and learning in a way that is peer reviewed and used 'by members of one's community' (Kreber 2002: 16–17). Such 'going public' need not involve *publication*, particularly where publication requires levels of expertise (in education) not available to those expected to go public in this way, given that their expertise lies elsewhere (in their own disciplines). Expecting peer reviewed publications and presentations would exclude 'a large proportion of the professoriate who wish to practice the scholarship of teaching' (Kreber 2002: 19; Mårtensson et al. 2011: 60).

To summarize: if teaching is always teaching *of* and teaching *in*, then *how* one teaches is connected with *what* and *whom* one teaches; and good teaching is always teaching in and across the disciplines. To teach well, one needs appropriate levels of expertise both in a discipline, and in teaching that discipline.

We now proceed to an overview of one institution's attempts to think through the difficult issue of education-focused employment pathways in relation to teaching achievement, focusing briefly on the history and rationale before concluding with a brief description of the way in which the university has sought to articulate key principles identified from the literature in its reforms.

Case study: National University of Singapore and the educator track

In the course of its relatively short history as a research-intensive university, the National University of Singapore (NUS) has, for the past two decades especially, attempted to foster excellence in the three interconnected pillars of education, research and service. For those fully immersed in its competitive institutional context, it is often hard to remember that NUS has not always been research-intensive.

For the greater part of its 112-year history, the institution was more teaching than research-focused, serving 'the local community' by offering a comprehensive curriculum dominated by an undergraduate body that today encompasses three campuses and seventeen schools. As a national university, a holistic, integrated education is a key mission.

NUS relies on good teachers to deliver its curriculum and in 2008 it officially launched a 'Teaching Track scheme' that catered explicitly to the group of faculty members whose primary mission was to teach. The official document that describes the scheme was more orientated toward administrative policies than teachers' academic career development in that it focused on paper qualifications for initial hiring and presented rules relating to issues such as length of contract. The purpose of the scheme was 'to attract and retain suitably qualified faculty members with focus and passion that are oriented towards teaching excellence, student learning, and pedagogical research and innovation'. With the exception of the English Communication and Language Studies Centres, appointments would make up 'no more than ten per cent of the total faculty size in an academic unit/department'. Criteria for appointment were vaguely expressed as 'demonstrated excellence and/ or obvious passion in teaching' without clearly articulating what the characteristics of teaching achievement might be. Instead of criteria, examples of evidence were provided, such as 'student and peer evaluation or case studies, textbooks, new teaching pedagogy and new course curriculum'. Progression depended on the highest academic qualifications attained and the number of years of relevant teaching experience, with the nature of achievement and the impact of work being left under-specified. All of this meant that there was no clear pathway for candidates to progress.

In 2014, in order to address the problems stated above, and in view of what the literature suggests about academic work, employment pathways, and teaching excellence, NUS decided to review the Teaching Track scheme and transform it into a more explicit and elaborated policy for the hire and retention of education-focused colleagues. It was then re-launched as the Educator Track in January 2015, with much of the work still currently in progress. Revisions emphasize scholarliness and evidence-based argument for excellence. The University has drawn substantively on work done by Graham (2015; 2016), who has synthesized the scholarship on teaching achievement and proposed an evidence-based framework, as well as frameworks that have been developed in Australia and elsewhere, such as the Australian University Teaching Criteria and Standards Framework, and Edinburgh University's Exemplars of Excellence in Student Education.

Given the importance of combining structural and cultural approaches that affect teaching quality at the level of the individual teacher, the NUS Educator Track is a hybrid: not a teaching only, but rather an education-focused track based on the following interrelated principles derived from the scholarship discussed above:

1. *Harmonization*: reducing the disparities between the tenure and educator tracks, including convergence in full professor with tenure.

2. *Integration*: research, whether in pedagogy or the discipline, is recognized and rewarded though not required; instead it constitutes one pathway for promotion, the other being educational leadership; a Campus Ad Hoc Committee will evaluate disciplinary research at higher levels, where applicable.
3. *Going public*: sharing SoTL work on the basis of a view of teaching as community property, hence emphasis on collegial sharing and, at higher levels, contributions to institutional improvement through educational leadership; documentation of achievement through a scholarly teaching portfolio; external review of teaching achievement, including where relevant education scholarship, through an External Review Panel.

Given the context-specificity of quality (Gibbs et al. 2008) and, in particular, the importance of disciplinary differences (Gunn and Fisk 2013; Brockerhoff et al. 2014), it was decided not to provide a prescriptive definition of 'teaching excellence'. Instead, a criteria broad enough to satisfy disciplinary nuances has been adopted whereby disciplines can formulate their own principles.

To progress through the track, candidates need to demonstrate widening impact. Two significant changes made in moving from the 2008 Teaching Track paper to the new Educator Track scheme testify to the *harmonization* principle, namely that (i) the rank of Associate Professor now operates on an open, as opposed to a term, contract; and (ii) the rank of Full Professor is a tenured appointment that is shared by both the Educator Track and the Tenure Track, thus reducing disparities between tracks and the perception that the education-focused track is inferior. This leads to another key principle, that of *integration*. The previous Teaching Track scheme was a teaching-only track that artificially disconnected teaching from other dimensions of academic work, (in particular research in the disciplines) for instance, by recognizing only 'pedagogical' research. Because of the importance of domain expertise for teaching excellence, as described in the previous section, the revised Educator Track scheme recognizes and rewards research – whether 'pedagogical' or in the discipline of the candidate – as a possible pathway for progressing through the track. In cases where the candidate elects to be evaluated on the basis of research in their discipline, a Campus Ad Hoc Committee will be constituted to review significant publications optionally submitted by the candidate to evaluate their impact. The third principle is that of *going public*. Nurturing and developing collegiality is seen as a means of spreading good teaching practices (see Roxå and Mårtensson, this volume), though care is taken not to make collegiality an explicit criterion given that doing so can create resistance to the idea of collegial sharing if it comes to be seen as a tool of managerialism (Kligyte and Barrie 2014; American Association of University Professors 2016). Instead, the emphasis is on documenting and sharing practices in an appropriately rigorous and scholarly way, an idea inspired by SoTL's emphasis on 'going public' so as to make teaching community property (Shulman 2004), thereby potentially enabling culture change for the benefit of the organization as a whole (Olsson and Roxå 2013). Since the purpose of scholarly investigation of practice is system-wide improvement, the sharing is intended primarily to be local. Progress through the track is not dependent on publication, whether in the discipline, in SoTL, or otherwise. Nevertheless, given the research-intensive context of the University and the close entwinement of disciplinary expertise with teaching achievement, and hence the desire to harmonize different employment tracks, research achievement may count and will be benchmarked against research of colleagues on other tracks. In line with the emphasis on collegiality, rather than an exclusive focus on pedagogical or disciplinary research, the track allows for progression on the basis of educational leadership as a second pathway.

The ongoing revision, and indeed reconceptualization, of the Teaching Track that has resulted in the Educator Track is driven in large part by the desire to make the criteria for appointment and promotion through the ranks much more explicit, transparent, scholarly, and rigorous. The reason for this has as much to do with providing a pathway for colleagues who are able to demonstrate strength in teaching and learning as it does with increasing the status and perceived value of teaching in a research-intensive context. In this way, the intention is to move the education-focused track beyond administrative details. The hope is that it will play a critical role in actively shaping the teaching and learning landscape in NUS, and in the process, help to work towards a more integrated approach by the University to teaching and research as joint, mutually reinforcing components of institutional excellence. The idea is to minimize the risks attendant upon teaching-only and education-focused employment tracks: namely, that they will further fragment academic work and thereby unwittingly reinforce the research-teaching divide. Whether these revisions will result in a more holistic, cohesive vision of learning, teaching, research and other dimensions of academic work within a university that works to integrate them, or will further fragment teaching and research, is something that will only become apparent in the years ahead as the new Educator Track is implemented alongside the more mature Tenure Track scheme.

A number of tasks remain, in particular the need to design strong support for colleagues by means of academic development initiatives (briefings, workshops, courses, communities of practice) as they seek to progress in their careers on the basis of teaching achievement, and with reference to the revised criteria. In addition, the university will need to evaluate the impact of the scheme by means of a process of continuing institutional quality improvement so as to consider whether a multiple-track employment system constitutes an appropriate response to the complexities of academic work today. Our case study illustrates one institution's attempt to foster teaching excellence through revising and enhancing an education-focused employment track, in the hope of thereby not only providing clearer pathways to colleagues on the track, but transforming the culture of the institution by concretely recognizing and rewarding high levels of teaching achievement. While we are conscious of the attendant risks involved in such a strategy, we argue that the institution has taken a positive step towards bridging the gap between research and teaching, and that these reforms have the potential to raise the status of teaching within a research-intensive institutional culture.

References

American Association of University Professors (2016) *On collegiality as a criterion for faculty evaluation.* Online. Available at www.aaup.org/report/collegiality-criterion-faculty-evaluation (accessed 19 June 2017).

Biesta, G. (2009) 'Good education in an age of measurement: on the need to reconnect with the question of purpose in education', *Educational Assessment, Evaluation and Accountability*, 21: 33–46.

Biesta, G. (2015) 'What is education for? On good education, teacher judgement, and educational professionalism', *European Journal of Education*, 50(1): 75–87.

Brockerhoff, L., Stensaker, B. and Huisman, J. (2014) 'Prescriptions and perceptions of teaching excellence: a study of the national "Wettbewerb Exzellente Lehre" initiative in Germany', *Quality in Higher Education*, 20(3): 235–254.

Chalmers, D. (2011) 'Progress and challenges to the recognition and reward of the Scholarship of Teaching in higher education', *Higher Education Research & Development*, 30(1): 25–38.

Cross, J. and Goldenberg, E. (2009) *Off-track profs: nontenured teachers in higher education*, Cambridge, MA: MIT Press.

Elton, L. (1998) 'Dimensions of excellence in university teaching', *International Journal for Academic Development*, 3(1): 3–11.

Finkelstein, M. J., Conley, V. M. and Schuster, J. H. (2016) *The faculty factor: reassessing the American academy in a turbulent era*, Baltimore, MD: Johns Hopkins Press.

Fung, D. and Gordon (2016) *Rewarding educators and education leaders in research-intensive universities*, York: Higher Education Academy.

Geertsema, J. (2016) 'Academic development, SoTL and educational research', *International Journal for Academic Development*, 21(2): 122–134.

Gibbs, G. (2008) *Conceptions of teaching excellence underlying teaching award schemes*, York: Higher Education Academy.

Gibbs, G., Knapper, C. and Piccinin, S. (2008) 'Disciplinary and contextually appropriate approaches to leadership of teaching in research-intensive academic departments in higher education', *Higher Education Quarterly*, 62(4): 416–436.

Graham, R. (2015) *Does teaching advance your academic career? Perspectives of promotion procedures in UK higher education*, London: Royal Academy of Engineering.

Graham, R. (2016) *Does teaching advance your academic career? Interim report on the development of a template for evaluating teaching achievement*, London: Royal Academy of Engineering.

Gunn, V. and Fisk, A. (2013) *Considering teaching excellence in higher education: 2007–2013: a literature review since the CHERI Report 2007*, York: Higher Education Academy.

Hattie, J. and Marsh, H. W. (1996) 'The relationship between research and teaching: a meta-analysis', *Review of Educational Research*, 66(4): 507–542.

Hattie, J. (2012) *Visible learning for teachers: maximizing impact on learning*, London: Routledge.

Hénard, F. and Roseveare, D. (2012) *Fostering quality teaching in higher education: policies and practices*, Paris: Organisation for Economic Co-operation and Development.

Kane, R., Sandretto, S. and Heath, C. (2004) 'An investigation into excellent tertiary teaching: emphasising reflective practice', *Higher Education*, 47(3): 283–310.

Kember, D. (1997) 'A reconceptualisation of the research into university academics' conceptions of teaching', *Learning and Instruction*, 7(3): 255–275.

Kirschner, P. A., Sweller, J. and Clark, R. E. (2006) 'Why minimal guidance during instruction does not work: an analysis of the failure of constructivist, discovery, problem-based, experiential, and inquiry-based teaching', *Educational Psychologist*, 41(2): 75–86.

Kligyte, G. and Barrie, S. (2014) 'Collegiality: leading us into fantasy – the paradoxical resilience of collegiality in academic leadership', *Higher Education Research & Development*, 33(1): 157–169.

Kreber, C. (2002) 'Teaching excellence, teaching expertise, and the scholarship of teaching', *Innovative Higher Education*, 27(1): 5–23.

Kreber, C. (2013) *Authenticity in and through teaching in higher education*, Abingdon: Routledge.

Locke, W. (2016) *Shifting academic careers: implications for enhancing professionalism in teaching and supporting learning*, York: Higher Education Academy.

Macfarlane, B. (2011) 'Prizes, pedagogic research and teaching professors: lowering the status of teaching and learning through bifurcation', *Teaching in Higher Education*, 16(1): 127–130.

Marsh, H. W. and Hattie, J. (2002) 'The relation between research productivity and teaching effectiveness: complementary, antagonistic, or independent constructs?', *Journal of Higher Education*, 73(5): 603–641.

Mårtensson, K., Roxå, T. and Olsson, T. (2011) 'Developing a quality culture through the scholarship of teaching and learning', *Higher Education Research & Development*, 30(1): 51–62.

Olsson, T. and Roxå, T. (2013) 'Assessing and rewarding excellent academic teachers for the benefit of an organization', *European Journal of Higher Education*, 3(1): 40–61.

O'Meara, K., Terosky, A. L. and Neumann, A. (2009) 'Faculty careers and work lives: a professional growth perspective', *ASHE Higher Education Report*, 34(3): 1–221.

Robertson, J. (2007) 'Beyond the "research/teaching nexus": exploring the complexity of academic experience', *Studies in Higher Education*, 32(5): 541–556.

Roxå, T., Olsson, T. and Mårtensson, K. (2008) 'Appropriate use of theory in the scholarship of teaching and learning as a strategy for institutional development', *Arts & Humanities in Higher Education*, 7(3): 276–294.

Ryegård, Å., Apelgren, K. and Olsson, T. (2010) *A Swedish perspective on pedagogical competence*, Uppsala: Uppsala University Division for Development of Teaching and Learning.

Shulman, L. S. (1986) 'Those who understand: knowledge growth in teaching', *Educational Researcher*, 15(2): 4–14.

Shulman, L. S. (2004) *Teaching as community property: essays on higher education*, San Francisco, CA: Jossey-Bass.

Skelton, A. (2007) *Understanding teaching excellence in higher education: towards a critical approach*, London: Routledge.

Smith, P. and Rust. C. (2011) 'The potential of research-based learning for the creation of truly inclusive academic communities of practice', *Innovations in Education and Teaching International*, 48(2): 115–125.

Vardi, I. (2011) 'The changing relationship between the scholarship of teaching (and learning) and universities', *Higher Education Research & Development*, 30(1): 1–7.

Willingham, D. T. (2008) 'Critical thinking: why is it so hard to teach?', *Arts Education Policy Review*, 109(4): 21–32.

Critical friend commentary

Roberto Di Napoli

The authors of this chapter cogently point towards current fault lines in academic work and practice: between teaching and research; teaching as 'practice' and teaching as 'scholarship'; disciplinary knowledge and pedagogical knowledge; and between different career progression tracks. The resulting picture is one of fragmentation and possible stasis because it seems to 'nail' academics to a given career and development path, denying them the flexibility to have different foci of interest and contribute to the good of an institution, discipline, and society in expansive ways over time. Against this trend, the authors argue for an integrative and integrated view of academic work and practice. They do this by anchoring career progression to two elements: a focus on the wider notion of 'education' (as opposed to simply teaching), and an emphasis on collegiality as a moral, integrative adhesive.

Arguably, integration is closer to the fundamental aims of a university: teaching, research and ensuring that students are given the best opportunities to learn professionally and ethically within and across disciplines. This is broadly the holistic spirit of the Humboldtian university (Habermas and Blazek 1987), which seems to have been lost in subsequent times of specialization. Yet knowledge, as much as learning and academic identities, consists of an intricate panoply of epistemological, ontological and ethical elements (Barnett and Bengtsen 2017). The authors are right in arguing against fragmentation in favour of integration in terms of academic work, practice and careers.

In line with this, I propose the notion of *modular profiling* in thinking about academic work, practice and careers. Academics should have the opportunity to orientate themselves to their careers in modular, expansive ways, where an activity may be predominant at one or more times in their lives but not necessarily over their entire professional life span, lest career tracks become inflexible paths that guide one's perceptions of progression possibilities and opportunities. Academics should feel free (and supported) to move in and out of activities as personal circumstances, abilities, foci of interest and professional contexts change. Consequently, academic evaluation should be more holistic, not simply articulated in terms of measurable impact and/or production in one activity. Rather, we should think in terms of the *contribution* individuals make for the *good* of an institution, knowledge and society at large. It is for this reason that I advocate a concept of modular profiling as a way of promoting academics for their overall impact over time and space: for an expansive view of higher education processes, activities, ethos and vision, beyond purely research or, indeed, teaching excellence.

References

Barnett, R. and Bengtsen, S. (2017) 'Universities and epistemology: from a dissolution of knowledge to the emergence of a new thinking', *Education Sciences*, 7(38): 1–12.
Habermas, J. and Blazek, J. R. (1987) 'The idea of the university: learning processes', *New German Critique*, 41: 3–22.

11

EXCELLENCE FOR ALL: INCLUSIVE TEACHING WITH A PASSION – A TEACHING EXCELLENCE RECOGNITION SCHEME

Michael Berry and Ross Guest

Introduction

This chapter discusses an innovative scheme for recognizing and rewarding excellence in teaching called the Teaching Excellence Recognition Scheme (TERS). This scheme has been applied in an Australian business school since 2015. The chapter provides in some detail the motivation for the scheme, focusing on the lack of existing incentives for academics to invest their time in teaching relative to research. The chapter then provides some context in terms of types of recognition schemes including potential issues with such schemes before going on to discuss the particular elements of the TERS scheme and the feedback received from academic staff so far.

Perceptions of the importance of teaching relative to research

A commitment to quality education lies at the heart of every academic institution. It shapes the student learning experience and occupies a significant proportion of academics' time and attention. It is best supported by excellent teaching. Yet the prestige of teaching continues to lag behind that of research in universities. It seems that teaching and learning are perennially undervalued activities within the tertiary sector. For more than thirty years there has been a growing and widely expressed concern that the efforts of teachers are not sufficiently rewarded and recognized in universities, particularly in comparison to those of researchers (Chalmers 2011).

A wide range of papers and reports (Kleinhenz and Ingvarson 2004; Andrews 2011; Aitken and Tatebe 2014) have confirmed that teaching and learning are undervalued as institutional activities when compared to research and that this situation has existed across an extended period of time (Ramsden 2009; Salmi 2015). In their study of 290 academic economists in Australia, Guest and Duhs (2002) found a strong response to the differential incentives for research and teaching performance. Similarly, from her survey of 152 academics across Australian universities, Taylor (2001: 53) found that 'most of the participants admitted to a shift from teaching towards research because of the rewards attached'. Furthermore, this situation seems to be universally represented across universities globally.

The reasons for this are varied and have been known for a long time. As far back as the Dearing Report (1997) from the UK, three reasons for the lower status of teaching relative to research were identified: (i) funding for teaching and development projects was often significantly less than other mainstream areas of research and this leads to a perception that there are more opportunities in research and it is more greatly valued; (ii) there were few national policy directions on the quality of teaching to guide universities (see also Gosling 2004 in Chalmers 2011) including the lack of an agreed, common definition or description of teaching excellence; (iii) promotion and career progression was often linked to research outputs rather than teaching accomplishments. The report also identified that an institution's prestige and status is often more closely aligned to the level of its research outputs than to its teaching outputs, with top tier universities across the world demonstrating a strong tendency to be more research focused, or 'research intensive', than teaching focused (Chalmers 2011).

These themes remain in play and have been echoed in subsequent studies. Guest and Duhs (2003) argue that a university's marginal income is virtually unrelated to teaching quality unlike research where research income, publications and higher degree completions are linked directly to funding. This provides no incentive for universities to allocate marginal resources to improving teaching quality relative to research. Instead universities adopt token rewards for teaching quality such as 'distinguished teacher' awards which are of the winner-takes-all variety. Evans (2005, in Andrews 2011) suggests that the number of awards provided for excellence in teaching are often far too few when compared to the number of potential recipients and staff. In his institution for example, where one 'outstanding teacher award' is provided each year, the number of staff who demonstrate high levels of teaching performance (perhaps twenty-five per cent) versus the number of awards available (one award) means that a high performing member of faculty within a pool of a hundred academic staff might have to typically wait up to twenty-five years to be formally recognized and rewarded for their achievements. In contrast, the access and availability for research grants is much higher.

Similarly, in Australia strategies to improve teaching quality typically take the form of schemes that reward relatively few elite staff (Beckmann 2016). Beckmann argues that this can lead other staff to 'disconnect' from the reward system and see outstanding examples of teaching practice as perhaps unobtainable and perhaps even unrealistic for their context and their particular students. Indeed, 'individual teachers of excellence' rewards schemes might inadvertently be robbing higher education in Australia of a broader focus on quality and lead to the reward of an elite few at the expense of the many (Crook 2014).

Survey-based research by Fairweather (2005) found that the time spent teaching was actually negatively reflected in salary outcomes, while time engaged in research was reflected in a higher salary and a greater range of employment options within the labour market. Fairweather also noted that globally all types of higher education institutions use similar 'research-oriented' criteria when hiring and rewarding staff. Andrews (2011) identified that only five per cent of staff were promoted to senior levels on the basis of their teaching, while the remainder received their promotion based on their research efforts.

Changing workplace practices in universities are another factor, with both Fairweather (2005) and Chalmers (2011) commenting that the increased use of part-time and non-tenured staff in universities and their role in undertaking a significant, and growing, part of the teaching workload is also contributing to the cultural perception that teaching is a more 'generalist capability' and a less-valued career role than research. They suggest that this has contributed to a culture in universities where teaching and learning is seen as the focus of early career academics, while research is seen as the domain of mid and later career academics where skills and capabilities in research, and a well-defined track record in publications, is needed for career progression. Hence, to pursue a long-term academic career, a focus on effective research skills and capabilities is seen as essential while teaching performance is recognized as a foundational 'given'.

This perception is also culturally supported across academic institutions through the language of their workload policy documents and guidelines, which often reinforce and highlight a role separation between research and teaching time allocations. Such documents often suggest that universities 'free up' the time of researchers by allocating more teaching to the non-research-intensive staff (Chalmers 2011). This is confirmed by Hardre and Cox (2008) who found that academics identified as being insufficiently research productive were often assigned increased teaching loads, while those who were sufficiently productive were 'spared' them. The very clear and consistent message that such practices send is that successful academics do research and less successful academics carry the bulk of the teaching load.

Teaching recognition and reward schemes

A review of reward and recognition schemes reveals that there are typically three types or categories of recognition schemes described in the literature which have been tried at tertiary institutions to improve the recognition and quality of teaching and learning. First are *institutional recognition* schemes which are typically built into an institution's leadership or 'reward and recognition framework'. Ramsden and Martin (1996) loosely refer to these as 'managerial schemes'. These require candidates to apply for recognition or be nominated by others. Typically, an annual process, applications are usually judged by a panel and a 'winner' in each of a couple of categories determined. Sometimes referred to as 'winner-takes-all schemes', non-winning candidates are typically not recognized (except perhaps with a commendation or encouragement certificate), but usually prompted to try again in the following year.

Second, *peer recognition schemes* are usually judged against a set of predetermined criteria by a team of 'peers' and are often initiated and managed by professional associations. Beckmann (2016) describes how tertiary institutions can establish and manage these processes. Such schemes require participants to write against an established set of criteria. If the applicant is judged to have met the criteria, then they are recognized (typically with a fellowship). This type of scheme allows a much broader number of candidates to achieve recognition and success than the institutional recognition schemes which typically only recognize one winning candidate per year.

The third category is a hybrid of these and could be described as a behavioural, or *rewards based,* approach. It asks candidates to demonstrate a range of behaviours which are seen as contributing to 'teaching and learning leadership' or 'teaching and learning excellence'. Each candidate maps their performance against the prescribed behaviours. The more they can demonstrate to the review panel, the greater their recognition or reward (typically drawn from a defined funding pool). Those candidates with more 'behaviours' demonstrated receive a larger slice of the available funds. The TERS falls into this class of scheme. It sets out indicators of excellence in teaching which reflect desired behaviours according to the strategic learning and teaching objectives of the institution, and provides rewards in proportion to achievement against the indicators.

The most predominate type of scheme is that of 'professional or peer recognition'. Under such a scheme, an example being that supported by the Higher Education Authority (HEA) in the UK, academics write against a set of common and well developed professional academic standards to demonstrate their suitability to join the HEA as a fellow, senior fellow or principal fellow. Applications are peer reviewed and academics are admitted at several levels depending upon the depth of professional experience and practice in the areas of learning and teaching, and the degree of leadership that they are able to demonstrate in these areas. This scheme is becoming well recognized and the Australian National University has now entered into an agreement in the form of a Memorandum of Understanding with the HEA to take this on, enabling more Australian educators to become recognized for their teaching excellence.

This type of scheme can contribute to the overall 'culture of excellence' recognition by promoting both an aspirational target for academics (shorter term and longer term at the higher levels), as well as by promoting professional discussion and dialogue about what constitutes 'sustained excellence' in teaching through the peer review process. Furthermore, many academics could potentially achieve this award over time (compared to the 'few elite' that are often rewarded through the institution reward or recognition schemes) if they apply their mind towards continuous achievement and the long-term documenting of their improvements in teaching and learning. However, the scheme does have some drawbacks. While it might work well for some of the more developed and expert teaching staff at a university, it is less likely to stimulate interest from earlier career academics who may have to wait several years to document and gather the evidence necessary to support their claims of excellence. Hence, unlike the rewards for research, which are directly linked to outputs that occur regularly and often come with monetary compensation or workload allowances, 'professional recognition schemes' take considerably longer to achieve, requiring academics to take a very long-term view of their teaching practice and development. Typically, such reward schemes can take years of consistent practice to gather the necessary data and experience to achieve effective professional recognition. The HEA scheme is also an organizational and administrative challenge; not only because it requires the potential awardee to commit significant organizational time to the gathering and generating of enough supporting evidence to submit a viable application, but also requires a high number of quality professional reviewers to support the peer review process and ensure that it is undertaken with sufficient quality and in a timely way.

A more systematic recognition and reward scheme

The Griffith Business School in Griffith University, Australia, introduced the Teaching Excellence Recognition Scheme (TERS) in pilot form in 2014, applying to one of six academic departments, and then across the whole School in 2015 covering approximately 220 academic staff.

Aims of the scheme

The TERS recognizes and rewards teaching excellence. Recognition is important because it showcases excellence in learning and teaching and helps to promote exemplar teachers who may become the future leaders and mentors in learning and teaching as well as potential future recipients of learning and teaching awards and grants. It also provides academics with a recognized evidence-base for their academic performance assessment and their promotion applications. The monetary reward element of the scheme is important too. It provides staff with financial resources to help build their capacity as an academic. For this purpose, the use of the funds is not restricted to learning and teaching activities. Academics may, for example, have invested a lot of time in their teaching and may need to 'back-fill' by buying some research time from a research assistant. The indicators of excellence serve as key strategic signals about the fields of learning and teaching activity and achievement that are valued most highly by the Griffith Business School. The intention is that these signals will steer the investment of time and energy into the fields of learning and teaching endeavour that are strategically important.

Operation of the scheme

Academics report against a range of indicators of teaching excellence on a two–year rolling average (in the first year the evaluation would be based on only that one year of data). The indicators are as follows (also see Table 11.1 for further detail on the indicators and the points attached to teaching):

1. Student evaluation of teaching (SET)
2. Student evaluation of course (SEC)

TABLE 11.1 Indicators of teaching excellence and points allocated under the TERS

Indicators	Maximum points	
	Non-sessional staff	Sessional staff
1. Student evaluation of teaching (SET)	10	10
Applies to SET scores that are above the 75th percentile cut-off, according to the formula:		
Points = (SET score − 75P) × 40, where 75P is the 75th percentile cut-off score above which the mean score falls into the 4th quartile band. This adjustment allows for known systematic variations in SETs for different types of courses.		
Example: SET score = 4.5, 75P = 4.3, therefore points = (4.5–4.3) × 40 = 8		
2. Student evaluation of course (SEC)	5	N/A
Applies only to the convenor of the course, since the convenor is usually responsible for the design, management and course oversight. This category applies to SECs on the overall satisfaction question above 4.0, according to the formula:		
Points = (SEC score − 75P) × 20 Or for OUA courses (using the 4 point scale): Points = (Overall sat score − 3.0) × 5		
3. Participation in Peer Evaluation of Teaching	5	5
Participation in formal peer evaluation as either an observer or subject. The evaluation must be conducted through the GU Pro-Teaching programme, the PACES programme, or a mentoring arrangement approved by, and reporting to, the HOD and/or Dean (L&T). Full points are awarded where the observation sheet and related documentation have been completed and submitted.		
4. Evidence of successful active learning methods and/or evidence of innovation in active learning	5	5
Building a culture of active learning is a key strategic priority of the GBS to achieve high quality learning. Evidence of successful active learning methods and/or evidence of innovation in active learning for recognition in the TERS scheme will consist of:		

- positive student comment(s) about active learning methods in the course, expressed in SET and/or SEC reports and/or other forms of written student feedback;
- innovations in terms of new learning activities or assessment where evidence is provided that the innovations are new to the course i.e. not present in earlier deliveries of the course;
- participation in the GBS innovation group, in which academics introduce new innovative ways of delivering a course; the additional criterion for recognition in the TERS scheme is that the innovation must involve active learning methods.

In order to reduce subjectivity in assessing returns against this category, any clear evidence of at least one of the above indicators will earn the full 5 points.

Indicators	Maximum points	
	Non-sessional staff	Sessional staff
5. Teaching awards or grants Applies equally to all listed team members on an award or grant. Group Learning and Teaching Citation 3 points Griffith Grant for Learning and Teaching 5 points Griffith Award for Excellence in Teaching: Commendation 3 points Award 5 points OLT award or grant 5 points	5	5
6. Scholarship of learning and teaching	5	5

6. Scholarship of learning and teaching

- *Author of text book publication (co-authored or sole-authored)*

  Each sole-authored textbook 5 points
  Each publication with one co-author 4 points
  Each publication with two or more co-authors 3 points

  Conditions for recognition are that a reputable publisher produces the book. The points are awarded in the year of publication. Second and subsequent editions accrue 2 points.

- *Learning and teaching publications*

  Each sole-authored publication (reputable outlet) 4 points
  Each publication with one co-author 3 points
  Each publication with two or more co-authors 2 points

- *Learning and teaching presentations*

  E.g. conference papers and invited internal presentations 2 points

- *Editorial board of business education journal* 2 points

7. Professional development — 5 — 5

- *Completing a T&L academic qualification* 5 points

  E.g. Grad Cert in Higher Ed. Each course in the Grad Cert accrues 1 point, plus a bonus point on completion of the fourth course.

- *Capacity building activities* 1 point

  The point applies to participation in each activity/event

  Activities here consist of: department seminars/retreats on L & T, Learning Futures events, external events/conferences on L & T, GBS TCOP meetings, teaching innovation projects organised through the Dean (L&T).

8. Early career teacher — 4 — 4

Earrly career teachers (first 5 years of university teaching in any capacity) will receive **4 bonus points**. This recognizes that they have not had the opportunity to build capacity that would allow scholarship or teaching awards, nor the sort of teaching experience that is likely be reflected in higher SETs or SECs.

3.   Participation in Peer Evaluation of Teaching
4.   Evidence of successful active learning methods and/or evidence of innovation in active learning
5.   Teaching awards or grants
6.   Scholarship of learning and teaching
7.   Professional development activities
8.   Early career teacher bonus points

There are two categories: Category A is for non-sessional (continuing part-time and fixed term, full-time) Griffith Business School academic staff; Category B is for sessional staff (on very short term casual appointments remunerated on an hourly basis). Points are awarded against each indicator up to the specified maximum.

Funding quantum

Funding is allocated at an Australian dollar ($) per point rate for all points above a threshold. The rate and threshold level is determined once all applications have been received and the total funding pool is known. The formula for allocating funding to a staff member is:

$$\text{\$ per academic} = \left(\frac{\text{points earned by academic above threshold}}{\text{Total points above threshold earned by all GBS academics}}\right) \times$$

$$\text{(total available funding pool)}$$

Example:
Suppose an academic earns twenty points; the threshold is fifteen points; the total points above the threshold by all Griffith Business School academics is 200 points; the total funding pool for the relevant scheme Category is $50k. Then the points earned by this academic are

$$\frac{5}{200} \times \$50,000 = \$1,250$$

Application and assessment process

A call for applications is announced early in the academic year, with the data applying to the previous two years. Academics enter data through the online tool, which is currently SogoSurvey. The survey tool organizes the data in a spreadsheet and an administrative support officer verifies the data where possible. The Dean for Learning and Teaching then makes any necessary judgements regarding points. A preliminary list of staff and their number of points is then sent to the respective Heads of Department for information for a 'reality check' to identify any obvious anomalies.

In 2016, a budget of $70k was allocated to the scheme and it was distributed over approximately thirty staff out of an eligible total of 220 (although most did not apply). Amounts awarded ranged from \$700 to \$3,500, depending on the number of points.

Other comments on the scheme

A number of aspects of the TERS scheme are worth highlighting. The TERS is unlike the institutional 'winner-takes-all' award schemes or even Fellowship schemes, in that it recognizes a larger number of staff with differential monetary rewards depending on their relative performance. The scheme does not preclude staff from seeking further professional recognition, through schemes at university, national and international level. The scheme is based on a clearly articulated and understood set of metrics or criteria, which are, along with the whole process, open to staff scrutiny, feedback and annual review. The two-year rolling average of achievements recognizes that performance is often uneven over time due to any number of personal and professional factors. Finally, there is no predetermined number of recipients – it depends on the number of academics who apply and their relative performance. That said, the minimum threshold number of points can be set to either increase or decrease the number of likely recipients.

Staff feedback and comment on the TERS scheme

Feedback was sought from a range of professional, academic and administrative staff during 2016. This has led to a few changes and modifications to the scope of the programme. For example, the points allocation for specific tasks was modified and the scheme was extended to casual academic teaching staff. The online submission platform is also being reviewed and will probably shift to Qualtrics. Through these changes it is hoped to ensure that the scheme is fair, balanced and accessible to a broad range of staff while continuing to support those who invest the most time and effort into refining their teaching and learning performance.

While the scheme is still in the early development stage of implementation, being less than two years old, it can be seen that the staff are overwhelmingly positive about the importance and value of the scheme. While the scheme is currently only open to academic and teaching staff, the possibility exists to potentially extend the scheme, through a new set of metrics, to include other support staff who have a semi-direct role in supporting the teaching and learning process. Such a group could include instructional designers, curriculum consultants, blended learning advisers, and so on. Such an extension would also need an additional and separate funding pool.

Administratively speaking, the programme is relatively easy to manage with applicant staff using an online application process which generates a summary and score for each staff member. Using a spreadsheet these can be sorted and the scores and rewards calculated relatively easily. This information is then communicated back to the applicants via a congratulatory email from the Dean, which includes the amount of funds provided and some feedback to applicants. Most applicants tend to use the money to support their professional learning development and teaching and learning processes.

The initial view from some staff is that it is simply a rewards and recognition scheme and that it helps to re-balance the rewards that are often seen as being attached to research:

> TERS is an excellent way of recognizing instructor efforts aimed at better learning experience and outcomes for students (senior Business School academic).
>
> . . . TERS gives formal recognition to excellence in teaching in a similar fashion to the 'Research and Conference Scheme' for recognizing research performance. Hence, it signals to academics the importance of teaching in the Business School by rewarding them for good teaching (experienced academic leader in the Business School).

Others started to look towards the longer-term impacts of the scheme in terms of its ability to shift the conversation towards teaching and cultural change:

> I believe the scheme has the potential to change both attitudes and behaviour regarding the importance of teaching. It may motivate academics to become more involved in professional development and they will be pleased to receive recognition for their effort (experienced academic leader in the Business School).

Other staff built on this idea of professional recognition and longer-term staff behavioural change as an overall way to create the cultural shift and motivation needed to deliver long term results and corporate goals:

> . . . it is critical to ensure that the design aligns with our priorities, which I think is already the case now. However, as priorities in the teaching and learning area change, the design of the scheme will need to be continuously reviewed to ensure that we are rewarding the behaviours we effectively want to encourage. Having said that, it seems to me that TERS does a good job in generally promoting a culture of innovation in teaching (Head of Department within the Business School).

The importance of rewarding both professional development and teaching innovation was recognized:

> TERS succeeds in promoting teaching excellence by not only rewarding excellent teachers per se, but also recognizing those teachers committed to continuous professional development as well as those innovative teachers willing to trial new methods to engage and motivate their students. By providing such recognition, the potential breadth of teaching excellence

within [the School] is maximized and the importance of teaching as a profession celebrated (Senior Lecturer within the Business School).

A small minority of staff had negative feedback which highlighted some important points to address in future:

> . . . one individual who was awarded almost the highest amount of money in the scheme is NOT considered an excellent teacher and was not present for a large portion of the year. Others who won multiple awards with national recognition received half the amount. This will backfire if a common sense approach to who should be recognized is not achieved. Formulas and maths don't always do that (leading academic and administrator within the Business School).

The above comment highlights how formula-based reward schemes can give a false sense of heightened precision and accuracy. Indeed, there is a view that, because our methods of identifying good teaching are imperfect, to rely too strictly on them would result in some good teaching going unrewarded, some poor teaching being rewarded and, crucially, some satisfactory teaching being deemed unsatisfactory with serious consequences for individuals. This is clearly articulated by Elton (2000), who claims that teaching quality cannot be automatically measured and that attempts to do so lead to unintended consequences. However, the alternative view is that we end up with a paralysis in that we know what good teaching is but we have not been able to find ways to systematically reward teachers according to the quality of their teaching. Our view is that it is better to acknowledge that schemes such as the TERS are imperfect and that it is important to improve them over time.

Conclusion

The Teaching Excellence Recognition Scheme has advantages over the more traditional reward and recognition schemes, although it can and does coexist with such schemes. The TERS rewards a broad number of individuals each year rather than recognizing and rewarding only a few outstanding individuals and asking the rest to try again next year. It actively seeks to promote a common and clearly identified set of criteria while still allowing individuals who are only demonstrating some of the criteria to potentially be recognized (depending upon the size of the funding pool). Furthermore, it does not require individuals to build a long-term teaching portfolio in order to be recognized, or require an overly cumbersome administrative process (like peer reviewed processes may). The annual nature of the programme also means that it can (and has) been modified and refined over time based on feedback. From the original pilot, through the first and second iterations, multiple refinements to the funding structure and criteria have been implemented. Such a programme can therefore respond to both staff feedback as well as the reshaping of the organizations key goals and values. Overall the success and general acceptance of the scheme to date could be based upon the fact that staff see excellence as a 'progressive and developmental journey' rather than a 'final destination', and that the majority of academic staff can locate themselves as being on this journey.

References

Aitken, G. and Tatebe, J. (2014) *Recognition of teaching excellence discussion paper*, Teaching and Learning Position Paper November 2014, Birmingham: Universitas 21.

Andrews, H. A. (2011) 'Supporting quality teaching with recognition', *Australian Journal of Teacher Education*, 36(12): 59–70.

Beckmann, E. A. (2016) *Teaching excellence: recognising the many as well as the few*, paper presented at HERDSA Conference, 4–7 July 2016, Fremantle, Australia.

Chalmers, D. (2011) 'Progress and challenges to the recognition and reward of the scholarship of teaching in higher education', *Higher Education Research & Development*, 30(1): 25–38.

Crook, R. (2014) *Analysis: slow progress on recognition of teaching excellence*, Times Higher Education, 10 July 2014. Online. Available at www.timeshighereducation.com/news/analysis-slow-progress-on-recognition-of-teaching-excellence/2014334.article (accessed 20 June 2017).

Dearing, R. (1997) *The Dearing Report: higher education in the learning society*, The National Committee of Inquiry into Higher Education, London: Her Majesty's Stationery Office.

Elton, L. (2000) 'The UK research assessment exercise: unintended consequences', *Higher Education Quarterly*, 54(3): 274–283.

Fairweather, J. (2005) 'Beyond the rhetoric: trends in the relative value of teaching and research in faculty salaries', *Journal of Higher Education*, 76(4): 401–422.

Guest, R. and Duhs, A. (2002) 'Economics teaching in Australian universities: rewards and outcomes', *Economic Record*, 78(241): 147–160.

Guest, R. and Duhs, A. (2003) 'Quality assurance and the quality of university teaching', *Australian Journal of Education*, 47(1): 40–57.

Hardre, P. and Cox, M. (2008) 'Evaluating faculty work: expectations and standards of faculty performance in research universities', *Research Papers in Education*, 24(4): 383–419.

Kleinhenz, E. and Ingvarson, L. (2004) 'Teacher accountability in Australia: current policies and practices and their relation to the improvement of teaching and learning', *Research Papers in Education*, 19(1): 31–49.

Ramsden, P. and Martin, E. (1996) 'Recognition of good university teaching: policies from an Australian study', *Studies in Higher Education*, 21(3): 299–315.

Ramsden, P. (2009) *Reward and recognition of teaching in higher education: a collaborative investigation*, York: Higher Education Academy and GENIE Centre for Excellence in Teaching and Learning, University of Leicester.

Salmi, J. (2015) 'New challenges for tertiary education: The World Bank report', *International Higher Education*. Online. Available at https://ejournals.bc.edu/ojs/index.php/ihe/article/viewFile/6659/5880 (accessed 20 June 2017).

Taylor, J. (2001) 'The impact of performance indicators on the work of Australian academics: evidence from Australian universities', *Higher Education Quarterly*, 55(1): 42–61.

Critical friend commentary

Bill Bosshardt

Although the chapter is written in an Australian context, many of the issues described would apply to an American context as well, across all sorts of departments or colleges. Harter, Becker and Watts (2011: 4) also document the importance of teaching and research rewards, in this case for economics, drawing on the results of surveys over a ten-year period and suggest that 'changing workplace practices in universities are another factor' for teaching being less valued. Their argument is that more part-time and non-tenured faculty bring the 'cultural perception' that teaching is a generalist capability. While I agree this is, for the most part, true, I think another trend is worth mentioning. In the United States, many larger, research-oriented institutions are now pursuing non-tenured academics to teach their large principle courses. The instructors are not tenured and expectations are extremely high. One of the non-tenured academics noted that he is expected to keep a high Student Evaluation of Teaching score. The non-tenured academics are paid very well, often exceeding the pay of researchers at lower ranked schools.

This contrasts with the past when excellent teachers took positions at liberal arts schools for lower pay. While this trend is not pervasive, it is becoming more common. Many participants at the 2016 Conference on Teaching and Research in Economic Education have such teaching positions and are required to pursue professional development opportunities. I was left with the impression that teaching is not rewarded at all in the regular annual evaluation/pay rise procedures in Australia. Many universities in the United States have (somewhat) regular merit pay rises. In many schemes, teaching performance is part of the review process and has some influence on pay rises. Of course, the weighting is such that research is the main contributor to the rise, but one could not say teaching received no weight. Another issue is that teaching performance is difficult to assess, so the ratings on teaching tend to be similar across faculty with the distinguishing characteristic being research output.

One contentious issue is the way in which the threshold is chosen. A high threshold reduces the number of staff included in the award, but increases the reward. I thought thirty out of 220 (about fifteen per cent) was low. A broader audience would benefit from a more extensive discussion of the trade-offs: what percentage is being targeted and why?

Reference

Harter, C. L., Becker, W. E. and Watts, M. (2011) 'Time allocations and reward structures for US academic economists from 1995–2005: evidence from three national surveys', *International Review of Economics Education*, 10(2): 6–27.

12

I HAD EXCELLENT TEACHERS – LOOK AT MY FABULOUS CAREER! PERSPECTIVES ON TEACHING EXCELLENCE IN THE PERFORMING ARTS

Scott Harrison

Introduction

Excellence in learning and teaching in higher education can be multifariously defined. Measures such as student evaluations of teaching and courses are common both for faculty performance and university/sectorial benchmarking, as well as providing feedback for personal and institutional improvement. Graduate destinations and employability are also increasingly popular benchmarks internationally, and the prolific use of league tables as a form of student recruitment and research esteem exercises cannot be underestimated. Other forms of recognition include internal and external awards, fellowships and grants. A further gauge of success is evident in the profile and career trajectory of alumni.

This chapter seeks to examine the role each of these measures play in the discipline of performing arts. Following a context scan that includes academic and grey literature, examples of teaching excellence in the performing arts are put forward, illuminating the various means by which performing arts schools in higher education promote teaching quality. From these cases, a series of themes emerged. Analysis of these data demonstrates a high degree of commonality across the examples, and the potential to ascertain appropriate and impactful measures of learning and teaching excellence in the performing arts is observed.

The findings reveal that excellence is largely defined through graduate success in the industry, and this consequently reflects well on the institution/s that provided the initial training. Other measures, such as the teacher/performer profile, external awards and teacher lineage are considered. Formal student evaluations are rarely a factor in determining teaching quality.

The research, while discipline-specific, has some implications for other domains within the higher education sector and perhaps assists in determining teaching quality in pre-tertiary settings. It also helps to expand the current thinking about the validity and reliability of teaching excellence measures. Suggestions for the adoption of innovative thinking and consideration of the definition of teaching excellence are posited, along with learning from other disciplines, particularly health and sport, as they might apply to the performing arts.

Background context

Excellence in teaching in the performing arts has historically been characterized by teacher lineage and/or adherence to certain schools. For example, in actor training one can claim to have learned from an esteemed performer, studied the Stanislavski system or Meisner technique or followed the teaching of Strasberg. Particular schools are noted for their 'excellence' – largely defined by their graduates: Central School of Speech and Drama, Royal Academy of Dramatic Art, Juilliard, National Institute for Dramatic Art, Guildhall School of Music and Drama, Tisch School of the Arts and the like. In music, it is common to have studied with a performer who claims to be able to trace their teaching back to Liszt, or Paganini. Dancers, similarly, belong to certain schools or adhere to particular traditions – French, Russian and so on. Reputation plays a significant role in the perceived excellence of the teaching, with biographies of famous performers scrutinized for their training experience. This is understandable, given the level of competition within the industry and the passion with which beginning performers approach their careers – any form of advantage is much sought after (see, for example, O'Bryan 2010). This makes the selection of an individual teacher and/or institution a critical decision for a beginning performer.

With recent aggregation of independent performing arts schools into colleges and universities in the 1990s and 2000s, typified by the Dawkins report in Australia (Australia, Department of Employment, Education and Training 1988), and similar movements in New Zealand and the United Kingdom, there was a shift in the perception and measurement of teaching excellence in this more formalized setting (see Abbott 1996). To align with parent institutional practices, evaluations of teaching and courses became de rigueur, with measurement through Likert scales and qualitative commentary used as evidence of 'good' teachers and teaching practices. In some instances, the mark of a good teacher is reduced to a single number or percentile. These measures persist, though their usefulness in many disciplines – including the performing arts – is frequently questioned (see, for example, Tang 1997; McCaffery et al. 2004; Stallings 2015). They contribute to league tables in many countries, and therefore potentially change the perception and standing of historically strong schools of performing arts.

A further measure of the standard of teaching can be found in university and national awards, grants and fellowships. Teachers are singled out for their excellence, assessed by their peers and acknowledged by their governments and institutions. In some cases, these individuals are outstanding practitioners, while in other circumstances they are simply able to write appropriate cases; in other words, they are capable at grants-writing. These accolades are subsequently used for promotion of the university and of the individuals concerned.

Perhaps more than any other measure, teaching excellence in performing arts is manifest in graduate success. Students and alumni who gain and sustain work in the industry reflect well on those who taught them (see, for example, Shirk and Miller 1994; Harrison et al. 2013): the student or alumnus who wins the reality television show, who is cast in a role on Broadway or the West End, takes to the stage at Covent Garden or the Kennedy Centre, brings glory to their teacher who must, by this definition, be excellent. Note, however, that teachers who produce other fine teachers, or graduates who work in marketing, front of house or backstage, are not as highly regarded. Performance teachers train performers, and the choice of any other career is frequently perceived as failure. This bias will be pursued further later in the chapter.

Literature context

Due to the paucity of literature in this discipline, the interface with related disciplines is included, along with reference to more generic literature regarding the nature of teaching in the performing arts. Reference to excellence is rarely noted in the standard writings on curriculum, pedagogy and assessment in the performing arts, though one notable exception is the work of Harrison et al. (2015). These authors explore assessment tasks in musical theatre and the ways in which they are perceived to be related to future career success by emulating the profession as closely as possible.

Skelton's (2005) work has particular resonance for this chapter in that it seeks to identify and examine teaching excellence and gives voice to the practical implications of said excellence. Of particular interest in this chapter are those that focus on the performing arts and, particularly, the uniqueness of alumni experience in this discipline. Moore and Kuol (2007) explore teaching excellence through the eyes of students and recent alumni. Their sample of 139 respondents found that students are more likely to invoke teacher attributes than actions, and recall positively such dynamics as a sense of belonging, the pleasure of community, the importance of being understood and cared about and the experience of having been welcomed and respected within their classroom settings. Other work on teacher attributes (Harrison 2003a; 2004) produces similar results with students in studio and classroom settings valuing teacher traits above knowledge and skills.

In the performing arts, Kadushin (1969: 14) dispels the myth that talent is sufficient, noting: 'Contrary to popular mythology, professional artists are made, not born. Though artistic techniques, especially in music, are often learned early, indoctrination into the culture of artists may come quite late'. This places further importance on the role of teaching in 'shaping', 'making' or 'enabling' learning in the student. Colwell and Richardson (2002) devote several chapters to the learning and teaching process in music, while little attention is focused on excellence. The exception is the work of McPherson (2016) who discusses the significance of the research, evaluates new developments and frames issues, theories and ideas with suggestions for future research. This volume features an expanded section on teacher education, some of which has limited relevance for the higher education setting. Reflections on teaching are relatively common in the literature, particularly in music and drama education. There is a scarcity of literature in the higher education domain, with some exceptions (Gaunt 2009; Gaunt et al. 2012; O'Bryan 2014; Carey and Grant 2015; Carey et al. 2016) where the inner workings of teaching practice are delved into with a view to illuminating and improving the student experience and, by extension, capturing and documenting exemplary teaching practice.

One of the leading figures in the crossover between performing artists and athletes is Hays (2010). Her paper 'The Enhancement of Performance Excellence Among Performing Artists' focused largely on performance enhancement, psychological skills training, developmental issues, injury and retirement, eating disorders and parallels and differences with athletes. While not about excellence per se, her implications imply excellent teaching practices. Harrison (2003b; 2005) also explored the synergy between teaching music and sport in the secondary school context, finding that some strategies could bring about excellent results in both disciplines. These included embracing team approaches, focusing on common goals and following similar pre- and post-game/performance rituals. There are some other tangentially-related publications in sport and sport psychology. The latter tend towards individual and team coaching which, while some clear parallels exist for the performing arts, the focus on winning means the findings do not have as much relevance for the topic under discussion here. Other disciplines with allied relationships to the performing arts include health and languages, both of which employ one-to-one tuition in a similar manner to that utilized in music. One recent example in this discipline is the Chinese Whispers project at University of Hull. This collaborative project involved academics from two disciplines (Music and Languages), diverse cultural backgrounds and international institutions (Tianjin Normal University and the Confucius Institute), various professions (for example: a Beijing Choir Master; composers and music conductors; teacher trainers; technicians) and different stages of the educational journey (students; trainee and qualified teachers; lecturers and professors). The project revealed similar strategies were employed across the two disciplines, and won a teaching excellence award – see Chinese Whispers (2016) at the University of Hull.

Within the performing arts in other geographical locations, the teaching material on band and choral excellence from the United States offers some useful ideas for ensemble and group teaching, as is common in orchestral training and ballet de corps work. The work of Lautzenheiser (1992) on *The Art of Successful Teaching* presents many inspirational ideas; however, many are reliant on the convivial and extroverted nature of the teacher, and are not always widely applicable. Also in the United States, the series 'Teaching Music Through Performance' (see, for example, Miles 1997) includes analyses of select pieces and insights from national leaders in the field and includes recordings by leading ensembles. This demonstrates the possible excellence that can be achieved, but this extensive series is more about repertoire choices for band, choir, orchestra and, more recently, jazz. The authors are largely university and college professors, so there is genuine authenticity in the teaching material, but the focus is more on pre-tertiary ensemble instruction. It is interesting to note that in the jazz series, Wynton Marsalis features as an author. Better known as a performer, Marsalis has recently crossed over into education with his leadership of Jazz at Lincoln Center. This trend of performer/teachers and what they bring to the teaching experience has recently been explored by Schindler (2010) and O'Bryan (2014; 2015).

Whether these practices result in excellent teaching practices is difficult to ascertain, as Norris (2002: 148) noted: 'Teaching excellence is virtually always determined by the whims, wants or opinions of those charged with making the determination of quality'. This notion of defining and classifying teaching excellence will be more fully explored in the findings and conclusions below.

Method and data generation

This study explores each of the notions of excellence espoused above and, using case studies (Stake 1995), seeks to illuminate the possibilities for defining and measuring teaching excellence. In so doing, it aims to enhance and expand the existing knowledge base in the performing arts and beyond. Each brief case has been anonymized, and conclusions about the efficacy of the teaching outcomes delivered. The study employed a convenience sample (Robson 1993) drawing on my own experiences as a leader in a higher education institution for the performing arts. Four short cases are presented as exemplars of teaching excellence, representing sub-disciplines in the performing arts and providing insights into the ways in which teaching excellence might be variously defined.

Case 1

This case reflects on a teacher of theatre performance who, over the course of three years, achieved consistently high teaching scores in individual tuition and in class-based settings. This resulted in a commendation from the university for outstanding work. The teaching commendation recognized repeated teaching scores in the top five per cent of the university. Two years later, the students of this teacher began to make their mark in the profession. As is often the case, training and mentorship extends well beyond the formal teaching environment, and into professional life. Performers, like teachers, typically take time to mature into fully-formed professionals who are adaptable, flexible and able to meet changing industry demands. This teacher had substantial performance experience, formal schoolteacher training, and had engaged in regular, ongoing professional development and completed doctoral studies in pedagogy. They published in their field, specifically on pedagogy.

Case 2

This case refers to a teacher who had substantial experience in the secondary sector before commencing teaching in higher education. The individual in this case undertook further postgraduate studies in higher education, despite already holding a doctoral qualification. After six years in full-time tertiary teaching in theoretical and historical aspects of performing arts, they were awarded a national teaching award. The award acknowledged the prior experience in pre-tertiary teaching, and drew on experiences and scholarship of teaching evident in the teaching practices which included class work, one-to-one teaching and doctoral supervision. Further grants followed this award and the impact of the work in assessment and pedagogy continues. This teacher had substantial professional performance experience and was closely involved in peak bodies and contributed to the establishment of professional development programmes for tertiary teachers of performing arts. They published extensively in this field.

Case 3

This case reflects on a voice teacher who, over the course of almost forty years, produced performers who consistently won competitions, worked with high-profile artists and undertook further study. The consistency with which their students received accolades is further evidence that performers do not succeed purely on talent, as noted by Kadushin (1969) above, but require teaching in order to develop sustainable careers beyond the formal learning stage. This teacher had a lifetime of performance experience and was closely involved in curriculum design for pedagogy courses. They had also been an office-bearer in professional associations, undertaken further study in their field and published and presented on their teaching. They were awarded a university teaching award.

Case 4

This case reflects on a teacher with more than twenty years of experience in higher education in music and drama who had successfully placed students into productions and enabled ongoing learning opportunities for her students. Students and graduates gained employment in highly competitive careers, with flexibility and adaptability as key planks in the undergraduate learning experience. This teacher came to teaching early in their career, with little professional on-stage experience but a capacity to enable others to achieve through both coaching and writing for the stage. They regularly perform with and for their students. The learning experiences were highly structured, time-intense and skills-based, and they closely resembled the professional setting. This teacher received consistently high teaching evaluations, and facilitated the receipt of awards for colleagues. They published and presented in their field and were the recipient of a university teaching award.

Findings

Each of these brief cases demonstrates some key, if not universal, commonalities. First, three out of four came to teaching the performing arts with substantial professional performance credentials. Second, most either had prior teaching qualifications or continued to undertake professional development, further studies and/or close involvement with the profession. Third, they were unafraid to make demands of their students, and to set realistic but high standards. Finally, they valued flexibility, agility, longevity, ongoing reflection and a lifetime connection with their discipline, and with their current and former students.

From these findings, albeit from a very small sample, it is possible to draw conclusions that may have resonance in other disciplines. Five broad themes emerge:

1. Obtaining qualifications and undertaking ongoing professional development.
2. Engagement with scholarship, including dissemination.
3. Commitment to longevity in the teaching profession and to students and graduates.
4. Valuing of flexibility, agility.
5. Prior and/or concurrent performance experience.

Of these, only the last – performance experience – is specific to performing arts. While it could be substituted for deep discipline experience in other domains, performance experience in the performing arts incorporates uniquely embodied knowledge. The two examples cited earlier, health and sport, have similarly embodied knowledge (a surgeon, for example, should know how to physically manage a scalpel in any context; a sportsperson should have muscle memory, etc.). The remaining four themes are not revolutionary or performance-specific by any means, but they do serve as foci for the development of teaching excellence frameworks in the performing arts.

Many existing teaching excellence frameworks focus solely on the student experience. While higher education institutions exist for their students, a focus on teaching excellence should, by definition, give voice to the enhancement of teaching for the benefit of the student experience. This approach, employing criteria such as those outlined above into the teaching practices, should result in better student and graduate outcomes as well as improved job satisfaction for teachers in higher education. Furthermore, these approaches are not restricted to full-time tenured faculty, or to the higher education sector per se. Rather, they are equally applicable for peripatetic staff, contractors, visiting artists and beginning teachers.

The broad impact of implementing these five themes is difficult to ascertain. They are true of this small sample, and are perhaps generic enough to prove impact. The significance of ongoing learning (for example, the teacher as learner) is well established in the literature, and the obtaining of qualification has become mandatory, at least in Australia where the Australian Qualifications Framework recommends university teachers have at least one qualification higher than the level they are teaching. Relatedly, engagement with and dissemination of scholarship implies rigorous peer review thereby guaranteeing both the quality and broad disbursement of ideas to influence teaching practice. Graduate tracking is becoming more commonplace in higher education settings, though the individual approach suggested in these themes is harder to quantify. Social media assists enormously in enabling institutions and individual teachers to stay in touch with their former charges and this, in turn, helps to provide data about alumni successes and destinations. Furthermore, the security of tenure means that teachers are likely to stay committed to an institution for longer, though the reverse is true for part-time and peripatetic staff. Institutions with a high proportion of casual faculty (as is often the case in the performing arts) run the risk of losing staff who are interested in greater job security.

The valuing of agility and flexibility in teaching – and instilling these qualities in students and graduates – is increasingly important in the fast-paced, 21st-century society. Teachers who value these qualities in their own teaching are likely to produce graduates who embrace these capabilities and are therefore likely to pursue more diverse career options and enjoy greater success. There is also a counter argument that references and values narrower, deeper skills sets. These graduates can potentially enjoy the heights of career success, but are likely to be fewer in number. Finally, the impact of teachers who have performance experiences is also difficult to measure. As Schindler (2010) notes, not all performers make great teachers, and conversely not all teachers are cut out for performance careers. The ideal combination for maximum influence is a collaborative approach to teaching performance, so that a student is exposed to a variety of excellent experiences that provide them with the greatest opportunity for success.

Further research could be undertaken into the notion of collaboration which is under-explored in the teaching of performing arts and which tends, for the most part, to emphasize the individual. One notable exception is the work of Gaunt and Westerlund (2013) in which international examples of collaborative learning in higher music education are explored. Group and team approaches, as noted in the literature above in relation to sport (Hays 2010; Harrison 2005), are also undervalued as the drive for success and impact in the profession becomes focused on individual achievement. This is perhaps most evident in music where individual tuition is the prime form of delivery, though acting and dance are no doubt faced with similar challenges. A further consideration, raised earlier, is that teachers are deemed to have failed if their graduates pursue careers in allied disciplines which are performance-related but not actual performance on stage. A collaborative approach might help to value these careers as performance students come to appreciate the skills involved in teaching, technical theatre, design, marketing and the like.

Conclusion

To the question of defining teaching excellence: as posited at the outset, teaching excellence is, and must continue to be, multifariously defined. Blunt measures, such as student evaluation scores where, for example, a rating above seventy per cent denotes good teaching, are no longer viable in isolation. While useful for institutional comparison, they do little to actually develop teaching practice, enhance the student experience or produce successful graduates. The cases provided here demonstrate that a nuanced approach that acknowledges teachers' embodied experience of their subject matter, their display of commitment to ongoing learning and knowledge dissemination, and their recognition through awards, citations, grants and graduate success (also variously defined) is more likely to be universally and externally recognized and validated as excellent.

In the light of this, perhaps a more apt approach to determining the nature of excellence would be to return to the etymology of the word itself: its Latin roots and archaic forms. The word 'excellere' implies a level of aspiration – to rise, be eminent and ever upward. This word and its derivation 'excelsior' – used to such good effect as an inspiration and motivator by David O. Russell (2012) in *Silver Linings Playbook* – provides the field with an active approach that assumes ongoing attention will be given to the ambition of producing excellent teaching for the benefit of the student experience. It is perhaps interesting to note that the ancient plural of the word is the term 'excellences', use of which could conceivably capture and acknowledge a plurality and diversity of approaches to this field to maintain a discourse amongst audiences including university managers, government bureaucrats, teachers and, most importantly, students. Ultimately, teaching excellences in performing arts are likely to be judged on the fabulousness of graduates' careers!

References

Abbott, M. (1996) 'Amalgamations and the changing costs of Victorian colleges of advanced education during the 1970s and 1980s', *Higher Education Research and Development*, 5(2): 133–144.

Australia, Department of Employment, Education and Training (1988) *Higher education: a policy statement* (Dawkins Report), Canberra: ADEET.

Carey, G. and Grant, C. (2015) 'Teacher and student perspectives on one-to-one pedagogy: practices and possibilities', *British Journal of Music Education*, 32(1): 5–22.

Carey, G., Harrison, S. and Dwyer, R. (2016) 'Encouraging reflective practice in conservatoire students: a pathway to autonomous learning?', *Music Education Research*, October 2016: 1–12.

Chinese Whispers (2016) *University of Hull*. Online. Available at www.heacademy.ac.uk/person-cate/hull (accessed 9 February 2017).

Colwell, R. and Richardson, C. (eds) (2002) *The new handbook of research on music teaching and learning: a project of the Music Educators National Conference*, New York: Oxford University Press.

Gaunt, H. (2009) 'One-to-one tuition in a conservatoire: the perceptions of instrumental and vocal students', *Psychology of Music*, 38(2): 178–208.

Gaunt, H., Creech, A., Long, M. and Hallam, S. (2012) 'Supporting conservatoire students towards professional integration: one-to-one tuition and the potential of mentoring', *Music Education Research*, 14(1): 25–43.

Gaunt, H. and Westerlund, H. (eds) (2013) *Collaborative learning in higher music education*, Farnham: Ashgate.

Harrison, S. (2003a) 'Who am I? Attributes of singing teachers', *Australian Voice*, 9: 7–11.

Harrison, S. (2003b) 'Music versus sport: what's the score?', *Australian Journal of Music Education*, 2003(1): 10–15.

Harrison, S. (2004) 'Identities of music teachers in Australia', in M. Chaseling (ed.) *Proceedings of the XXVth Annual Conference, Australian Association for Research in Music Education*, 198–206.

Harrison, S. (2005) 'Music versus sport: a new approach to scoring', *Australian Journal of Music Education*, (1): 56–61.

Harrison, S., O'Bryan, J. and Lebler, D. (2013) 'Playing it like a professional: approaches to ensemble direction in tertiary institutions', *International Journal of Music Education*, 31(2): 173–189.

Harrison, S., Sabey, P. and O'Bryan, J. (2015) 'Are we there yet: the role of assessment in musical theatre training', *Studies in Musical Theatre*, 8(2): 159–175.

Hays, K. (2010) 'The enhancement of performance excellence among performing artists', *Journal of Applied Sport Psychology*, 14(4): 299–312.

Kadushin, C. (1969) 'The professional self-concept of music students', *American Journal of Sociology*, 75: 389–404.

Lautzenheiser, T. (1992) *The art of successful teaching: a blend of content and context*, Chicago, IL: GIA.

McCaffery, D., Lockwood, J., Koretz, D. and Hamilton, L. (2004) *Evaluating value-added models for teacher accountability*, Santa Monica, CA: RAND Education.

McPherson, G. (2016) *The child as musician: a handbook of musical development*, Oxford: Oxford University Press.

Miles, R. (ed) (1997) *Teaching music through performances in band, Vol. 1* (2nd edn), Chicago, IL: GIA.

Moore, S. and Kuol, N. (2007) 'Retrospective insights on teaching: exploring teaching excellence through the eyes of the alumni', *Journal of Further and Higher Education*, 31(2): 133–143.

Norris, N. D. (2002) *Perspectives on the mistreatment of American educators: throwing water on a drowning man*, Lanham, MD: Scarecrow.

O'Bryan, J. (2010) 'Eminent singers' recollections of learning to sing: the importance of "fit" between singer and singing teacher', in S. Harrison (ed.) *Perspectives on teaching singing: Australian vocal pedagogues sing their stories*, 47–65, Bowen Hills, Queensland: Australian Academic Press.

O'Bryan, J. (2014) 'Habits of the mind, hand and heart: approaches to classical singing training', in S. Harrison and J. O'Bryan (eds) *Teaching singing in the 21st century*, 21–34, Dordrecht: Springer.

O'Bryan, J. (2015) '"We ARE our instrument!": forming a singer identity', *Research Studies in Music Education*, 10(1): 25–41.

Robson, C. (1993) *Real world research*, Malden, MA: Blackwell Publishing.

Russell, D. O. (Dir.) (2012) *Silver Linings Playbook* (motion picture), USA: Weinstein.

Schindler, M. (2010) 'Performers as teachers: a tertiary perspective', in S. Harrison (ed.) *Perspectives on teaching singing: Australian vocal pedagogues sing their stories*, 31–46, Bowen Hills, Queensland: Australian Academic Press.

Shirk, J. and Miller, M. (1994) *Linking the faculty recognition process to teaching excellence*, paper presented at the National Conference on Successful College Teaching, February 26–28, Orlando, Florida.

Skelton, A. (2005) *Understanding teaching excellence in higher education: towards a critical approach*, London: Taylor and Francis.

Stake, R. E. (1995) *The art of case study research*, Thousand Oaks, CA: SAGE Publications.

Stallings, V. (2015) 'The challenges associated with the implementation of the New Teacher Evaluation Model, Achieve NJ: a building-based administrators' perspective', *Seton Hall University Dissertations and Theses (ETDs)*, Paper 2131.

Tang, T. (1997) 'Teaching evaluation at a public institution of higher education', *Public Personnel Management*, 26(3): 379–389.

Critical friend commentary

Celia Duffy

This chapter throws new light on defining excellence in higher education in the performing arts. In my own institution's recent Curriculum Reform, in which we interrogated just about every aspect of our work very thoroughly, the element that, surprisingly, probably received the least critical attention was the notion of excellence – although the word was liberally bandied about, including as our first red-line, non-negotiable curricular principle (Duffy 2013). This is not unusual in the conservatoire sector, where professional-level student achievement, high technical standards and advanced training (rather than education or research) are bundled together in the 'excellence' wrapper. It is a useful tag, but it is somewhat taken for granted.

Many of Harrison's remarks on the external higher-education, metrics-driven management environment ring true, in particular the sometimes perverse results of league tables and blunt-instrument national student surveys in the performing arts sector. The unreliability of national schemes for rewarding teaching, where those schooled in bid writing (a skill not generally found among conservatoire teaching staff) win the plaudits and quality assurance processes that rely on paperwork with little or no observation of practice are familiar too.

The case studies of exemplars of teaching excellence cite obtaining qualifications, ongoing professional development and engaging with scholarship as two of five broad themes of indicators of excellence in teaching. From my perspective, there is still a great deal of cultural shift needed to transform the conservatoire's population of visiting sessional staff into qualified, research-informed teachers – and some resistance. Progress has been reported, however, by the most recent Centre of Excellence in Music Performance Education (CEMPE) at the Norwegian Academy of Music (CEMPE 2015) in involving artist-teachers in research activities.

I have argued elsewhere (Duffy 2016) that to a busy professional musician already juggling playing and teaching commitments, the time demanded by pursuing teaching qualifications is a real obstacle. It is also difficult for institutional managers to engage an elusive cohort of part-time sessional staff in professional development and change. Structural conservatism and uncritical acceptance of notions of excellence linger, both in our institutions and in the profession. Professional and leadership development is, however, increasingly being addressed by institutions, by large-scale projects such as CEMPE and by the Innovative Conservatoire initiative (ICON). ICON challenges these notions and creatively interrogates and transforms conservatoire teaching practices, including supporting the arguments of this chapter for championing collaborative and group-based approaches.

References

Centre of Excellence in Music Performance Education (CEMPE) (2015) 'Interview with Ingrid Maria Hanken'. Online. Available at http://cempe.no/en/news/cempes-first-lady-steps-down-our-goal-has-been-to-share-knowledge-across-disciplines-and-traditions/ (accessed 24 April 2017).

Duffy C. (2013) 'Negotiating with tradition: curriculum reform and institutional transition in a conservatoire', *Arts and Humanities in Higher Education*, 12(2–3): 169–180.

Duffy, C. (2016) 'ICON: radical professional development in the conservatoire', *Arts and Humanities in Higher Education: An International Journal of Theory, Research and Practice – Special Issue 'The Reflective Conservatoire'*, 15 (3–4): 376–385.

ICON (the Innovative Conservatoire), Guildhall School of Music and Drama. Online. Available at www.innovativeconservatoire.com/about-icon/ (accessed 24 April 2017).

13

THE THRILL OF THE UNEXPECTED

James Derounian

Introduction

Lewis Carroll, best known for *Alice's Adventures in Wonderland* (1865) also wrote a poem, *The Hunting of the Snark*, in 1876. The elusive nature of the Snark depicted in the following extract reflects that of teaching excellence and how it may be harnessed for the benefit of students and staff:

> For the Snark's a peculiar creature, that won't
> Be caught in a commonplace way.
> Do all that you know, and try all that you don't:
> Not a chance must be wasted today!

Teaching excellence in higher education has become something of a Holy Grail and – like the Snark – 'won't be caught in a commonplace way'. There is much noise and talk about what it comprises, its importance to student recruitment, employability, marketing courses, and the generation of new insights and personal and societal progress. In this chapter, however, I want to argue that excellent teaching at universities and colleges cannot be manufactured on a production line, like cars or biscuits. In doing so, I will elaborate on two overarching purposes of this book as a whole: to add to the discourse about teaching excellence; and to explore one meaning of teaching excellence and how it might be delivered. Starting with a discussion on the purpose and intentions attached to teaching excellence, I will then move on to explore the 'thrill of the unexpected' – in particular, positive disruption as a powerful approach to teaching and assessments, for staff and students.

The Higher Education Funding Council for England website asserts that:

> Teaching excellence must be at the heart of a world-leading higher education system. For students, who now invest substantially in their higher education,

it is critically important. We are committed to funding excellent and innovative teaching, to sharing excellent and expert practice, and to supporting the interests of students.

And – I strongly suspect – if you turn to virtually any higher education institution worldwide, you will find variations on these themes. The University of South Florida, for example, has an *Academy for Teaching and Learning Excellence* that offers 'ideas on how to adjust, innovate, and expand your teaching horizons'. It goes on to cite lecturers from its different disciplines, such as sociologist Dr Elizabeth Hordge-Freeman, who is 'motivated to persuade students to challenge their worldviews and critically re-evaluate commonsense notions about the structure of society as well as relationships and interactions that they take for granted'. Switching continents, the Higher Education Research and Development Society of Australasia works to 'facilitate and promote the enhancement of teaching and learning', while the University of Birmingham (UK) boasts a 'cutting-edge teaching pro-gramme built on a foundation of over a hundred years of research and teaching excellence'.

Beyond these general commitments and rhetoric in support of excellent teaching for students, are a string of pearls – or skills – that higher education teachers seek to engender including critical analysis, problem-solving, creativity, original thinking, exploration, and questioning that leads to new insights and possibilities. Murphy (2001: 6) articulated six core abilities from the UK Qualifications and Curriculum Authority including 'Problem Solving' and 'Improving Own Learning and Performance'. Murphy (ibid.: 10) goes on to argue that an 'entirely different approach to assessing key skills in HE is to pass the responsibility for such assessment to the students themselves'. We cannot 'teach' skills, or 'impart' them, but can help learn-ers to develop them, particularly if students assess them for us, and demonstrate them in assignment submissions. This chimes with Steventon's (2016: 98) idea that self-actualization, where an individual realizes their full potential, 'occurs as a result of the student making decisions and taking responsibility for their learning and in the process becoming less reliant on the teacher as 'expert' provider of knowledge'; in other words, stressing the co-dependency of excellent teaching and excellent learning (Roxå and Mårtensson this volume).

Principles for teaching excellence – a personal story

In 2002 I became the University of Gloucestershire's first *Teaching Fellow*, and used this award as a launch-pad to successfully bid for a National Teaching Fellowship to the UK's Higher Education Academy (HEA). A running theme across my university and sector-wide awards was recognition of personal teaching excellence. My case for the initial teaching fellowship was built on the back of blended learning approaches for distance learners – many part-time, mature students – working for local councils across England and Wales. Distance and blended learning delivery was much more unique in 2002, but has become increasingly mainstreamed since then.

University recognition enabled me to apply for a National Teaching Fellowship; these were open competitions, first to be put forward by my own institution, and second to be assessed by peers as worthy of a National Teaching Fellowship that 'celebrates excellent practice and outstanding achievement in learning and teaching in higher education' (HEA 2015: 1).

The connection with disruption came with advice from a National Teaching Fellow colleague, Professor Mick Healey, who suggested either that I present a written application conventionally as a chronological story, or I adopt what he termed a higher risk strategy of being 'different' and 'disruptive' by setting down my credentials in such a way as to stand out. I took the latter route, using a fairy tale opening: '*Once upon a time there was a young man who was brought up in North London . . .*', and writing about myself in the third person, which somewhat perversely distanced my written self from my writing self; so sentences read along the following lines: '*His goal has been to provide enjoyable, innovative and engaging opportunities for teaching and learning in higher education*'.

This device enabled me to look more objectively at myself, my career progress and achievements. I also enjoyed the challenge of communicating in this way. And in one sense this is a highly conventional academic writing device in that many journal articles refer to 'the author', 'the research shows . . .', so in fact I used an accepted academic style, but in an unfamiliar context, to write about the self. It obviously succeeded since I was awarded a fellowship, complete with £10,000 towards future teaching and learning development. However, the two reviewers articulated very different conclusions about my application. The first reviewer stated: 'there is strong evidence of your commitment and enthusiasm for providing students with the best learning experience with the goal of developing a cadre of committed community developers', but 'found the use of the third person in the written submission detracted from the sense of personal ownership and commitment that could have been conveyed by writing as yourself'. The second reviewer, on the other hand, 'truly enjoyed reading this application due to its biographic approach and its content highlighting an impressive career and contribution to teaching and learning both within and outside the applicant's discipline'. This divergence draws us back to the delicacy and sensitivity of disruptive practices that, for some, may lead towards revelation, whilst for others could be irritating, frivolous, discombobulating or upsetting.

It seems to me that just as a mountain will look different depending on where you stand, so too the view of excellent teaching may well differ, from student to student, teacher-to-teacher or teacher to student! In previous research, I presented 'three clear elements of inspirational undergraduate teaching' as judged by some UK undergraduates (Derounian 2017: 1). First and foremost, they believed it to be motivating – which can be seen as a form of disruption, moving people on from the status quo; second – and related – inspirational teaching is deemed encouraging, and third, it flows from teachers' passion for their subject. Later in this chapter I will suggest practical means by which we, as teachers, can foster these three ingredients.

The ambiguity of teaching excellence

In 1985 on *Road to Nowhere*, American band Talking Heads sang the following tantalizing lyrics:

> Well we know where we're goin'
> But we don't know where we've been
> And we know what we're knowin'
> But we can't say what we've seen
> And we're not little children
> And we know what we want
> And the future is certain
> Give us time to work it out.

This quotation indicates the sort of ambiguity attached to teaching excellence and how to trigger it: '. . . we know where we're goin'' – in pursuit of excellent teaching– but we need '. . . time to work it out' in determining meanings and ways of delivering it. In a global context, this journey for universities and colleges has become urgent. The introduction of the UK Teaching Excellence Framework (TEF) is, according to the HEA website, intended to inform student choice of courses based on recognition of excellent teaching. However, 'where we're goin'' in the TEF is hotly contested by academics, not least on the basis of how excellence will be measured. For example, the TEF links wonderful teaching to students' securing suitable graduate employment, but while teachers can nurture students' skills for employability through quality teaching and assessment, there are too many other variables influencing employability that lie largely beyond the control of the teacher (such as individual personality, commitment and aptitude – not to mention the general state of the national and global economy). But rather than focus on the direction of teaching excellence, I want next to turn to the 'time to work it out' by going back to the principles through an exploration of disruption as a means of achieving excellence, but a mechanism for learning that will not be a panacea for all.

Disruption as a pedagogic strategy

Paulo Freire (1972) argued that the purpose of education is to awaken the consciousness through the release of the creative imagination. In order to do that teachers should endeavour to stimulate 'the power of thought to negate accepted limits and open the way to a new future' (ibid.: 11). Similarly, Race and Pickford (2007) suggest disrupting students' equilibrium in order to trigger their learning and movement towards new understandings. The argument goes that from discomfort comes wrestling to make sense of what is presented; and from such active thought emerge new insights, developments, knowledge and skills. Feldman (2008: 1) writes in praise of 'mavericks and risk-takers . . . because to be dangerous and fearless goes hand in hand with genius and without it we're stuck'. She throws down the gauntlet to teachers in suggesting that 'unless we incite our students to push the boundaries, scale unclimbable walls, seek the invisible stars, question and challenge, defy and test limits, we won't be truly serving them' (ibid.).

Positive disruption can come from the skills, knowledge and experience that students bring with them to their studies and fits with the idea of co-produced learning. As King (1993: 30) contends, 'the student is like a carpenter (or sculptor) who uses new information and prior knowledge and experience, along with previously learned cognitive tools (such as learning strategies . . . and critical thinking skills) to build new knowledge structures and rearrange existing knowledge'. The sculptor or carpenter respectively takes stone or wood in a raw form and disrupts the material to create something quite different. For Ausubel (1968: 235), 'the most important single factor influencing learning is what the learner already knows. Ascertain this and teach him accordingly'. Claxton (2006: 360) agrees that a 'creative breakthrough . . . often comes as a reordering of what one already knows'.

But there is a tension in seeing the role of education as to stir up independent thought and non-conformity and, at the same time, maintain order and people's utility to society at large. The state has a vested interest in students becoming compliant, law-abiding citizens, workers and non-disruptive contributors. In a societal context, students who question, criticize, defy and test limits, as Freire (1972) advocated, challenge the very foundations of the system, its authority and established power bases. In a teaching context, disruptive students can be a nuisance if their challenges interrupt the efficient flow of the session. Yet, according to Moon (2009: 4), inculcating and facilitating academic assertiveness and disruption – in the sense of not taking information from lecturers as given – is precisely what academia should be about. For Moon (ibid.: 4), academic assertiveness is broadly 'a set of emotional and psychological orientations and behaviours that enable a learner appropriately to manage the challenges to the self in the course of learning and their experiences in formal education and personal development work'. She contends that such assertion is key to behaving as a good critical thinker, since this requires an individual to stand up and be capable of defending their viewpoint. A means by which to engender assertiveness amongst students is to first make them aware of their own capabilities and the value of these.

It is important to acknowledge, however, that often this approach to teaching and learning will be challenging and uncomfortable for the student, and that can be challenging for the teacher too in the form of negative evaluation of their teaching (Hughes et al. 2009; Steventon 2012). As Steventon (ibid.: 91) notes, liberating pedagogies take both 'out of their comfort zone', leading to worries for students about impact on grades and degree classifications, and for teachers untried practices that carry risks for which they will be called on to justify. Palmer (2001: 4) notes that an 'insight may be a pleasant awakening or rob one of an illusion . . . the quicksilver flash of insight may make one rich or poor in an instant'. So the disruptive toolbox carries a health warning – 'handle with care'.

Notwithstanding such concerns, mechanisms like the TEF risk stifling creativity and innovation and promoting passive and conservative approaches to learning. Naidoo and Jamieson (2005: 272) agree that such market driven teaching in higher education is 'not sufficient for high quality learning which is based on intrinsic and hard to measure factors such as commitment, professional responsibility, empathy and knowledge and enthusiasm for the subject'. And yet, in a world of 'wicked' intractable problems – such as climate change, migration, global terrorism, and addressing poverty – that seem to kick up as many questions as answers, Martin Luther King Junior's (1963: 27–28) exhortation that such problems are more likely to be solved by a creatively maladjusted, nonconforming minority than a conforming majority seems as crucial as ever. Without such questioning and disruption of the accepted order we would still believe that the heavens revolve around the Earth, our planet is flat, and humans have nothing in common with apes.

So far, I have tried to draw a thread through teaching excellence as an important and topical focus for pedagogy, to understanding the principles underlying and challenging excellent teaching in higher education. I now want to move from the principles to the practice of disruption for excellence.

Disruptive practices for teaching excellence

Here is a case for positive disruption to spark teaching and learning excellence: A soap-opera on television, radio, or online, invariably employs the 'hook' of a cliff-hanging end to an episode, so that you are keen to find out what happens next. And in the first minutes of the following encounter, you recall a lot of detail about where the story left off. This can be described as purposefully unfinished learning, and may be much more effective in helping us remember, than if a programme ended with everything resolved. 'Unfinished business', whether issues, concerns or opportunities nag at your consciousness, occupy and disrupt your thoughts, and demand to be addressed. A student contact session strikes me as similar. If we tie off all the loose ends, then there is little appetite and anticipation for what follows. Whereas, if there are a few unresolved issues or possibilities, then there is a chance that students' memory of the week's content will return during the opening minutes of the next class. Reflection includes pondering and ruminating on outstanding matters, and this can be highly purposeful and productive in that the process of reaching for solutions makes it your own, and sticks in a way that passively receiving does not. So there is a benefit to finishing while the majority is engaged in discussion or disagreement, so as to tee them up for more. This can be more productive than neatly delivering all the intended learning outcomes.

Cohen and Jurkovic (1997: 66) turn to art for teaching inspiration and disruption: 'Masterpieces move us, intrigue us, and remain in our thoughts well beyond the ordinary admiration we have for a good, solid piece of work'. They suggest a number of 'surprise packages' for student learning and teaching to answer the question what 'can we do creatively to give life to . . . information?' (ibid.: 68). On a parallel track Steventon (2012) highlights the transformative potential of podcasts in providing a means by which students become producers of knowledge, where voice is a means of expressing themselves differently. Cohen and Jurkovic (1997: 68) advocate teaching practices that utilize 'the element of surprise to make us see, hear, and experience the world anew'. We might, for example, require students from one discipline (say, sociology) to look at an issue through an economic lens, and then see how that plays out in practice – perhaps exploring financial impacts on mental health provision by talking this through with practising therapeutic counsellors. Or ask social work students on a module about disabilities, to work in pairs with one pushing and the other occupying a wheelchair. The lived experience of wheeling another human around is far from textbook.

Cohen and Jurkovic (ibid.) also encourage teachers to get out of order, so that 'by shaking up the accepted sequence of things, people see processes in a new light and become open to fresh approaches'. An example of this kind of disruption would be to dive in at the end point of an idea or class, and then with students work back to the beginning; rather like the Greek myth of Theseus and the Minotaur in which the hero kills this monster and finds his way out of its labyrinth by following a length of string back to the entrance. This approach is in opposition to the conventional route of starting at the beginning and moving towards an ending. The Creative Teaching Site's 'Shake up the teaching process' web page reinforces this approach, noting that periodically something comes along that is so exciting or compelling that it makes sense to use it as an aid to teaching, even though it may be tangential to the methods already planned.

Or what about 'breaking the rhythm'? In discussing with students how to present in public, I acted out a series of cardinal errors that were plausible enough so that they nodded in acknowledgement: 'Yes, I do that!'. This short, disastrous and disruptive presentation involved turning my back on the class, coming in late, quoting without sources, crossed arms as defensive body language, picking my nose, avoiding eye contact and ending abruptly. Using similar techniques Cohen and Jurkovic (1997: 68) noted that 'by the time they realized that the examples were don'ts rather than do's, they had been disarmed into recognizing their own mistakes, and they became more open to change'. Another simple mechanism that I practice and encourage students to do likewise, is what might be termed 'strategic opportunism' (Isenberg 1987), namely putting yourself in the way of opportunities to advance understanding of something; for example, by attending an event concentrating on the topic, a networking gathering of specialists in your field, or an opportunity to present at a conference. This proactive serendipity can operate as positive disruption to increase the chances of gaining new insights, understandings, information and ways forward.

Finally, Cohen and Jurkovic (1997) encourage the use of fun as a mechanism for disruptive learning, running with our imaginations, and adopting a lightness of being – put on a good show, create shock value, compose a soundtrack, tell a story – rather than succumbing to technical aridity! I recall a lecture on rural poverty by my old professor Gerald Wibberley at London University's Wye College, when I was a student, in which he described a Welsh farmhouse he grew up in during the 1940s; and the fact that in winter he would wake to frost on the *insides* of the windows and over his bed covers. It was a highly personal, immersive and dramatic story to communicate the realities of country life for many experiencing disadvantage.

However, Hughes et al. (2009: 31) caution that fun can be applied in two ways: one (which they refer to as *plaisir*) is where a session is enjoyable for students but superficial in terms of learning gain, while the other (*jouissance*) represents the pleasure gained from a 'light bulb moment' when a complex problem is solved, or enlightenment occurs. This represents deep learning and should be the aim of disruptive teaching practices to achieve excellence.

Assignments to demonstrate excellent learning

Brown (1997, in Rust 2002: 145) states that assessment 'defines what students regard as important, how they spend their time and how they come to see themselves as students and then as graduates. If you want to change student learning then change the methods of assessment'. If we accept this, then there must be room for assignment tasks beyond the regular suspects of essays, presentations, group work, exams seen and unseen, portfolios, and reflective diaries. So long as creative and inventively 'disruptive' assessment methods and approaches appropriately demonstrate intended learning gain and that learning outcomes have been met, then why not?

The thrill of the unexpected must be purposeful and not merely frivolous or indulgent. I talked about the value of serendipity, happenstance, fluke and 'strategic opportunism' (Isenberg 1987) in stimulating learning and teaching, and well remember sitting in an assessed politics group presentation, listening to undergraduates talking about the ills of a centralized state, citing North Korea and China and a litany of their drawbacks as examples. On momentarily checking the assessment brief with my colleague, to our horror we realized a typographical error had shifted the focus from what should have been a 'Unitary County', where a single local authority operates, to a 'Unitary Country', completely changing the nature of the presentation. Despite much hilarity ensuing, an unscheduled conversation took place that also resulted in the award of a decent mark. While intended learning outcomes are important, there should be room for emergent and unexpected ones too, which may turn out to be more beneficial than the originals.

On another occasion, colleagues from my university took final year undergraduate Countryside Planners on a residential field trip to Spain to look at aspects of rural development. Instead of a more conventional reflective log and portfolio, they were asked to produce a *museum artefact* that had been unearthed and exhibited by future archaeologists, to illustrate country life in the 2000s. I still remember receiving (and smelling) a charred, battered and tea-stained sepia manuscript, purporting to have been dug up in an archaeological excavation, that explained social, environmental and economic conditions in Catalan villages, liberally illustrated with carefully selected scorched photographs, brochures and other ephemera – disruptively engaging.

As part of my own teaching practice, I was faced with the problem of how to get a scattered and disparate group of learners to compile an online group essay with the remit to explain the key principles of community development. The answer was to allocate a mix of about fifty campus-based and distant students randomly into small groups. The assignment mirrored key aspects of community development (which was the focus of the module) around inclusion/exclusion, collaboration, ownership, and individuals sharing complementary skills to agree on and deliver the content of their group submission. Finally, each individual briefly reflected on the process, with reference to key community development principles: joint working, participation trust and so on. Invariably the process *was* the product: the extent to which members cooperated to produce the essay was generally reflected in the group mark. I was delighted, therefore, to read one of my National Teaching Fellowship reviewer's comments: 'The applicant's approaches to enhancing learning are pedagogically innovative and wholly student-centred'.

Of course, 'left-field' or disruptive assignment tasks need to be fit for purpose and enable the learner to meet required learning outcomes. Like humour, assessments should be treated with care and sensitivity. Or as Rust (2002: 156) puts it: 'ensure that all assessment tasks, and assessment criteria, clearly and directly relate to the learning outcomes . . . [and] engender intrinsic motivation (and reduce plagiarism) by encouraging assessment tasks which resemble 'real-world' tasks and involve active engagement by the student, and by providing choice of tasks'.

And finally . . .

I return to Sally Feldman (2008: 1) and her cri de coeur, that if 'there's one quality I hope our students will hang on to, it is courage in the face of wimpishness and cravenness. Foolhardiness is underrated'. To this end she advocates 'mischief with a purpose', which I would extend to staff in their disruptive teaching as well as students in their learning. Hughes et al. (2009: 37) articulate their desire 'to make a space for the student in higher education who engages with, and enjoys, intellectual work not simply because it will lead to a higher mark or because it will lead to a better job (though we would not of course discount these aspects) but rather because the wider experience of intellectual work enables the student to more fully and deeply engage with issues of concern in their lives and the lives of others'. As mentioned at the start of this chapter, I have endeavoured to connect with several of the overarching goals of this book: to encourage a conversation amongst different audiences about teaching excellence, and to explore a range of pedagogical approaches and interventions that, I argue, beneficially impact on teaching excellence. These form the basis on which I was judged by others for the award of National Teaching Fellow.

So as UK universities face the implementation of the TEF, we would do well to remember the words of philosopher Bertrand Russell (1950, in Woods 1993: 6), that the 'teacher, like the artist . . . can only perform his work adequately if he feels himself to be an individual directed by an inner creative impulse, not dominated and fettered by an outside authority'. Put another way, the warning is reinforced by Naidoo and Jamieson (2005: 275) who conclude that 'constant threat of student litigation and complaints, together with the requirement to comply with extensive external monitoring procedures, may encourage [teachers] to opt for 'safe teaching' which is locked into a transmission mode where pre-specified content can be passed on to the student and assessed in a conventional form'. Is that really the way to achieve teaching excellence?

References

Ausubel, D. P. (1968) *Educational psychology: a cognitive view*, New York: Holt, Rinehart and Winston.

Carroll, L. (1876) *The hunting of the snark*, London: Macmillan. Online. Available at www.poetryfoundation.org/poems-and-poets/poems/detail/43909 (accessed 23 June 2017).

Claxton, G. (2006) 'Thinking at the edge: developing soft creativity', *Cambridge Journal of Education*, 36(3): 351–362.

Cohen, S. and Jurkovic, J. (1997) 'Learning from a masterpiece', *Training and Development*, 51(11): 66–70.

Derounian, J. G. (2017) 'Inspirational teaching in higher education: what does it look, sound and feel like?', *International Journal of the Scholarship of Teaching and Learning*, 11(1): article 9.

Feldman, S. (2008) 'Clear and present danger', *Times Higher Education*, 4 December 2008. Online. Available at www.timeshighereducation.com/comment/columnists/clear-and-present-danger/404598.article (accessed 23 June 2017).

Freire, P. (1972) *Pedagogy of the oppressed*, London: Penguin.

Higher Education Academy (2015) *Are you TEF ready? The Teaching Excellence Framework*. Online. Available at www.heacademy.ac.uk/institutions/consultancy/TEF?utm_source=Google&utm_medium=PPC%28Grant%29&utm_campaign=Consultancy&gclid=CPSO2dmh-9ECFcS37Qode4cH1w (accessed 23 June 2017).

Hughes, C., Perrier, M. and Kramer, A.-M. (2009) 'Plaisir, jouissance and other forms of pleasure: exploring the intellectual development of the student', in iPED Research Network (ed.) *Academic futures: inquiries into higher education and pedagogy*, 28–41, Newcastle-upon-Tyne: Cambridge Scholars Publishing.

Isenberg, D. (1987) *The tactics of strategic opportunism*, Harvard Business Review, March. Online. Available at https://hbr.org/1987/03/the-tactics-of-strategic-opportunism (accessed 23 June 2017).

King, A. (1993) 'From sage on the stage to guide on the side', *College Teaching*, 41(1): 30–35.

King, Jr. M. L. (1963) *Strength to love*, Minneapolis, MN: Fortress Press.

Moon, J. (2009) *Making groups work: improving group work through the principles of academic assertiveness in higher education and professional development*, York: Higher Education Academy/Subject Centre for Education ESCalate.

Murphy, R. (2001) *A briefing on key skills in higher education*, Assessment Series No. 5, Learning and Teaching Support Network Generic Centre. Online. Available at www.economicsnetwork.ac.uk/handbook/assess5.rtf (accessed 23 June 2017).

Naidoo, R. and Jamieson, I. (2005) 'Empowering participants or corroding learning? Towards a research agenda on the impact of student consumerism in higher education', *Journal of Education Policy*, 20(3): 267–281.

Palmer, R. E. (2001) *The liminality of Hermes and the meaning of hermeneutics*, MacMurray College. Online. Available at www.mac.edu/faculty/richardpalmer/liminality.html (accessed 23 June 2017).

Race, P. and Pickford, R. (2007) *Making teaching work: teaching smarter in post-compulsory education*, London: SAGE Publications.

Rust, C. (2002) 'The impact of assessment on student learning: how can the research literature practically help to inform the development of departmental assessment strategies and learner-centred assessment practices?', *Active Learning in Higher Education*, 3(2): 145–158.

Steventon, G. (2012) 'Finding their voice: podcasts for teaching, learning and assessment', in L. Clouder, C. Broughan, S. Jewell and G. Steventon (eds) *Improving student engagement and development through assessment: theory and practice in higher education*, 86–98, Abingdon: Routledge.

Steventon, G. (2016) 'Authentic learning: a route to student attainment?', in G. Steventon, D. Cureton and L. Clouder (eds) *Student attainment in higher education: issues, controversies and debates*, 98–110, Abingdon: Routledge.

Woods, P. (1993) *Critical events in teaching and learning*, Abingdon: Routledge.

Critical friend commentary

Phil Race

Teaching excellence is ineffable seems to be my thought for the day. Too great or extreme to be expressed or described in words is the gist of definitions of ineffable, so this sets a challenge for a compilation about teaching excellence. Derounian's opening reference to 'the Snark' crystallizes the challenge by stating 'do all that you know, and try all that you don't'. And his extract from the Talking Heads lyrics of 'Road to Nowhere' is excellently chosen and relevant. For the last few decades, we have described our curriculum carefully in terms of intended learning outcomes (so that students might better know where they're going), without enough attention to finding out 'where they've been'. And we've been too blinkered to leave room for emergent learning outcomes (which are often far more important).

My turn to diverge: my other life – outside academia – has always been music. Teaching excellence is perhaps all Wagner and Liszt. Roughly contemporaries, these two composers were interconnected for a long time (including Wagner's second wife being Liszt's daughter), but who influenced whom most – Wagner or Liszt? Did *they* know? Can *we* ever know? I'm sure we'd all agree that it is *learning* excellence we all want to happen, so how much might this depend on – or be quite separate from – *teaching* excellence? We seem to have been set off on the Holy Grail of the latter, but will it help or hinder the former? Sir Peter Scott (2017: 1) in the Guardian Online comments that 'the Teaching Excellence Framework (TEF) . . . claims to measure the quality of teaching, but won't and can't' – words of wisdom.

In classical music, 'sonata form' prevailed for ages, where everything fitted nicely into an expected pattern, and was found 'satisfying' thereby like assessment criteria neatly addressing the evidence of achievement of intended learning outcomes – 'constructive alignment' perhaps. But the great composers (Beethoven, Mahler maybe) gave us the 'thrill of the unexpected' (already played with by Haydn often enough). They did not just 'maintain order' but rather embodied 'creative maladjustment of a nonconforming minority', to borrow again a few of Martin Luther King's words.

I love the chapter's emphasis on 'happenstance' and 'serendipity'. Reflecting on the chapter, I found that most of the important directions in my own life and career have been 'happy coincidence'. One example: after offering me my first full-time job (Lecturer in Physical Chemistry), the Deputy Director drove me back to the station and asked if I might also like to be Warden of their hall of residence for a while? That then led me to grow, over ten years, into an educationalist rather than just a scientist, and to devise what Derounian calls 'left-field' assignments such as the following:

> **Devise, prepare and reflect on a question-bank:** based on the five other modules you are studying now. This enables you to make a 'learning tool' which you can use to quiz yourself (and others) preparing for the exams in these other modules, and could be done on paper, in a notebook, or electronically.

Specification and assessment scheme

- 400 numbered, short, sharp questions, e.g. one-liners: 'name 5 causes of the corrosion of iron' (20 marks)
- 400 numbered 'clues' or prompts towards answers to questions, e.g. 'not just water or oxygen' (20 marks)
- Innovative or attractive design, e.g. 'not just on sheets of paper' (10 marks)
- Short reflection (no more than 100 words) on how your question bank worked for you (10 marks)

Emergent learning outcomes

There were many great question banks, some in lovely little pocket books with questions at the front and clues in the back, and the odd electronic one; students reported that it was one of the most useful things they had ever done, and that they had used it actively and successfully to revise their other modules for exams; many had collaborated productively, learning by quizzing each other with their questions; students repeatedly said they would build a question bank along these lines in future studies.

For me, this was 'the thrill of the unexpected' and perhaps a step towards achieving students' *learning* excellence.

Reference

Scott, P. (2017) 'Ideological shakeup will create a "squeezed middle" of universities', *The Guardian*, 7 March 2017. Online. Available at www.theguardian.com/education/2017/mar/07/ideological-squeezed-middle-universities-higher-education-bill (accessed 23 June 2017).

14

GLOBAL PERSPECTIVES ON TEACHING EXCELLENCE

Caroline Wilson and Christine Broughan

Introduction

This final chapter provides a space to reflect on the changing higher education landscape and examine teaching excellence's role within it now and in the future. While recognizing that teaching excellence remains a contested issue, we aim to drive forward debate about its definition and purpose by drawing on multiple perspectives from around the globe. We interviewed experts from the international higher education sector to engage in dialogue around how teaching excellence will be defined, measured and valued in the future (see the list of contributors in Table 14.1). A schedule for these discussions was designed around the current and future context of higher education and what higher education institutions might do to adapt physical and institutional structures and expectations of 'teaching' in order to facilitate teaching that will be considered 'excellent' by tomorrow's students and other stakeholders. These contributors were also asked to consider what attributes and skills will be required of those academics tasked with delivering excellent teaching in the future.

Four key themes emerged from the discussions and these form the structure of this chapter. These are by no means intended as an exhaustive list, but instead offer a framework from which to explore the issues. Contributors' comments cluster around: delivering teaching excellence in light of the internationalization and expansion of provision to meet global demands; the need to produce graduates for jobs yet to be envisioned; an exploration of the environment and type of academic required to produce excellent teaching and the governance required which balances autonomy and accountability. As we work through the contributors' reflections, we consider how these align with issues identified in earlier chapters of this book.

This chapter questions the extent to which the sector really is facing a new era: is it undergoing a fundamental and disruptive paradigm shift? Or is what we are witnessing just part of the continuous cycle of adaptations that higher education has

TABLE 14.1 Contributors to the chapter drawn from the international higher education sector

Aieman Al-Omari	Professor in the Faculty of Educational Sciences, Hashemite University, Jordan
Nadia Badrawi	Vice President of Arab Network for Quality Assurance in Higher Education (ANQAHE), Egypt; Board Member National Authority for Quality Assurance and Accreditation of Education (NAQAAE); Professor of Paediatrics, Cairo University
Simon Bates	Senior Advisor for Teaching and Learning and Academic Director in the Centre for Teaching, Learning and Technology, University of British Columbia, Canada
Jennifer Branch-Mueller	Associate Professor and Teacher in Librarianship Education, Department of Elementary Education, University of Alberta, Canada
David Carless	Professor of Educational Assessment, University of Hong Kong
Jenni Case	Professor at the University of Cape Town, South Africa
Valile Dwayi	Director of Centre for Learning and Teaching Development, Walter Sisulu University, South Africa
Maaroof Fakhri	Director of Education Partnerships at Labster, Copenhagen, Denmark
Alain Malette	Senior Director of Recruitment, Admissions, and Market Development, University of Ottawa, Canada
Lance de Masi	President of The American University in Dubai (AUD)
Racquel Warner	Assistant Professor and Researcher in Education, Mohammed Bin Rashid School of Government, Dubai
Harvey Weingarten	President and CEO of the Higher Education Quality Council of Ontario (HEQCO), Canada

always faced in preparing for, and responding to, constant societal and technological change and a future whose demands and needs remain unclear?

Internationalization and expansion of provision

Higher education has experienced unprecedented growth over the past few decades. The demand to produce more graduates in order to provide the workforce of the future has led to greater diversity of provision, both in terms of internationalization and the range of background and ability of students. From an international perspective, two main drivers are at force: universities exploiting opportunities to recruit international students, and the need for students to experience an authentic international experience in order to thrive in a global society. One of our contributors, Nadia Badrawi, highlights how students are already able to study wherever they want as technology allows structural boundaries of universities to fall away. She and her colleagues are working on the basis that most universities will move to distance learning in order to provide an international student experience.

Another contributor, Alain Malette, argues that the sector is caught somewhere in the middle of 'experiencing' internationalization and 'managing' it. Institutions should, and must, he argues, collaborate to offer a variety of qualification routes. This could include two universities in different jurisdictions (for example one in North America and another in Europe) combining to offer a joint course whereby students are exposed to a discipline in two very different settings. Maaroof Fakhri agrees and goes further to suggest that while students of all types tend to be very well networked, they need infrastructure to capitalize on this:

> The networks that students have access to outside university are now clearly stronger, more interconnected and more global than universities can hope to achieve. If universities want to tap into these networks to better engage students and help them achieve the most positive contribution, they need to work in distributed teams to develop and deliver courses that can support students to have an impact globally at scale. Traditionally this has been through branch-campuses and international exchange programmes, but this is no longer the most effective way. Intercultural workings and collaboration will need to be seamlessly integrated into all courses.

The authors of Chapter 3 are cautious about the universal availability of a truly international experience. Lynne Hunt and Owen Hicks suggest that international/transnational provision has been dominated by the privileged, leading many to argue that this type of activity may simply reinforce disadvantage. Whilst it is theoretically true that students need no longer be shackled by geographical location, Hunt and Hicks point out that a potential chasm exists between the global elite who enjoy such opportunities and the majority of the population who are still restricted by geographical and financial constraints. Excellent teaching, therefore, cannot just happen in the elite institutions, but the internationalization of the sector should serve as an opportunity to deliver and reward excellence globally. In Chapter 4, Glenda Crosling identifies the potential for transnational education to deliver enhanced educational programmes. She does suggest, though, that this requires a careful balance between setting standards of teaching excellence and recognition of local factors in order for higher education institutions to be spaces where individuals can reinvent themselves, developing and exploring the global environment via a myriad of means. A truly internationalized provision has the potential to disrupt the inculcation of outdated practices and drive higher education into a new era that keeps pace with the accelerated change we are witnessing in society.

Teaching excellence also has a role in ensuring that the demand to produce more graduates to provide the workforce of the future goes hand-in-hand with the opportunity for higher education to act as a vehicle for social mobility: 'all young people who aspire to realize their potential through higher education must be given fair opportunities for access and success' (Valile Dwayi). This equity of opportunity should be both in terms students' choice of institution and their experiences when studying once at the institution. Racquel Warner advocates that our role as educators is to model a human value system that is based on equity and fairness but she suggests that this is typically not the case across the university sector: 'The "othering" that is often institutionalized within universities is shocking, with elitist sentiments becoming acceptable as open discourse'.

Reflecting on this challenge, Aieman Al-Omari argues that the sector still needs to have a comprehensive strategy around making excellence inclusive:

> Faculty must be provided with the means to autonomously engage in planning for and implementing inclusive excellence as a comprehensive, campus-wide process, particularly when the issues under discussion are fundamentally academic in nature, such as equity in hiring, curricular change, tenure/promotion, and student educational outcomes across racial and ethnic groups.

According to Alain Malette, this requires a cultural shift within the higher education sector where institutions delineate and prohibit behaviors that do not support inclusivity: 'Each actor on campus has a part to play, and institutional management must demonstrate the required leadership to develop an inclusive vision where no one feels left behind'.

If social mobility and inclusive teaching are defining principles of excellence, then Valile Dwayi argues it should be judged according to the learning gain of all its students at an individual level rather than by traditional student outcomes. This suggests that teaching excellence should be considered alongside learning gain in order to ascertain the true value offered by higher education:

> Learning, rather than teaching, is the true currency of universities; and the true test of the worth and depth of learning is what students can do with what they've learned (Lance de Masi).
>
> Ideally, the graduate attributes, or learning gains, should empower students to be able to develop new knowledges, skills and attributes as demanded by new contexts, which will keep on evolving even after their graduation. The key is not about 'the being' of a graduate, the status quo, but 'the becoming' thereof, which can only be achieved through lifelong learning (Valile Dwayi).

Related to this is the notion that teaching excellence adopts the 'concept of co-determination' (Aieman Al-Omari) such that higher education becomes emancipatory and empowering, rather than serving to reproduce inequalities by promoting the dominant culture which would widen, rather than reduce, inequality.

The need to produce graduates for jobs yet to be envisioned

So far, our contributors have argued that the new era for higher education requires, at its heart, the need for a truly authentic international and equitable educational experience in order to achieve social mobility. This represents a seismic shift in terms of the scope of higher education provision, but also places under scrutiny the purpose of higher education. Of particular relevance for teaching excellence is the shift in both *what* is delivered and *how*. Many traditional vocations such as engineering, administration, healthcare and marketing will continue to be further computerized in the future meaning there is little point in educating a future workforce in the same ways as previously. By way of compensation, new industries are emerging constantly, such as big data, mobile internet, internet of things and robotics. Also, traditional disciplines are merging, with one contributor suggesting teaching excellence will be required to deliver the:

> . . . fusion of many subjects together and the main part of the teaching will be the competencies needed for work. . . . For example, in medicine the basic sciences of pathology, anatomy and physiology are dissolved in the clinical sciences. In the future, the workforces will drive curriculum. Graduating students will be motivated to innovate and create new jobs and new untraditional companies (Nadia Badwari).

These exponential advancements in technologies and the changing expectations of society mean that we are now required to prepare our students for careers that have yet to be envisioned, leaving much of our content-driven provision looking tired and out of date. This necessitates a deconstruction of the disciplines in order to lay down the appropriate foundations from which to deliver excellent teaching.

Not only are industries and job roles changing, but the manner in which our future graduates engage with the world of work is also evolving rapidly with the rise of peripatetic labour, portfolio careers and remote working. Successful graduates will need to be armed with skills to enable them to adapt with chameleon-like ease to workplace adhocracy. Excellent teaching should be delivered within a framework that is sympathetic to, and to some degree emulates, these new styles of working. Potentially this will require a substantial shift from the hierarchical and bureaucratic systems often associated with higher education to those more associated with emerging global successes such as Uber and Airbnb. From an ontological perspective, Racquel Warner suggests that current curricula rely heavily on traditional ideas about the structure of the global economy but its future needs to prepare students for alternatives: 'Universities that are able to educate and develop creative, innovative and entrepreneurial students are going to be the successful ones'.

As higher education embraces the challenges set out by a world that is accelerating at an unprecedented rate both in terms of scope (emerging industries and jobs) and reach (globalization), the currency of teaching excellence will need to adapt to these new drivers. As such, it was suggested that teaching excellence needs to continually evolve:

> It should be iterative, seeking to build on existing strengths, and yet fearlessly look beyond borders: whether disciplinary; institutional; or other. To prepare

students for a world we cannot predict, institutions should seek to constantly destabilize students throughout their academic journey (Alain Malette).

James Derounian in Chapter 13 agrees, and hopes that the drive towards frameworks and rewards for teaching excellence still leaves space for the unintended consequences, surprise and fun within the learning environment.

Does the shift from the discipline content driven knowledge base of teaching excellence suggest a new era for higher education or is this part of the continuous cycle of reinvention that higher education has always experienced? One aspect of teaching and learning that has undisputedly witnessed accelerated change is that of technologies. Maaroof Fakhri, argues that a key part of student learning will need to be around harnessing the 'industrial explosion' of tools emerging in the areas of artificial intelligence, nanotechnology, biotechnology, robotics and virtual reality:

> Higher education institutions need to fully understand these new tools, curate them, and help students understand how they can achieve their goals using the tools they have access to in an ethical and moral way. From a curriculum stand-point, this fundamentally means teaching students how to analyse and solve problems, and then providing them access to the tools to allow them to train and refine those skills. . . . If we can get this right, then we'll be able to produce students who can operate not just in a world we cannot predict, but one that will over their lifetime throw complex challenges at them at an unprecedented pace.

Technology acts both as the driver and solution to new ways of working, he says, especially as students operate and identify with virtual spaces in their everyday lives and expect their learning to be delivered in the same fashion:

> If teachers wish to foster a sense of belonging, they need to go to where the students are, and where they feel like they belong. With the heavy investments in virtual reality, collaborative virtual reality already exists, with some experiences allowing you to socialize, converse and play together in a virtual space. We're already exploring whether teachers can 'teleport' into virtual reality to meet and interact with their students in the virtual laboratory to maintain and develop the elements of teacher-student relationships which add so much value to a programme.

Racquel Warner agrees that remote access to academic support through the use of videos, online quizzes and tasks should be a central feature on all student portals and available when students need it. Harvey Weingarten goes further, highlighting that concepts of time and place become increasingly less significant in the teaching and learning process thanks to technology. While the fundamental principles of engaging students and developing a sense of belonging remain constant, the opportunities for achieving this are no longer bounded by physical location or the need for synchronous engagement.

Whatever the resolution to issues around curriculum and the impact of technology, a key feature of teaching excellence should be the scope to transform students both within and beyond the classroom by '. . . enabling students to take charge of their own learning. This is key to the formation of the professional citizenry of the future' (Lance de Masi).

This idea of students seeing their learning primarily as preparing them for the workplace is picked up in Chapter 5, with Mary Runté and Robert Runté cautioning that students with this outlook are less likely to view 'knowledge as its own reward', and so may be less open to definitions of teaching excellence that do not emphasize immediate relevance to practical skills. Faculty, by contrast, may draw a distinction between training and education in its broader sense, and wish to define teaching excellence as the ability to elevate course content beyond the acquisition of discrete knowledge and skills, to enculturation into professional judgement, attitudes and passion.

The transformative learning which should be a hallmark of teaching excellence can be achieved through the development and promotion of skills that facilitate 'learning how to learn'. While 'what to learn' might be elusive, Harvey Weingarten argues that 'how to learn' is more constant:

> Yes, the specific content required to navigate life and jobs will change. But, there are a set of skills that all would agree are critical to individuals navigating this complicated life – skills like the ability to think critically, to communicate well, to be able to work with others. These are the essential skills that HEIs say they foster. The key thing now is to measure whether in fact these skills are acquired and, if not, how we could do a better job of teaching them.

It is clear that the globalization of higher education, driven by markets and technology, has stretched both the scope and reach of teaching excellence. However, while there may be reduced geographical boundaries to higher education in the future, the desired outcome should remain constant in that excellent teaching:

> . . . will encourage students to develop confidence in their own creative abilities, strong community engagement and a sense of ethical responsibility allied to the humility that comes from understanding that learning is a lifelong phenomenon that demands a lifelong curiosity and commitment (Aieman Al-Omari).

In the next section we build on Siara Isaac, Ingrid Le Duc, Cécile Hardebolle and Roland Tormey's focus in Chapter 9 on the pivotal role of staff training and development in supporting teaching excellence. They argue that teaching excellence should be about the *process* of scholarly improvement rather than *outcome* focused. They further suggest that to meet the needs of the 21st century, learner analytics should be core to informing decisions and supporting academics.

The environment and teacher required to deliver excellent learning

The transformation in scope and reach of higher education has implications for those tasked with delivering its provision. In this section, our contributors reviewed teaching excellence both in terms of the curriculum and environment needed and the capabilities and skills required by the teacher. The switch away from 'transferers of content' to 'curators of knowledge' is expressed by Racquel Warner:

> For the past two decades or more, educators have been preparing students for a world that was in constant change. Once knowledge was no longer resident in the heads of a few scholars and was widely available on the internet, the obsolescence of teaching content was apparent.

As earlier set out in this chapter, Jennifer Branch–Mueller similarly identified that technology will enable students to learn anywhere, without meeting their tutors or peers in person, and this identifies a skill required of teachers in building communities of learners:

> I believe in high structure/high touch with distance students. I think you need to provide a clear plan for learners so they know what is going to happen and then you need to ensure that they are communicating with others a lot. That enables them to feel connected to each other. With the large volume of discussion posts required to build community, the instructor needs to use technology efficiently to 'keep up' and be a part of the learning. I find that the instructor needs to be present, share stories and anecdotes and do short videos so that students see the instructor as a real person.

Along the same lines, Racquel Warner suggests that:

> Faculty will require 21st century skills of communicating effectively, being creative, innovative yet being masters of their craft of teaching. Being adaptive and being able to problem solve. All the skills that students require should be modelled by the faculty. Being able to use technology not just for the sake of it, but as a way of connecting students with wider resources and teaching them how to optimize their learning using online resources are what teachers will be doing in the future.

Furthermore, Nadia Badrawi saw excellent teachers harnessing technology to follow the portfolios of each student and their milestones until reaching full maturity and graduating, a point endorsed again by Maaroof Fakhri:

> Great teachers will be able to utilize personalized student learning data (that has been analysed using machine learning and similar algorithms), to select the best tool-kit for each learner. This is actually made much easier through

flexible learning environments, as they naturally can monitor and analyse every aspect of student behaviour, and learning styles.

While the promise of technology dominated many commentaries, an alternative position was offered by Jenni Case who argues that there will still be a requirement, albeit reduced, to share physical space:

> High quality higher education will retain the substantial face-to-face dimension. Young people want it, surprisingly; students from less advantaged backgrounds particularly so. People criticize universities for still carrying on practices such as sitting together to learn. I do not think that is lack of imagination on our part. Powerful learning happens when people physically share a space. Now, obviously, there is the online space, which supplements that, so we can use our time more intelligently and that is what we will have to do. We will have less contact time because it is expensive. I can imagine some kind of hybrid between online and face-to-face, but I do not see an end to face-to-face learning in quality provision.

In terms of the curriculum design, there are different visions of how to build learning packages fit for an unpredictable future but also for professions with specific requirements. In medicine for instance, there is a requirement for the curriculum to be highly correlated with the requirements of the students' future profession:

> . . . the curriculum will be more flexible in the future and the assessment will depend and coincide with the flexibility of the curriculum. I believe that even in the same degree, there will be flexibility and students will have the ability to choose and even change some of the curriculum according to the present job market. The role of the teacher will be to ensure that these flexibilities and changes in the curriculum do not affect the competencies needed in the job market and that the changes . . . are aligned with the competency standards of the programme (Nadia Badrawi).

Simon Bates concurred with this concept of 'managed flexibility':

> Flexibility for students in terms of curriculum choices is generally a positive element of a programme of study. However, flexibility without structure can lead to a patchwork of curriculum taken without coherence. The right balance seems to be in providing degree pathways that are flexible and offer choice rather than being prescriptive, but are still coherent.

With the endless possibilities for curricula offered by accessibility of content there is a risk of students, and to some extent teachers, becoming 'lost' and this does appear to represent a fundamental issue in the delivery requirements of 21st century global higher education. Accordingly, David Carless says another skill identified for the excellent teacher is to ensure there is a clear framework of learning for students to navigate through:

> Good teaching enables students to work towards clear goals with rich learning outcomes embedded in a coherent, integrated curriculum. Students are supported in the development of capacities to appraise work so that they are effectively self-evaluating their progress towards these learning outcomes. Student assessment literacy is developed so that learners understand the purposes of assessment and their active role in its processes. Similarly, student feedback literacy is evolving so that students can become active generators and users of feedback.

Picking up on the requirement to balance student personal direction in their learning with the need to continue to meet current and future discipline knowledge, Nadia Badrawi recommends a key part of teacher education is how to integrate courses with the competencies needed in the different job markets, given future professionals were likely to move flexibly between job types.

It is clear from the above that the demands for new ways of working and the potential offered by technology to deliver flexible and personalized learning pathways will drive a change in the way that teaching excellence is defined. We have explored the environment and curriculum changes required in this new era, but *who* will be the deliverers of teaching excellence in the future? If we think back to historical examples of excellent teachers, an image of the great orator, a lone speaker on the podium, sharing knowledge and presenting carefully choreographed arguments hitherto inaccessible to the audience, springs to mind. Yet the future of teaching excellence is more akin to the analogy of the Formula 1 team where the driver, and in our case teacher, is the more visible part of a team of experts having distinctive and complementary roles with a single focus, to win races or enhance learning gain through excellent teaching. Jenni Case expressed it as the teacher being a critical lead in formulating a 'relational space', which creates energy that both teacher and students feed off.

Jennifer Branch-Mueller saw that within many institutions, guiding students through a flexible curriculum is a shared responsibility between learning professionals:

> . . . educational developers and instructional designers who can support instructors to 'build' courses and programmes that meet the learning needs of students. These support people can keep up with learning and assessment trends, technology innovations while faculty members and instructors keep up with research and content in their specialized areas. I don't think the average instructor can do both – and many won't want to.

It was recognized that excellent teachers will need to be open to collaboration; willing to seek advice from experts in student learning, course design or learning technology to help them meet their teaching and learning goals. They will also be more likely to be involved in team teaching in the future:

> . . . teamwork will be more needed in the future. I believe that most of the courses will be integrated and the educational strategies will move to be problem based (Nadia Badrawi).
>
> Consider a team of teachers where one understood how to use machine learning and personalized student data to quickly identify problem areas for individual students, or unique pathways for their learning, while another could easily navigate the digital social sphere to engage students and develop projects that allowed them to collaborate across borders (perhaps using virtual reality), and another that acted as a personal coach. In the same way students connect and collaborate across borders, teachers will need to in order to keep up (Maaroof Fakhri).

Simon Bates agreed that changing opportunities and challenges requires:

> . . . a broader set of skills, habits and values for the 21st century educator. This set of skills does not necessarily have to reside within a single person (but often can, in leaders occupying teaching and learning-focused academic roles) but rather across the team. The sorts of skills required include:

- Collaborator: committed to sharing and enhancing one's own educational approaches within and between disciplines.
- Teacher for learning: an understanding of how people learn and how to design effective activities for learning.
- Experimenter: an openness to try, reflect on and learn from new approaches, pedagogies and technologies to support student learning.
- Scholar: an awareness and appreciation of effective, research-based and discipline-appropriate pedagogic strategies.
- Technologist: fluency using learning technology in educationally effective ways.
- Curator as well as producer: a producer and consumer of educational resources, through sharing and co-development.

When the contributors were asked to describe the attributes and traits of an excellent teacher, their comments suggested that teachers needed to be more robust and agile than ever before. They also needed to be able to deal with diversity and change in order to remain excellent. So, while there is recognition that some roles will need to be specialized, Johan Geertsema, Chng Huang Hoon, Mark Gan Joo Seng and Alan Soong (Chapter 10) found no evidence to suggest that 'teaching only' contract staff are better at teaching than other staff. As such, they warn against the segmentation of academic roles and raise concerns regarding the fragmentation of work due to non-tenured positions. Teaching excellence, for these authors means retaining the principles of academic citizenship that enables academic freedom and the promotion of a community of learners.

Cognizant to this, David Carless summarized the skillset of the excellent teacher as a rounded academic citizen:

> Excellent teachers communicate high expectations and interact skillfully with their learners both online and face-to-face. They have empathy; put students' best interests at heart; and imbue cultural sensitivity and an international outlook. They have a passion for their subject, for students and for intellectual inquiry. Excellent teachers have a varied pedagogic repertoire which they access selectively for a particular teaching situation. Effective teachers are also skillful at managing challenging issues, such as assessment and feedback. They use well-designed authentic assessment methods to stimulate deep approaches to student learning, help students understand what good academic work looks like, and design sequences of assessment tasks which facilitate student action on feedback. Most importantly, excellent teachers are resourceful and determined: they fight against contextual constraints and don't allow themselves to be diverted from their goal of providing an inspiring student learning experience. They have at heart a generosity of spirit and a concern for student well-being.

Simon Bates echoed many of these points and reflected that:

> The teachers I have admired most and have learned the most from have all had the following traits in abundance. There may well be others, but this seems like a good start:

- Above all, a genuine interest in working with learners, supporting them on a pathway from novice to expert.
- Empathy and sensitivity, and the ability to create a climate that motivates learners, sustains their engagement and drives them to succeed.
- An awareness of one's own expert blind spot: it is all too easy as an expert with decades of experience in a field or discipline to forget what it was like not to know.
- A self-confessed lifelong learner, willing to see teaching itself as part of their own learning journey, a constant curiosity and desire to learn.

Both contributors concur that despite the ontological shift facing higher education through supercomplexity, exogenous contingencies, uncertainty and the pace of change, many teacher attributes will remain constant with perhaps only a few, notably harnessing technology and becoming curators of knowledge, being qualitatively different from the past.

Governance which balances accountability and autonomy

In Chapter 2, Caroline Wilson reflects on the value and challenges involved in measuring excellent teaching. Valile Dwayi points out that while good governance must, at least to some extent, rely on good metrics, there is concern that it:

> . . . becomes a numbers game that can always be structurally subverted . . . Instead, we need to disrupt the notions of teaching excellence and guard against skewed systems of reward that bedeviled global banking systems.

Concern was expressed that metrics have become a tool of symbolic power and control and distort the very thing they aspire to measure. This is akin to Goodhart's law, the adage that once a measure becomes a target, it ceases to be a good measure. Metrics have gained such power that they are at risk of becoming 'truths' in their own right, masquerading as teaching excellence. Contributors suggest that we should guard against such reification and avoid any drive for the conclusion that there is one aspirational version of excellence, measured by hard outcomes of student achievement, as this will mean that the majority of institutes, tutors and students will always fall short.

Some contributors contend that, whatever metrics are chosen, they can never do justice to the richness, plurality and diversity of our activities and risk being inimical to good teaching. An alternative version suggested by Racquel Warner is that:

> Teaching excellence should be measured by the degree of engagement, the learning process and the attainment of outcomes. The extent to which students' learning has been scaffolded to make them ready for the next big learning adventure, is the extent to which teaching excellence is demonstrated. A teacher who can strike a balance between cognitive, affective and behavioral needs in the students is demonstrating teaching excellence. It is holistic.

Sandeep Gakhal (Chapter 1) suggests these debates not only question the ontological assumptions elucidating teaching excellence and its measurement, but also highlight how current structural practices can serve to undermine the pursuit of excellence. This would suggest the need to avoid repeating more of the same, and instead disrupt the current system of higher education in order to make significant progress. Otherwise we risk that the metrification, consumerism and structures of universities may encourage bland styles of teaching that are 'safe' where 'pushing students outside their comfort zone may not be seen as good teaching' (Jennifer Branch-Mueller). Further, this climate might encourage students to adopt a 'just good enough' mentality that views their learning journey along some predefined pathway rather than providing circumstances to see how much they can achieve. Consequently, Harvey Weingarten cautioned against students being the only source of measuring teaching excellence:

> Regrettably, in my experience, students do not exert the power they have, or should have, in insisting on a higher quality academic experience. They are very instrumental – every student survey I know of shows that the dominant (not necessarily the only) reason students attend postsecondary is to get the credential to get a good job. That means they are prepared to jump through whatever hoops and barriers we place in front of them to get that credential.

This resonates with the earlier argument by Aieman Al-Omari for an acknowledgement that teaching excellence is 'co-determined' by the student, with institutional governance which encourages students to find their learning emancipatory and empowering in which questioning and challenging the dominant culture is not just condoned but encouraged.

The space for excellent teachers themselves to be involved in forming and challenging policies and practices in higher education is also lacking according to Mark Israel and Dawn Bennett (Chapter 8) and Michael Berry and Ross Guest (Chapter 11). The latter authors suggest recognition schemes can go some way to ensure that excellent teaching receives similar plaudits to research and urge the sector to do more to involve teachers publicly recognized as excellent in practice and policy development. An overwhelming view expressed was the need for proxy measures of teaching excellence to act as critical, creative and credible drivers rather than pejorative propaganda agents that stymie progress.

This concept of governance, embracing many interests and voices, corresponds with the arguments found in Chapter 6, where Torgny Roxå and Katarina Mårtensson conclude that teaching excellence thrives in organizations where collegial governance is the dominating principle. In Chapter 7, Denise Chalmers and Beatrice Tucker also point to the importance of the values which should underpin teaching excellence being in line with an institution's vision.

The points raised in this section resonate well with those of Scott Harrison, who contends in Chapter 12 that teaching excellence is, and must continue to be, multifariously defined and used alongside other measures in a nuanced approach, this also includes acknowledgement of teachers' embodied experience of their subject matter, and a commitment to ongoing learning and peer review (also variously defined).

Conclusion

This chapter has been forward-looking, seeking predictions on the sector's need to adapt to deliver, *and continue to deliver*, teaching excellence through the challenges on the horizon and beyond. It has also reflected on the attributes and skills that academics, who will be required to deliver excellent teaching in the future, need to possess and develop. It has done this in the context of rising internationalization and expansion of provision in order to meet growing global demand, the accelerated change in the job market and the make-up of future graduate jobs, and the governance required for higher education institutions to thrive and deliver excellent teaching amidst such change.

Finally, as with the whole of this book, we consider the extent to which we really do face a new era in higher education, and whether a fundamental paradigm shift is required as universities look to the future. Our contributors, with experience of higher education drawn internationally, have offered a vision of how to ensure future excellence, which requires higher education institutions, and those working within them, to adapt in order to embrace diversity in both the global makeup of student populations and also in their abilities. At the institutional level and in the governance of higher education institutions, a front foot approach is advocated, in which all learning is recognized as empowering, not just that of the high achievers (Valile Dwayi), in which difference of cultural or educational background is not just accommodated but embraced in order that all students are better networked and integrated, leading not just to more equitable outcomes but better outcomes for all in terms of producing graduates who can thrive in a globalized world (Maaroof Fakhri; Racquel Warner). Higher education institutions need to focus on being a spur for social mobility in order that greater numbers of students than ever before are able to reach their full potential, and support a future global landscape with its many well documented challenges ahead (Aieman Al-Omari; Valile Dwayi; Alain Malette).

Another key feature of teaching excellence at the institutional level is embracing the fact that *learning* is what will fuel the future, not *education* (Lance de Masi), and dominant metrics currently measuring performance need to adjust to acknowledge individual learning gain. The requirement for future students to be better learners rather than better educated (Lance de Masi), and in charge of their own learning, feeds through to excellent teaching practice. Innovative portfolio, or 'fluid' careers, working across disciplines, requires a flexible curriculum (Nadia Badrawi; Alain Malette) with teachers focusing not on *what* is taught but *how* learning is achieved (Lance de Masi; Harvey Weingarten).

Remote delivery will be a key feature of learning (Nadia Badrawi), partly to continue to make learning affordable, and partly due to technology making this possible. This means employing teachers who, in pursuit of excellence, will need high level communication skills in order to develop and maintain contact with students and to create the environment for engaging interaction between peers (Simon Bates; Jennifer Branch-Mueller). Such teachers also need to be able to operate as role models (Racquel Warner) for their students in providing inspiration and to demonstrate interest in working with learners (David Carless).

Does all of this represent a paradigm shift? The pace of change in technology, expectation and policy reflected in this chapter and in others which precede it, can leave many individuals, institutions and sectors struggling to keep up. Looking back, one can perhaps point to other radical changes that have needed to be accommodated, but the contributors to this chapter were in clear agreement that change impacting on the sector currently is doing so at an unprecedented rate. Added to this, adapting and keeping pace is made exponentially more difficult when aligned to the challenge of preparing structures and people for an uncertain future, when little of the future can be predicted from the past. In this respect, perhaps we can truly say that we *are* experiencing a new era for teaching excellence.

Valile Dwayi argues that the task of preparing students for an uncertain future lies at the heart of the current situation faced in higher education, which is precisely why it needs a transformational shift rather than an adjustment if it is truly to provide excellent learning as defined by the contributors to this chapter:

> Planning for the future runs the danger of being framed in rationalistic and technical terms while the dynamics of our social world remain mired in un-predictabilities of cultural, social and political tensions. . . . Our current practices, including the notion of teaching excellence, remain historically and socially constructed, and the future can be understood in the dialectical and reflexive relations of social structure.

This chapter has offered a timely critique of teaching excellence at a point where its format is still being developed and operationally defined in many countries and against a backdrop where higher education is experiencing fundamental change. Though the core purpose of higher education remains, it is in a form barely recognizable to most of its alumni. Defining, measuring and rewarding teaching excellence continues to be exquisitely elusive but our profound belief in higher education will ensure its enduring and significant contribution to the future of a better society.

Acknowledgements

We wish to express our gratitude to the contributors to this chapter for the expertise, knowledge and insight they have so generously given.

INDEX